LANGUAGE AND STYLE
SERIES

General Editor
STEPHEN ULLMANN
IV

W. M. FROHOCK
STYLE AND TEMPER

Studies in French Fiction,
1925–1960

OXFORD

BASIL BLACKWELL

1967

First printed 1967

Printed in Great Britain
in the City of Oxford
AT THE ALDEN PRESS
and bound at
The Kemp Hall Bindery

FOR
NATALIE AND DAVID
TARBET

Contents

Acknowledgments

Such specific debts as I am aware of having incurred are indicated in the notes. I repeat my thanks here to the individuals concerned. I should like to thank, also, the editors or former editors of *Romanic Review*, *Yale French Studies*, *Accent*, and *Bucknell Review* for permission to reprint material that appeared first in their publications.

In addition, I have also to thank the following for permission to quote works to which they hold copyright:

The William Faulkner Literary Estate, and Chatto and Windus Ltd., for permission to quote from *Intruder in the Dust* (1948, p. 238) and from *Absalom, Absalom* (1936, p. 214);

Librairie Plon for permission to quote from two works of Georges Bernanos, *Les Grands Cimetières sous la lune* (1939, pp. 12–13) and *Monsieur Ouine* (1953, p. 1514);

Editions de Minuit for permission to quote from *La Modification* (1957, pp. 190–1) by Michel Butor, and from *Le Vent* (1957, pp. 68–9) by Claude Simon;

Editions Gallimard for permission to quote from *Les Caves du Vatican* (1958, p. 787) and *Les Faux-monnayeurs* (1958, pp. 974–5) by André Gide; *Pilote de Guerre* (1959) and *Terre des Hommes* (1959) by Antoine de Saint-Exupéry; *Les Noyers de l'Altenburg* (1945, pp. 104–5 and 105–6) by André Malraux; *La Nausée* (1938, pp. 127–8) by Jean-Paul Sartre; *Noces* (1950, pp. 31–2), *L'Etranger* (1962, pp. 1164–6 and 1209), and *La Peste* (1962) by Albert Camus; and from *Les Célibataires* (1959, pp. 766, 903 and 905) and *Les Bestiaires* (1959, pp. 561 and 559) by Henry de Montherlant.

The names of frequently quoted periodicals
have been abbreviated as follows:

Introduction

Such unity as an indulgent reader may find in the following papers results less from design than from a continuing concern with their general subject. None was originally conceived as part of a future book; in their first form they were meant for presentation to groups of specialists or for publication in specialized journals. The suggestion that they be made available in more durable form led to their becoming the matter of my seminar at Harvard during 1964 and 1965. They were afterwards rewritten and amplified. As a collection they might best be described as a series of efforts to help define a number of major talents.

But why these particular talents—André Malraux, Jean-Paul Sartre, Albert Camus, Henry de Montherlant, Antoine de Saint-Exupéry, Georges Bernanos, Louis-F. Céline, Jean Giono—and not others? Simply because critical opinion of them continues to vary, has not yet solidified. At one point, under the influence of Ramon Fernandez[1] we searched them for 'messages'. Later we were praising them for having 'changed the character of French fiction', since in their hands a form long oriented toward the social and psychological had mutated into something we called 'metaphysical', devoted to 'creating an image of man for their age'.[2] Today we are perhaps most aware of them as literary artists. It

---

[1] See his *Messages* (1924). Readers in England and America will remember his contributions to Eliot's *Criterion* as well as to *La Nouvelle Revue Française*. My statement here is based upon personal reminiscence. The unpopularity of his later political views and conduct may have obscured his historical importance in the years 1920–40.

[2] The formula itself is taken from Germaine Brée and Margaret Guitton, *An Age of Fiction*, p. 3, but the position reflected is one which few critics would have disowned at the time. The publication date, 1957, is somewhat misleading, the manuscript having been prepared considerably earlier, at a moment when emphasis still fell heavily upon the philosophical aspects of fiction. The influence of Existentialism was still strong even when indirect, and the curious hyper-intellectualism in vogue in France since the end of the war had not lost its force. (For an example of this mood in France see Claude-Edmonde Magny, *L'Age du roman américain* [1948], with its

is relevant, for example, that after years when critical attention focused on the 'thought' of Albert Camus, the annual bibliographies now show that interest has shifted to his art.[3]

Yesterday's perspectives inevitably seem distorted. So long as we were reading novels for their messages, Jean Giono's modern pastorals dwarfed the work of other men whose stature has waxed, while his has waned, in the time since. And so long as we had not tired of images of man, the novelists who had dwelt most explicitly on the human predicament—Malraux, Saint-Exupéry, Camus, and Sartre—in their turn dwarfed the others. Even today one is not disposed to quarrel about the 'image' formula or the epithet 'metaphysical' as descriptive terms. But the difficulty is that they have taken on normative values as well. 'Metaphysical', in this context, acquires a meaning much more restricted than the one proposed originally (I believe) by Jean Hytier.[4] To him all literature seems to be a metaphysics of one sort or another, and the novel, more specifically, a metaphysics 'of the intelligence'. In contrast, the restrictive meaning implicitly denies metaphysical value to some novels while authorizing us to attribute a certain superiority to the kind which have been most selfconsciously holding up an image.

The restricted concept may also have had a part in encouraging critics to choose among the images offered, some of which would appear to be deemed more 'for their time' than others. One detects a strong critical

---

[3] E.g., *Bibliography of Critical and Biographical References for the Study of Contemporary French Literature*, published annually by Group Seven of the M.L.A. Professor Brée's *Camus* (1959) was instrumental in restoring critical balance.

[4] *Les Arts de littérature* (1946); cf. Gaétan Picon, *André Malraux* (1945), in which the adjective is applied repeatedly, in the restricted sense, to Malraux's work. My debts to Professor Hytier are too many and varied—as well as too obvious—for enumeration here. It is, however, the pleasantest of obligations to pay homage, on the eve of his retirement, to this erudite and modest man whose voice, for a generation of American scholars, has been indistinguishable from that of sanity itself (see 'La Méthode de M. Leo Spitzer', *RR*, XLI, no. 1 [Feb. 1950], 42–69).

---

highly symptomatic translation, p. 163, of Hemingway's sentence in which Mme Magny's French turns his 'timeliness' into 'temporalité'.)

Henri M. Peyre, in *The Contemporary French Novel* (1955), takes a similar view, exposed somewhat less systematically.

The present introduction expresses a mild dissent first registered in reviews of Professor Peyre, *Yale Review*, XLV, no. 1 (Sept. 1955), 151–4, and of the Brée-Guitton volume, *RR*, XLIV, no. 3 (Oct. 1958), 198–202, and here developed at greater length. I should not want my disagreement to hide my admiration of these studies or my extensive debt to them.

preference for the 'tragic' and 'humanist' image found, for example, in Malraux and Saint-Exupéry, to the exacerbatedly Roman Catholic one of Bernanos or the one proposed by Céline, who makes a protagonist say that the only reason for telling his story is to show what vermin men can be.[5] In our present perspective with its heavy emphasis on the art and craft aspects of literature, such a view needs correction, not because it credits the 'tragic humanist' novel with too much but because it does not recognize the full value of the others.

This too will pass. Today's perspective we know to be part of the literary climate of the moment. The emergence of the 'new novel' in France has emphasized the importance of form and technique and taken as basic the notion that the 'image of man' novel was poorly informed about its special subject.[6] And the success of the work of critics like Georges Poulet and J.-P. Richard[7] in establishing a criticism of literature considered as temporal and spatial form cannot but have heightened our awareness. Our very exclusiveness should make us confident that ours is not the ultimate word.

But this is exactly the point. The fact of such critics contributing to a continuing dialogue is what justifies—if anything does—offering such a collection as this to students of form and style.

How much did these novelists hold in common?

Such confirmed individualists can hardly be thought of as a group. One of the embarrassments of discussing them is the absence of a common label for easy reference. The age spread is too broad to permit calling them a literary generation—Bernanos's eldest child was hardly younger than Camus. No term in '-ism' is inclusive enough to encompass the diversity

[5] *Voyage au bout de la nuit*, Editions de la Pléiade, pp. 27–8. The French word translated by 'vermin' is 'vaches'.—Henceforward, all page references to novels of which a Pléiade edition exists will be to this edition, and will be incorporated in the text unless the quotation is the subject of incidental comment in a footnote. The choice of the Pléiade editions is prompted by the relative durability of their paper and availablity to readers.

[6] See esp. Nathalie Sarraute, *L'Ere du soupçon* (1965), 10–11: 'Chacun savait maintenant, instruit par des déceptions successives, qu'il n'y avait pas d'extrême fond . . . Celui que l'analyse de Proust avait dévoilé n'était déjà plus qu'une surface'.

[7] M. Poulet's influence seems to have been gradually cumulative; it is impossible to say which of his three volumes of *Etudes sur le temps humain* has had most impact. In the case of M. Richard, despite the excellence of his other studies, *Poésie et profondeur* remains the essential work. In indicating his affinity with M. Poulet I do not, of course, mean to overlook what he owes to the seminal works of Gaston Bachelard.

of their work. Yet theirs were the first new names to achieve importance after the apotheosis of the novel (*c.* 1925–27) which was the publication of Gide's *Faux-monnayeurs* and of the final volume of *A la recherche du temps perdu* and they wrote such significant new fiction as was written in France between that time and the inception (*c.* 1953) of the 'new novel'.

Clearly they saw little future for the novels of the rise and decline of middle-class fortunes which had been the stock of immediate elders like Georges Duhamel, Jean Schlumberger, Jacques de Lacretelle, Jules Romains, and François Mauriac. The multi-volume chronicles, sagas, or *romans-fleuve*, as represented by *Les Thibault, La Chronique des Pasquier, Les Hauts-Ponts,* and *Les Hommes de bonne volonté* had no worthy successors. Malraux, Sartre, and Montherlant contemplated such enterprises at one time or another, but two of these long novels were never finished and the third, Montherlant's *Jeunes Filles,* approximates the type only with respect to length.[8]

As compared with writers like Mauriac and Martin du Gard, the younger men were less wedded to the novel form. Only Giono made fiction a steady, almost lifelong, pursuit.[9] Bernanos began no new novel after 1936, although he went on writing actively for another decade; but for his having found *Monsieur Ouine* so hard to finish all of his fictions would belong to the same ten-year period. Saint-Exupéry discovered a kind of essay that was more hospitable to his talent than was the novel. Malraux finished his last fiction in 1943 and has never returned to the projected volumes of *La Lutte avec l'ange.* Céline's powers declined rapidly after *Mort à crédit.* Sartre seems unlikely, after so long a lapse, to fill out the promised tetralogy of *Les Chemins de la liberté.* The only fiction Camus conceived as longer than a cautionary tale, after the war, was *La Chute.* Nothing in these facts suggests that the novel was in special esteem.

There is even some suggestion that these novelists found the form inadequate for what they wanted to express; they seem to have been

---

[8] For the clarification of a number of ideas regarding symbols of continuity, and the recurrence of familiar myth-patterns, not only in the multi-volume novels mentioned but also in shorter fictions like *L'Immoraliste* and *Saint-Saturnin,* I have profited from conversations with Professor John Keith Gilbert, whose Harvard doctoral dissertation, *Symbols of Continuity in recent French Fiction,* is still unpublished.

[9] Such, at least, is the testimony of Pierre Robert, *Jean Giono et les techniques du roman.* In the debate as to whether or not this novelist changed enough to justify our speaking of a first and a second 'manner', he argues persuasively that there was no break in Giono's development and that we should think not of radical change but of normal growth.

urgently moved to give the same materials, themes, and ideas more than one mode of statement. *Les Voix du silence* re-orchestrates the themes of Malraux's novels, and thus we read *Le Mythe de Sisyphe* with *L'Etranger* and *Caligula*; *L'Etre et le néant* with *La Nausée*; *Les Grands Cimetières sous la lune* with *La Nouvelle Histoire de Mouchette*. This is true not only of the more 'philosophical' minds, but also of writers like Giono, whose *Vraies Richesses* reworks the matter of *Que ma joie demeure*. We have to conclude that (except in Giono's case) the commitment to prose fiction is far from exclusive and perhaps weak.

On this point, the contrast with both slightly earlier and slightly later writers needs little emphasis. For Mauriac and his coëvals the novel was surely the central element of the literary life; excursions into other forms appear both digressive and momentary. Similarly, when Madame Sarraute and the other 'Midnight Novelists' depart from fiction, they do so in essays on professional problems of form, style, and technique—something as different as possible from saying over in a second mode what has already been said in a first.

There is also a suggestive difference in attitudes toward the literary life itself. Medicine, politics, religion, archeology, aviation, art study, and athletic sports competed for the attention of the writers who concern us. Our common stereotype of 'the literary man' tends to break down.

Should we attribute such differences merely to the turbulence of their particular time? Perhaps: some kinds of literary activity must lose their charm when Armageddon is just over the horizon; one is unlikely to embark on long aesthetic undertakings when life itself is so insecure. This, by itself, might explain why, in contrast with the practice of other generations, their fictions are so frequently brief. Even for ordinary men, sedentary occupations can become intolerable when the rest of the world is in agitated motion. And these were far from being ordinary men.

Their restlessness, the utter inability to heed Pascal's warning about sitting still in a room that took some of them as far from home as Tierra del Fuego and Indochina, suggests strong tensions and an excess of nervous energy: one thinks of Rimbaud's *fugues*, and wonders whether so much moving about was not somehow compulsive. We have documentary evidence of emotional disturbances such as the 'crisis' in the life of Montherlant and Bernanos's recurrent need to be treated for anxiety states. Camus was subject to moments of 'ecstatic lucidity' and Giono to periods of reclusion. Saint-Exupéry frightened his comrades in arms with his increasingly suicidal daring. Malraux has accepted the adjective 'shamanistic' as describing his own conduct. Milton Hindus pictures

Céline as little less than a victim of chronic mental illness.[10] Various kinds of anxiety state (*angoisse*, *Angst*, *anxiété*) are studied in their writings.

It is tempting, also, to think of them as *révoltés*. The word *révolte*, itself, has been used so much in recent years and in so many contexts that its meaning has become elusive; there is also an obvious danger of assuming that because a man writes of anxiety and revolt in his books he must be speaking from personal experience. This we must avoid—but not to the point of failing to see that these men were markedly nonconformist, extremely critical of their own culture, and alienated not only from the middle class but also, at least at times, from the totality of European life.

If they had lived at another time such men might not have written novels at all. One can easily imagine these intense personalities expressing themselves in one or another sort of poetry, one which permitted a more direct revelation of the ego without requiring prolonged observation of the other egos that make up the external world. But their fortune was to live when the prestige of the novel, and the audience the novel commanded, made the choice almost mandatory; even autobiography appears to have demanded to be disguised as fiction.

The extent to which they were obliged to strain and wrack the form is attested by the labels the critics so quickly attached to their work: Malraux's 'tragedies', Giono's 'epics', Saint-Exupéry's chivalric 'poetry of flight', Camus's 'allegories'. Further testimony, of a somewhat different kind, is at hand in the tendency of several—Montherlant, Malraux, and

[10] Montherlant's 'crisis' is mentioned by most of his interpreters, and most recently by John Cruickshank, *Montherlant*, pp. 22 ff., discussing *Les Voyageurs traqués*. Bernanos was treated repeatedly for 'angoisse nocturne' and Albert Béguin, in *Bernanos par lui-même*, reports attacks of paralyzing anger also. Saint-Exupéry's fellow officers in World War II became seriously concerned by his compulsive conduct; see 'Indications biographiques', Editions de la Pléiade, p. xxx. For an analysis of Malraux's tendency toward 'shamanistic behaviour' see my *Malraux and the Tragic Imagination*. Simone de Beauvoir reports Sartre's experience with hallucinants in *La Force de l'âge*, p. 216. Camus's periods of 'exaltation lucide et amère' (see 'Biographie', in *Théâtre, Récits, Nouvelles*, Editions de la Pléiade, pp. xxxi ff.) suggest a manic-depressive condition. Milton Hindus's *The Crippled Giant* is an account of a series of conversations with Céline that took place while the latter was still in exile in Denmark; it makes no pretense of scholarly objectivity, but leaves no doubt that the author felt himself to be dealing with a case of mental illness. Students of style and form have tended to pass over the possibility of a relation between mental tensions and style. Stephen Ullman's discussion of Sartre's hallucinated imagery (*Language and Style*, pp. 186–8) is an exception to the rule more or less represented by Pierre Maubrey (*L'Expression de la passion intérieure dans le style de Bernanos romancier*) who attributes to 'internal passion' what may well have been owed to psychic disturbance. See my review, *RR*, LI, no. 2 (Feb. 1960), 152–4.

Céline in particular—to write about heroes curiously like themselves and to surround this central figure with recurrent character-types, such as Malraux's Mythomaniacs, Terrorists, and Policemen or Bernanos's Priests. We may find even more in the difficulty they often experienced in bringing off their most characteristic work, as for example Bernanos with *Monsieur Ouine*.

It is thus not very hard to understand why the disposition of criticism toward their work should be so varied. Their novels frequently violate all our cherished preconceptions about the limits of the form. Their styles are often oracular, prophetic, and—using the word to describe not condemn—incoherent. Imagery is called upon to perform functions rarely required of it in other fiction. Syntactical structures and narrational procedures alike are at times remarkably discontinuous. They challenge, in particular, the interpreter who would like to practice the *critique féconde des beautés* which the late Leo Spitzer[11] said should be the special business of students of form and style.

To deal with the art of such individualistic, not to say idiosyncratic, writers, a position of extreme nominalism urgently commends itself to the student. We are diffident when we refer to their writings as 'novels' and even more so in affirming that they belong to a literary genre with its own history; we admit using such terms mostly for convenience and because we lack better. But our confidence returns when we regard each book as a unique work, the expression of an individual talent less obedient to the laws of a genre and amenable to its norms than capable of generating laws and norms of its own—an object to be studied in itself. The title of this collection, *Style and Temper*, is meant to acknowledge the inherent appeal of this critical position. It is consoling, and mitigates a lingering sense of loss, to think that the author of the *Stilstudien* might perhaps have approved.

But an extreme Crocean, or idealist, attitude ill befits a procedure which proposes to take into account form as well as style and bases analysis on the assumption of a difference between them. 'Style *is* literary form', writes Dr. R. A. Sayce,[12] and in one way his view is unexceptionable. But at the same time, form is style organized for a special purpose and we analyze the organization. Some of the concepts used in analysis are

[11] *Linguistics and Literary History*, p. 128, n. 10: 'Indeed, any *explication de texte*, any philological study, must start with a *critique des beautés*, with the assumption on our part of the perfection of the work . . .'

[12] *Style in French Prose*, p. 6. The full statement is: 'Style is literary form, its values are formal values.'

derived from the contemplation, by many students, of numerous fictions and this, logically, assumes that they have a common character. To talk of point of view (or perspective), distance, characterization, psychological notation, and of techniques like 'free indirect discourse', implicitly admits that the issues of optics, individuation, motive, and so forth recur persistently. For a nominalist of the strict obedience to use them would constitute a paradox, at least on the level of theory.

In practice, when one is actually confronted by the literary work itself, the paradox evaporates. We can see the uniqueness of the work only if we look beyond the work. How, indeed, recognize its uniqueness without comparing it with others? In other words, the awareness of trends and tendencies that attentive reading produces makes us realize that even such various writers as these we are dealing with were faced by similar problems of technique and tended to solve them in similar ways.

What trends and tendencies do we see?

To our present hindsight it appears that a change took place in the typical human situation the novel exhibits: one figure is now allowed to fill the stage, and interest focuses on him and his destiny, rather than on groups, families, or *unanimes*. The individual works out his fate not in rebelling against his clan or, alternatively, in defending it, but in conflict with life itself: even when he takes part in revolution he cares less about changing the world than about his personal relationship with the universe. This is most clearly the case of Sartre's Roquentin, Céline's Bardamu, and Camus's Meursault, but is almost as true of the priests of Bernanos, Saint-Exupéry's Rivière, and Malraux's Kassner. (The latter is the only character in *Le Temps du mépris* permitted to have a name.) The Jamesian formula equating the novel to 'felt life' here contracts to the 'felt life' of a single human being.

The crowning event of such a story is less likely to be an act, though an act is sometimes its consequence, than a moment of particularly acute perception in which hero and reader become aware of the real nature of their human situation. As do all novels, this one works by stripping away appearance and revealing reality; but now the reality is cosmic in implication—whether the hero is Bernanos's *Curé d'Ambricourt* discovering that 'all is Grace' or Sartre's man identifying his own nausea in the park of Bouville. Such terms as 'epiphany' or 'illumination' describe these episodes. It is the combination of this insistence on epiphanies with the narrowing of focus mentioned above which occasions the development of new technical strategies by changing the position of the artist in relation to his materials.

Already before the end of the twenties, although seeming only to exercise the gifts of a sharp satirist with affinities for the role of ironic observer, Montherlant modifies the old formula of romantic-ironic fiction. We still hear a voice, purportedly uninvolved in the action and keeping the distance and detachment of comedy, as it guides the reader in understanding what happens. Often his interventions are direct and undisguised: the narrator-author speaks out in his own voice. But others are produced by variations in tone; indeed, at the end, the juxtapositions of varying tones reveal another and quite different distance, and a sympathy for the character, which are essential to the meaning of the novel. In other words, interventions here are becoming a matter of style.

Underlying such a practice is, of course, the issue of the extent to which the author is to be 'present' in his novel. No law of nature, of course, decrees that he can not be present and speaking in his own name in a novel that eventuates in epiphany, but by and large the novels we are studying tend to make the presence very discreet, through one or two available strategies: either a rigorous restriction of point of view, with such interventions as must occur handled in an inconspicuous style (Malraux, the later Bernanos) or else entrusting narration to the protagonist himself.

The tendency toward the latter solution is marked, and renewed interest in first-person narration becomes increasingly apparent. Céline in *Voyage au bout de la nuit* and *Mort à crédit*, Sartre in *La Nausée*, Bernanos in *Le Journal d'un curé de campagne*, exploit it with noteworthy success; Malraux finally adopts it in the last of his fictions, *Les Noyers de l'Altenburg*; Giono uses it on occasion despite the inherent restraint imposed on his incontinent metaphor-making; Camus never uses anything else, even in *La Peste*—Dr. Rieux, telling his own story as if he were someone else, speaks in a *pseudo*-third person. The relationship between character and reader becomes one of sympathy in the root sense: the latter 'feels life' *with* the narrating character.

This sounds as if there had been a revival of the tradition which extends from Constant's *Adolphe* through Fromentin's *Dominique* to Gide's *Immoraliste*, but the differences from the older *roman de l'individu* are conspicuous. Gide's unhappy hero tells his own story with an elegance of expression which reveals a literary gift and perhaps creates a certain distance between him and the reader. The same can be said of *Dominique* and *Adolphe*—with some allowance made for additional distance which may be owed to changes in sensibility over the intervening years. In contrast, the more recent examples of the 'confessional mode'[13] appear to avoid the formal and literary, as if a human being weighed down by his own humanity could not search for rhetorical effects without sounding insincere, or stuffy, or both. The hero-narrators are far from being literary men. In particular, hero-narrators who are openly represented as writing their accounts (Dr. Rieux, Bernanos's *Curé*) repeatedly disclaim literary intentions.

This brings to light another new stylistic problem: the moments of intense perception which we call epiphanies are moments of intense emotion, also; and since the intensity would naturally be reflected in the language used, the novelist intent on a fiction which involves an epiphany is placed in a truly unique situation: viz., he can hardly hope that the 'zero degree of writing' will lend itself to the essential effect.

Thus we return to one of the oldest critical concepts: 'levels' of style. Writers who may never have heard of Virgil's Wheel are still confronted by the problem of appropriateness. We no longer think of 'high', 'middle', and 'low' styles, and words are no longer banned from the vocabularies associated with specific subjects (as the currency of obscenities in recent writing amply attests), and the one enduring criterion for the use of a given word is that it should not sound strange in the mouth of the user or in the context; but in spite of all this the author must contrive, by manipulation of syntax and figure, appropriate rises and lowerings of tone. Camus's notes are explicit regarding his concern with this subject during the writing of *L'Etranger* and *La Peste*; there is ample evidence, though less direct testimony, of a similar concern in Sartre, Céline, and Bernanos, and at least matter for speculation about it in the case of Malraux.

Baudelaire's old contention, that any writer sets up for himself an obstacle which he must subsequently surmount, provides a pertinent metaphor. The obstacle confronting our novelists was their conception of the novel as the story of a man who by nature would not use a heightened language, yet who tells in his own voice of an experience whose nature requires elevated expression—in achieving which he must not step 'out of character'. It would be simplistic to say that the question was how to be literary without being 'literary', but the phrase is suggestive: they had to attain elevation without resorting to the grand manner.

These trends and tendencies reveal the common concerns of writers

[13] This term is appropriated from Northrop Frye, *The Anatomy of Criticism*. Acceptable as approximate equivalents would be 'roman de l'individu' and even 'pseudo-autobiography'. The older term, 'roman d'analyse', does not describe the modern product accurately.

who in respect to other, less essentially literary matters were frequently miles apart and differed from each other radically. They often differed, also, in their solutions of the literary problems. (Again we are reminded of the uniqueness of each writer and of each work.) The nature of their literary situation, itself, made it inevitable that they should converge repeatedly, and the student who commits himself to any protracted examination of the works finds himself returning again and again to the same issues.

The order in which the papers appear here was dictated by the considerations outlined above. A general discussion of the 'presence' of the novelist in his work and of some of the kinds of intervention which are possible—illustrated in the instance by an examination of a passage from Gide—seemed a useful opening. It is followed by a study of Montherlant both because virtuosity in intervention forms an important part of his immense talent and because scrutiny of his talent throws light on this method of an author's being present in his work.

The paper on the imagery of Saint-Exupéry follows the one on Montherlant because it involves another mode of the author's being present: a highly personal kind of poetry is already visible in the novels, even when Saint-Exupéry avoids intervention, and becomes dominant as soon as he turns from the novel to the personal essay. I believe I am right in recognizing, in connection with his more overt practice of poetry, a preoccupation with recording something like the moments of deep, intense, intuitive, and often irrational perception so important in the work of Proust and Joyce.

The chapter on Malraux then pursues the subject of such epiphanies somewhat further. I have discussed elsewhere[14] this novelist's tendency to tell a story pointing a given moral lesson but to juxtapose with this conclusion a symbolic picture that denies its relevance. Thus, in *La Condition Humaine*, the story itself teaches the rational and prudent reader that the cost of participating in revolution is the ultimate frustration and death of the revolutionary, but the juxtaposed scene of the last moments of Katow's life reveals, even so, that his is the only fully acceptable way to die. The chapter in *L'Espoir* in which the peasants carry the wounded aviators down from the wreck on the mountain has a similar effect. And in *Les Noyers de l'Altenburg* such epiphanies follow one upon another. They are the subjects of the paper.

Bernanos presents certain similarities with Malraux, through a certain incoherence on the level of rational discourse and a certain coherence on the level of image, symbol, and atmosphere, even though his identification

[14] *André Malraux and the Tragic Imagination*, pp. x–xii and *passim*.

of the moment of ultimate perception with the happy death of the Catholic leaves him no room to develop the epiphany. Once again we are aware of the poet's work as well as the work of the novelist.

As a very dramatic example of the writer who discovers a special advantage in first person narration, Bernanos appears again as the subject of one section of the chapter on uses made of this device. So do Céline, Giono, Sartre, and Camus. The topic is one which naturally brings up again the matters of tone, tonal variation, elevation of language, and dramatic characterization, as well as the inevitable one of imagery. And just as inevitably, considerations regarding discontinuity of style and of vision demand attention.

The final paper, on style in the 'Nouveau Roman' and especially the styles of Michel Butor and Claude Simon, is meant to point a contrast, and in doing so reveal to what extent the styles of the slightly older writers had become discontinuous.

Such theorizing and speculation as seemed out of place if included in earlier chapters has been relegated to the place of an epilogue.

CHAPTER ONE

Intervention:
The Presence of the Author

Intervention is not a wholly satisfactory term because it brings to mind the novels of authors who intrude obviously in their stories: those who invite the reader to join in watching the puppets dance and insist that what he is watching is art not life, even when they intend him to feel that if this is art it is life also. Such a term deflects attention from the important truth, verifiable by inspection, that there are other ways for an author to take up a position somewhere between the reader and the action. Not even Flaubert, with his remark about wanting to be in his work only in the sense that God is in creation—present everywhere but nowhere visible—disappeared from sight completely.

We know what he meant: he intended nothing to obtrude from the texture of his fiction that could be attributed directly to the author; no opinion, affirmation, or explanation was to divert attention from creation to creator. Yet what he was really talking about was the *effect* produced upon the reader of *Madame Bovary* or *L'Education sentimentale*. Minute inspection of the texts reveals his 'failures', those openings in the fabric where the worker shows through: no one takes as anything but the expression of the author's private feelings that last line of the description of the old peasant woman called up before the crowd at the agricultural fair to receive a medal (value: twenty-five francs) for faithful drudgery—'Ainsi se tenait devant ces bourgeois épanouis ce demi-siècle de servitude'.[1] But, at the same time, few readers would feel that this remark about a half-century of bondage compromised Flaubert's effect of non-intervention.

Marcel Proust sums up Flaubert's achievement very happily without using the word intervention at all: 'Dans le style de Flaubert, par exemple, toutes les parties de la réalité sont converties en une même substance, aux surfaces d'un miroitement monotone. Aucune impureté n'est restée.

---

[1] Ed. du Centenaire, p. 163.

Les surfaces sont devenues réfléchissantes. Toutes les choses s'y peignent, mais par reflet, sans en altérer la substance homogène. Tout ce qui était différent a été converti et absorbé'.[2] Proust is speaking in tropes, of course. This substance and these surfaces are aspects of what Flaubert thought of simply as style. The words describe the *effect* of the style on a perceptive and attentive reader.

He becomes more literal and explicit when he turns from what Flaubert did not do to what Balzac, he affirms, did habitually: intrude in his own name and voice upon the action of his novels. Proust says that Balzac is forever explaining something or proffering some comment and that the explanations and comments are especially regrettable because they so often unmask Balzac's fundamental, naive vulgarity.[3]

The aesthetic ideal in question here, of unbroken 'surfaces' and 'substance', was doubtless Proust's as much as it was Flaubert's. Germaine Brée has written very felicitously of 'the arresting continuity of the solitary and persistent voice which out of the night creates a world'[4] and what she means is entirely clear: this voice *is* Proust's narration and *is* his style; it is never interrupted, and the critical concept of intervention has no purpose here. He is 'absent' from his work in Flaubert's way, present but invisible because everywhere present in the same degree.

It is doubtless an index of Flaubert's long-lived prestige that the ideal should have persisted as long as it did, that it should have haunted the Naturalists, and that we should be so aware of occasions when some novelist appeared to discard it. Yet the opposite procedure, of the artist's calling attention in some way or other to his presence in the work, offers too many possibilities for it to remain forever unexploited. Thus it may be an index of the decline of Flaubert's prestige that André Gide should

[2] *Contre Sainte-Beuve*, p. 207. See also 'A propos du "style" de Flaubert', *NRF*, 7e année, no. 76 (Jan. 1920), 72–90, reprinted in A. Thibaudet, *Réflexions sur la critique*, pp. 249–63. For an account of the background of these articles, see Douglas W. Alden, 'Proust and the Flaubert controversy', *RR*, XXVIII, no. 3 (Oct. 1937), 230–40.

[3] Compare Joseph Warren Beach, *The Twentieth-Century Novel*, p. 328: 'He relies too much on formal exposition. He imagines that if he has described a character we can see him; that if he spends three or four thousand words telling us about a character, then we know all about him . . .' This was written not about Balzac but about Dreiser, but Dreiser himself has recorded (*A Book about Myself*, pp. 410–12) learning to write novels by reading Balzac in the Pittsburgh Public Library. It is also relevant that the late Geoffroy Atkinson could prepare the five volumes of his *Idées de Balzac d'après la Comédie Humaine* by clipping with scissors, so little was the material sunk into what Proust calls 'the surface'.

[4] *Marcel Proust*, p. 4.

make capital of his own presence in his two most considerable fictions, *Les Caves du Vatican* and *Les Faux-monnayeurs*.

For present purposes, at least, we may apply the term intervention to any instance of the novelist's revealing his presence, by whatever means, so long as he does so intentionally and in view of attaining some literary effect.

Addicted readers of Gide's prose probably remember best such interventions as the one in *Les Caves du Vatican* where the author breaks in to remonstrate with his hero: 'Lafcadio, mon ami, vous donnez dans un fait divers et ma plume vous abandonne. N'attendez pas que je rapporte les propos interrompus d'une foule, les cris . . .' Such an intervention stands out among the myriad others in *Les Caves* simply because the author addresses his character rather than the reader himself; the use of the apostrophe[5] is inherently comic and thus stays in the memory. More often the device is, more simply, to address a rhetorical question to the reader and then answer it directly: 'Ces paroles si mesurées, si sages, sauront-elles calmer Anthime? Oui, pendant les deux premiers services (au reste le dîner, bon mais simple, n'a que trois plats) et tandis que la conversation familiale musardera le long des sujets non épineux'.[6]

These are far from being isolated examples. Several others[7] are almost equally conspicuous. We remember that the story ends with a truly egregious one, in which the author professes not to know what Lafcadio, after the night spent with Geneviève and having now to decide among surrendering to the police, submitting to the discipline of the Church, or running away, will bring himself to do. Such interventions stand out against a stylistic background that admits numerous less immediately noticeable ones; the fundamentally conversational tone makes small asides, parentheses, adjectives that express a judgment on the part of the author seem entirely natural.

[5] p. 723. The comic mechanism is, probably, inherent in the form itself: in a novel of the kind which, since *Vanity Fair*, has treated its characters as puppets, now one of these creatures has suddenly to be reproved for generating an energetic life of his own.

[6] p. 694. Gide's facetious tone has momentarily disappeared. See, in contrast, p. 702: 'Arrête, ô ma plume imprudente! . . .'

[7] For example, pp. 685–6: 'Ici, malgré tout mon désir de ne relater que l'essentiel, je ne puis passer sous silence la loupe d'Anthime Armand-Dubois. Car, tant que je n'aurai pas plus sûrement appris à démêler l'accidentel du nécessaire, qu'exigerais-je de ma plume sinon exactitude et rigueur?'

Up to this point in the discussion it has seemed appropriate to refer to the intervening voice as that of the author or of Gide. But what, exactly, do we mean? Surely this is not Gide the much exhibited, private personality of the *Journal* with its familiar uncertainty and tentativeness. The jaunty tone, the friendly but essentially critical disposition toward the characters, suggest a sort of assumed *persona*, a role. One thinks occasionally of a *Prince des Sots*, leading the revels and showing the audience what attitude to take toward the characters, who will resume his own everyday, bourgeois character when the fun is over. This speaker says 'je' but he is neither the 'je' of the *Journal* nor, as we shall see eventually, in all respects the 'je' of *Les Faux-monnayeurs*. The more we contemplate it, the more we see that Gide is exploiting a device of considerable, and varied, literary value.

He calls his book, we remember, a 'sotie', and everything about this *ad hoc* form makes intervention appropriate. It serves notice on the reader that he is being offered an illusion of reality, not an 'absorbed' and re-created one, and that the author intends to capitalize upon the organic relation between fiction and comedy. In form and purpose these interventions are as unlike as possible those Proust complains about in Balzac. The latter's do not define a special attitude toward the materials, one out of many which could equally well be taken. What the reader is told to see in the portrait of Sophie Gamard[8] is what any observer should see—with Balzac's help—in the archetype of the *vieille fille*; his intention, Balzac insists repeatedly, is to make his exterior world more completely real by relating it more fully to the life going on around the reader. Gide's mockery sets a tone and invites the reader into a gallery of grotesques.

But this maneuvering, at the same time, serves a purpose considerably more complex than has so far appeared.

> Je ne sais trop que penser de Carola Venitequa. Ce cri qu'elle vient de pousser me laisse supposer que le cœur, chez elle, n'est pas encore trop profondément corrompu. Ainsi parfois, au sein même de l'abjection, tout à coup se découvrent d'étranges délicatesses sentimentales, comme croît une fleur azurée au milieu d'un tas de fumier. Essentiellement soumise et dévouée, Carola, ainsi que tant d'autres femmes, avait besoin d'un directeur. Abandonnée de Lafcadio, elle s'était aussitôt lancée à la recherche de son premier amant, Protos— par défi, par dépit, pour se venger. Elle avait de nouveau connu de dures heures—et Protos ne l'avait pas plus tôt retrouvée qu'il en avait fait sa chose, de nouveau. Car Protos aimait dominer.

[8] *Le Curé de Tours*, current Garnier ed., p. 55.

Un autre que Protos aurait pu relever, réhabiliter cette femme. Il eût d'abord fallu le vouloir. On eût dit, au contraire, que Protos prenait à tâche de l'avilir. Nous avons vu les services honteux que ce bandit réclamait d'elle; il semblait, à vrai dire, que ce fût sans trop de reluctance que cette femme s'y pliait; mais une âme qui se révolte contre l'ignominie de son sort, souvent ses premiers sursauts demeurent inaperçus d'elle-même; ce n'est qu'à la faveur de l'amour que le regimbement secret se révèle. Carola s'éprenait-elle d'Amédée? Il serait téméraire de le prétendre; mais, au contact de cette pureté, sa corruption s'était émue; et le cri que j'ai rapporté, indubitablement, avait jailli du cœur.[9]

Gide's harlot has just told her lover, the arch-crook Protos, that he is not to harm the feeble little Amédée Fleurissoire. 'A celui-ci je ne veux pas que tu fasses du mal'. Her breaking the normal syntactical order to begin the sentence with 'à celui-ci' makes it clear that not only is there some danger of his being harmed, but also that she knows of others whom Protos has in fact harmed already. This is the cry that prompts the two paragraphs quoted.

Just previously Gide has referred to the girl simply as Carola; here she is called by both Christian name and surname, and the effect is one of disengaging the narrator, as if he were moving away from the action in order to contemplate it; his relationship to her has become more formal. At the same time, mention of the surname emphasizes her status: only a whore could be named Venitequa. And the narrator also emerges from the anonymity of the third person to become the 'je' we have already recognized in other interventions.

But this *persona* is by no means simple; speaking in turn are an uncertain and somewhat puzzled psychologist who is in the dark as to motives, a moralist not a bit in the dark as to moral values, and someone whose role is confined to stating facts. Thus the first two sentences profess the uncertainty of the moralist who does not know what feeling has brought out Carola's cry. Then the moralist speaks, out of a knowledge of human nature, with marked confidence, observing that sensitivity of sentiment can turn up in the strangest places. And next the stater of facts brings us up to date about how Carola happens to be here and under the domination of Protos. This speaker gives way to the moralist at the beginning of the new paragraph: the ordinary human (as he knows humanity) would have been able to redeem the girl. But the psychologist

---

[9] p. 787. I am grateful to Miss W. Jane Bancroft for suggestions regarding the analysis of this passage.

again expresses uncertainty: *one would have said* that Protos was making a conscious effort to corrupt her. The moralist now judges as evil what Protos has made her do and calls him a bandit, but the psychologist adds that Carola's resistance has *seemed* low. Now the moralist's general knowledge of humanity prompts his remark that the first steps toward virtue are often unconsciously taken, but the psychologist has the last word: love may not have been Carola's motive, although the cry had without doubt come from the heart.

Here a reader whose mind tended toward the literal might protest. If the novelist can permit himself to know what kind of people his characters are, why can he not also concede himself enough insight to understand the meaning of what they do? Is not Gide being excessively arch? If he knows that right is right, wrong is wrong, and Protos is a bandit, why shouldn't he know also whether Carola was moved by love for Amédée? It is at this point that the complexity of Gide's tactic reveals itself.

Beneath the elegant fooling there lies Gide's deep conviction that the traditional French novel does not tell the truth about human nature. The character is established for what he is in the first chapter, and his behavior then must be consistent with what was there revealed about him, forever after. He is the prisoner of his own psychology and as entrapped by it as are the people in Zola's novels by the determinants of environment and heredity. Tradition requires him to behave 'in character', and in so doing denies the fullness of human freedom.

Seventy pages after the passage quoted, Gide has Lafcadio push Amédée off the train for no better reason than that a light flashes in the darkened countryside before he finishes counting to twelve. His hero is obedient only to the whim of his own free nature, and there is an arbitrariness about his action which often surrounds those of ordinary human beings— but never those of the characters of Stendhal or Paul Bourget. He was finally to admit that the so-called 'gratuitous act' is possible only in the imagination and that one does not find completely unmotivated conduct in human nature. But this does not imply the concession that the motive must be rationally comprehensible. Freedom for the human being remains that of being inconsistent or unpredictable in the way that, according to Gide, the characters of Dostoevsky are so.[10]

A sharp ear is probably not deceived in hearing differences in tone in the various roles of the passage we have been inspecting. It is the moralist who unwinds the somewhat sententious remark which ends with the figure about the flower growing from the dunghill. The adjective, attached to the

---

[10] See Mischa Harry Fayer, *Gide, Freedom, and Dostoevsky, passim.*

flower, 'azurée', may strike one as over-elegant; the simile itself is clearly more elegant than pristine; the double inversion in the syntax: 'ainsi parfois, au sein même de l'abjection ... tout à coup se découvrent d'étranges délicatesses sentimentales, comme croît une fleur azurée ...', would seem to be intentionally elaborate.

The total effect, surely, is one of considerable formality and perhaps of stiffness. This is already suggested in the leisurely rhythm of the opening of the sentence, with the obligatory pause after 'ainsi' and the lengthening of the vowel in 'même', both re-enforced by the sense as well as the phonetics. It is also the moralist who uses a noteworthy anacoluthon—'mais une âme qui se révolte contre l'ignominie de son sort,/souvent ses premiers sursauts demeurent inaperçus'—which again strikes a note of portentousness. The reader who suspects Gide of intending to make his moralist sound somewhat over-solemn, and of thus revealing thereby a somewhat satirical disposition toward him, may not be entirely wrong.

One would be ready to admire such strategies even if their whole value lay in being funny. *Les Caves du Vatican* is, after all, a comic piece.[11] The irony that inheres in it requires a certain psychic distance between characters and reader, and one effective way of opening such a space is for the novelist to insert his own *persona* between the two.

But no experienced reader needs be told that there are further reasons here for admiration. We have seen the novelist, even in his playful mood, connecting this cry of a prostitute with his own concern about human freedom. Despite his antic disposition we discover his characteristic seriousness: he still knows a hawk from a handsaw. In short, his intervention connects an incident in a frivolous tale of a character unable to tell a hotel from a whorehouse with one of the informing ideas of his own life's work.

In *Les Faux-monnayeurs* various new factors complicate our discussion. By the kind of uncertain count which alone is possible in such matters, instances of direct, overt intervention are no more numerous than in *Les Caves*. And the reader is perhaps less aware of them, although this may mean only that he is distracted by other aspects of the fiction and does not notice them. But in any case, the structure of the novel introduces additional ways for the author to be present in his work, and so does the style in which the narration is occasionally conducted.

The most conspicuous of these additional ways is, of course, the inven-

[11] The fact is one which critics have almost unanimously overlooked. A luminous exception is Albert Guerard (*André Gide*, p. 128): 'Perhaps only the maligned casual reader sees that *Les Caves du Vatican* is above all a very funny book'.

tion of the character Edouard. Gide's longstanding delight in a novel that is, in part, about a novelist who is treating the same materials—and meeting difficulty in doing so—is as old as *Paludes*, and the novelistic usefulness of the device is clearly visible in *Les Caves du Vatican*. But Edouard is permitted to be a surrogate for the author instead of a caricature of the kind of writer the author would not care to be. He is often entrusted with the point of view and, through the excerpts from his diary, with the actual narration. Some of the ideas he expresses, for example the one about the 'pure' novel, we know to have been on Gide's mind also.[12]

But he is a disavowable surrogate. We cannot say that Edouard 'is' Gide: among other differences, he does not bring *his* novel off. The consequent ambiguity multiplies the perspectives opened up by construction 'en abîme'. As an autonomous character Edouard brings about much that takes place in the story; at the same time, the misfortunes that might never have happened but for his curiosity about people, his willingness to meddle in their lives, and his wanting to influence the young, make him look from time to time like an instrument devised for self-criticism by a particularly elusive creator. It is thus hardly easier to affirm, without qualification, that he 'is not' Gide than that he 'is'.

Meanwhile the style of the parts of the story narrated by the anonymous 'je' has its own peculiar quality. It falls frequently into the kind of present tense that reports an action at the moment when it takes place. It places the reader upon the scene, and he is not there alone: at his shoulder he hears a voice using the first-person plural repeatedly, saying for example that since father and son have no more to say to each other *we* may as well leave them or that even though a character is walking rapidly *we* should follow him.[13] In these moments the voice is likely to be conversational rather than literary, or to mix the tones.

C'est l'heure où, dans une triste chambre d'hôtel, Laura, sa maîtresse d'hier, après avoir longtemps pleuré, longtemps gémi, va s'endormir. Sur le pont du navire qui le ramène en France, Edouard, à la première clarté de l'aube, relit la lettre qu'il a reçue d'elle, lettre plaintive et où elle appelle au secours. Déjà, la douce rive de son pays natal est en vue, mais, à travers la brume, il faut un œil exercé pour la voir. Pas un nuage au ciel, où le regard de Dieu va sourire. La paupière de l'horizon rougissant déjà se soulève. Comme il va faire chaud dans Paris! Il est temps de retrouver Bernard. Voici que dans le lit d'Olivier il s'éveille.[14]

[12] See *Journal des faux-monnayeurs*, p. 62 ff.

[13] p. 959: 'Encore qu'il marche vite, suivons-le'.

[14] pp. 974–5. The tone may be explained in part by the fact that the passage occurs at the end of a chapter.

The passage is very often quoted as illustrating the ubiquity of Gide's narrator—who enjoys a freedom unavailable otherwise even to God, since he has both the power to be everywhere at once and see everything, but only if he so pleases. But the way it moves from one place and character to another is hardly more revealing than the movement of the prose itself. Most of the sentences are, almost ostentatiously, literary. The parentheses and repetitions are clearly not part of the spoken language, and neither are the figures involving the smile of God, and the eyelid of the horizon. But in the exclamation about how hot it will be in Paris we return to spoken language and are reminded that we are listening to a voice. The effect of 'comme' is to make what would otherwise be a neutral and impersonal statement into a personal, though banal, remark. The literary tone has been broken off long enough for the narrator to call attention to himself before restoring somewhat the other tone by displacing the adverbial phrase in the final sentence.

At other times, the narrator is very aware that he, like Edouard, is writing a book. He remarks, in a passage inserted between long excerpts from the latter's diary, that its principal purpose is to let in a little air.[15] In another he explicitly recognizes the presence of a reader.[16] Elsewhere he produces a novelist's reason for cutting short a scene: since the conversation continued to be witty there is no point in reproducing it.[17] Finally, this tendency culminates in the chapter, amply discussed in every commentary on Gide, where he puts his task aside for a space and, addressing the reader, discusses various possible ways of bringing his story to its end.[18]

In addition, most of the varieties of intervention appearing in *Les Caves du Vatican* recur in *Les Faux-monnayeurs*, serving the same purposes. The narrator has his moments of asserting his ignorance, or uncertainty, about a character's motives. One difference must be noted: although in several instances this is the case, this convenient 'nilscience' is also called into play in matters of fact.[19] We are thus no longer justified

[15] p. 1023: 'Passons. Tout ce que j'ai dit ci-dessus n'est que pour mettre un peu d'air entre les pages de ce journal. A présent que Bernard a bien respiré, retournons-y...'

[16] p. 1045: 'Je veux indiquer, pour l'édification du lecteur...'

[17] p. 1050. The scene involves Passavant and Lilian, for both of whom the narrator professes distaste.

[18] pp. 1108-11. For a particularly perceptive discussion of the passage see Justin O'Brien, 'Gide's Fictional Technique', *YFS*, no. 7 (Spring 1951), 81–90.

[19] For example, p. 960. The term 'nilscience' I owe to Justin O'Brien, although I am unable to find it in his writings on Gide.

in insisting on a connection between the practice and his ideas about the psychological freedom of fictional characters.

At least on one occasion he suspends his story long enough to apostrophize a character, Bernard, just as in *Les Caves* he apostrophizes Lafcadio.[20] Once he turns aside to remark to the reader that he finds another character, in the instance Lady Griffith when she is in a certain mood, extremely irritating.[21] In his own name he passes summary judgment on the perverse nature and behavior of Passavant.[22] He also contrives to intrude his own judgments through the choice of an adjective inserted in an otherwise neutral context.[23] One character, Laura, he judges by quoting a passage from Montaigne.[24]

The procedures themselves have not greatly changed; the reader who feels a difference in his own response to the interventions in *Les Faux-monnayeurs* must look for the reason in the contrast between the fundamental moods of the two books. Although he may be a bit frivolous from time to time, the narrator is not this time in any clowning mood. This is not to accuse him of solemnity, of course; but we do have to observe that he is not so intent, in this later story, to add a performance of his own to those offered by his characters. In a book of broader canvas, his one final attempt to write a full-scale novel, it is probably to be expected that Gide would not treat intervention as an exclusively comic device. His fundamental seriousness, hidden below the fooling in *Les Caves*, is here much nearer the surface.

This might be enough to explain why one is more prone to identify the narrating *persona* of *Les Faux-monnayeurs* with Gide than is the case with the narrator of *Les Caves*. But another factor strengthens the temptation to do so. We recognize, as we read the second book, devices which are already familiar from the reading of the first; both are Gide's; we can hardly help feeling them Gide's own rather than those of a *persona* invented in view of one specific work. And we can only wonder how we would have been affected, as readers, if Gide had held to his original plan of putting the narration of *Les Faux-monnayeurs* in the mouth of his old hero, Lafcadio.

[20] p. 995. In both cases the tone may be described as pseudopaternal.

[21] p. 973: 'Lilian m'agace un peu quand elle fait ainsi l'enfant'.

[22] p. 1046: '. . . . ce suppôt damné qu'est Passavant'.

[23] For example, p. 1239: '. . . dans cette abominable histoire, ce qui me paraît le plus monstrueux . . .'

[24] pp. 1076–7: ' "Les bienfaits, dit Tacite à travers Montaigne, ne sont agréables que tant que l'on peut s'acquitter"; et sans doute cela n'est vrai que pour les âmes nobles, mais Laura certes était de celles-ci'.

It is easy to forget that when Gide published *Les Faux-monnayeurs*, Paul Bourget was still alive, that Maurice Barrès, like Anatole France, had been dead hardly two years, and Marcel Proust only four. Yet some awareness of the historical context is needed to reveal the nature and dimensions of Gide's accomplishment. The same society that Barrès and Bourget defended in their demonstrations was the one, in all major respects, that Proust pictured in its accelerating decline and that Gide's novels helped liquidate. All four have a place in the history of the so-called 'novel of ideas'. (If Proust's banishment of ideas from the novel were to be taken literally no one would read him. As a matter of fact Walter A. Strauss has extracted a generous number from the matrix of *A la recherche du temps perdu* for use in his study of Proust as literary critic.[25]) In the novels of Bourget, as in the *Déracinés* of Barrès, the central idea becomes something to write *about* and somehow to be exemplified: the *Déracinés* proves that it is better to stay on home soil than to come to Paris. With Proust the idea of, say, involuntary memory is absorbed in incidents like the one of the *madeleine*. And we have seen Gide's idea of one kind of human freedom expressed simply in the way he lets a character behave, and in his disposition—one of partial ignorance or of uncertainty— toward the sources of the behaviour. The usefulness of intervention, in this respect, would be hard to contest.

Most of the novels to be mentioned in the remaining chapters of this discussion testify to the continuing power of ideas and to their continuing importance to the novelists. But, with one exception, the authors will not permit themselves to be openly present in their works; instead, their presence will be felt through a persistent, often dominant poetic tone (Saint-Exupéry, Bernanos) or else through the use of a protagonist whose character incarnates and interprets their feeling of the relationship between the self and the cosmos. They do so in a manner which has implications as to both form and style.

Meanwhile, the exception just noted is Henry de Montherlant.

[25] *Proust and Literature, passim*. It is, however, true that the bulk of the material Professor Strauss has used comes from the nonfictional, more or less incidental writings.

C

CHAPTER TWO

Montherlant's Interventions[1]

Yves Gandon's study of Montherlant in *Le Démon du style*[2] long ago recognized the opening pages of *Les Célibataires* as a pastiche of the typical nineteenth-century novel before Flaubert and, more specifically, of the novel as practiced by Balzac—something which the title Montherlant gave his work also vigorously suggests. The identification is too persuasive to be in danger of serious challenge. The picture of old Elie de Coëtquidan, standing on one foot like a crane while he reads his newspaper by the light from a shop window, is presented as being what any observer whosoever would have seen if only he had been in the right place at the right time; the detailed enumeration of the contents of the old man's pockets assumes both an omniscient and an omnipresent author; and the novelist's procedure constitutes one of those extended metonymies that Roman Jakobson has identified as characterizing traditional realism.[3] If M. Gandon's reader experiences any hesitation at all in accepting his conclusion it centers around the question of why Montherlant should have gone to the trouble of elaborating a pastiche of Balzac: the latter, after all, has been the subject of no few pastiches before this one, some of them very distinguished performances, and one wonders how the novelist expected to profit.

A plausible answer, which at least has the merit of not contradicting M. Gandon, is that through the pastiche Montherlant was able to establish a fundamental tone for the novel as a whole, corresponding to the mood which the reader is supposed to accept, a kind of basis for orchestration: all the other tones the novel achieves are to be understood as departures from this one and in reference to it—the total orchestration to be understood as containing the meaning of the novel.

---

[1] Some of the material of this chapter first appeared as 'The Climax of Montherlant's *Bestiaires*', *RR*, XLIII, no. 4 (Dec. 1952), 266–71.

[2] pp. 189–201.

[3] 'Two Aspects of language and two types of aphasic disturbance', in Roman Jakobson and Morris Halle, *Fundamentals of Language*, pp. 80–1; the chapter is by Professor Jakobson alone.

The conventions of the novel as Balzac understood them permit and almost require constant, one-way communication between author and reader. *Les Célibataires* is one of those novels which derive their vitality from the presence of their author. His interventions vary from those in which the speaker is identified as the authorial 'nous' to the kind, far more frequent of course, contrived simply through manipulations of style. At times, the latter take the form of a comment, made such by the choice of an adjective, of the type: 'Il eut plus tard un autre mouvement *de bonne race*' (p. 767), or by a phrase suffixed to the main sentence such as: 'Ce sacrifice fut entièrement perdu, *en bon sacrifice qu'il était*' (p. 767). Most of Montherlant's interventions, though effective in keeping the reader constantly aware of their author's general philosophy, are as brief as these; only a few are long, like Balzac's. And while most are overt, in Balzac's manner, there are some whose nature is not readily apparent and require a certain alertness in the reader if he is to recognize them. One of these last is of signal importance for understanding the story:

Dehors continuait la nuit sans histoire. Toute la forêt craquelait sous le vent et le froid. Les crapauds endormis battaient au fond du feuillard secoués par leur cœur trop fort. Les renards dormaient dans leurs tanières, le museau sur l'échine l'un de l'autre, ravis par leur puanteur; et les sangliers dans leurs bauges, rêvant à la glace étoilée qu'ils avaient léchée à la lumière du soir. Dans les souillats récents l'eau se congelait à nouveau, et la boue durcissait, alentour, sur les troncs d'arbres où les biches et les cerfs s'étaient frottés. Mais au fond du ciel clair, au-dessus des immobilités tapies, les oies sauvages passaient toujours, les pattes collées au ventre, soutenues par le vent, parmi les myriades d'insectes des hauteurs, le long de la grande route migratrice, semblable aux routes invisibles qu'il y a sur la mer pour les vaisseaux, ou à celles que suivent les astres. Ces bandes-ci volaient en V, chacune des passagères touchant presque l'autre, sauf trois d'entre elles qui volaient isolées, sans qu'on comprît pourquoi. La force incroyable de leur vol faisait là-haut le bruit de trombe que fait un peloton cycliste sur la piste d'un vélodrome. Quelquefois le V se fragmentait, et les tronçons continuaient dans le même sens. Puis ils se ressoudaient, attiré les uns vers les autres par une sorte d'attraction magnétique, tandis qu'un autre courant d'attraction entraînait tout le volier vers le sud, comme l'aiguille de la boussole ou la baguette du sourcier. Mais toujours les trois dissidentes volaient à l'écart, singulières et rebelles, pareilles à des pensées profondes (p. 903).

This passage unexpectedly interrupts the narrative toward its end, in the penultimate chapter of the book, after the much down-trodden Léon de Coantré has discovered that he is ill. During the afternoon he has been to see his doctor and has closed the door on his last chance of being helped, by walking out of the doctor's waiting room in a rage of injured dignity because he has been made to wait endlessly with the peasants who are his fellow patients. He has also been abandoned by his rich uncle, who has sent him out to live in this hostile countryside so that the family will not be embarrassed by his poverty and his eccentricities. After he has returned from the doctor's to the porter's lodge of his uncle's estate, where he has been allowed to live, he has found the fire out, has eaten poorly from tin cans with his coat and hat still on, and then crawled into bed, still fully dressed, because he is cold. He does not yet know how soon he is going to die.

On the way home he has seen the first flock of migrant geese and stopped to watch their passage. He has followed them out of sight and the thoughts have gone through his mind that they are free, that they have no worries about money, and that they are on the way to lands of sunshine.

From this point to the end of the chapter, passages narrating his last hours there in the hovel alternate with others in which successive flights of geese pass overhead in the night. Léon has been so stirred by the passage of the first flock that before he goes to bed, as we have seen him do, he listens for more. He hears none, and the second flock goes over after he has fallen asleep. He awakes after a while with the idea of putting himself in the hospital at Le Havre and then lies thinking vaguely of how comfortable he will be there. And then his mind turns back to the flock he has seen, confusing his own hope with theirs.

There follows another description of the migrating birds, almost a page in length, which is *not* represented as being imagined by the dying man.

> Elles s'étaient assemblées il y avait deux jours, dans une agitation sacrée ... Elles savaient la dureté épuisante du voyage ... Mais rien de tout cela ne les rebutait ... Car au-delà il y avait les cols des Pyrénées, où la pluie et la brume cesseraient brusquement, comme si une paroi aérienne leur faisait obstacle; au-delà il y avait l'Espagne odorante; au-delà les eaux vertes et les eaux bleues de Gibraltar, se côtoyant sans se confondre; et Tanger à la gorge bleuâtre, tourterelle sur l'épaule de l'Afrique; et plus loin les étangs chauds et roses, dormant leur paresse enflammée. Et elles allaient, ne voulant plus s'arrêter, s'arrêtant tout juste le temps de boire et de lustrer leurs plumes dans un point d'eau, pressées, pressées, comme si elles savaient bien qu'on peut mourir pour une minute de trop qui n'est pas du bonheur (p. 905).

In the paragraph following this one, Léon, now referred to as *M. de* Coantré rather than by his Christian name, sits up in bed with his eyes dilated, 'like a bat nailed against a wall', and dies.

One may hesitate over the question, whether these passages make up one unified but twice interrupted whole or three smaller compositions on the same general theme. One observes a development in treatment: there is a marked decrease in the immediacy of the imagery as they proceed. In the first appearance of the geese, when Léon stops on his way home to watch them fly over him and on out of sight, the visual element is very strong: as the flight changes direction and pivots as if around the fixed part of a hinge, so that the birds display their bellies instead of their side-plumage, their dominant color changes from a brownish to an ashen gray. The next return to the subject is less about the birds than about the straightness of their flight; the visual becomes correspondingly less compelling, and although there is an auditory image—'le bruit de trombe', etc.—the comparison evokes not so much the geese as an indoor bicycle race; to know what they sounded like we need never have seen a goose. And the third passage deals so largely with the animal instincts of the flock, and the delights toward which they are flying, that no direct perception of the geese is present at all. Admittedly, the difference in treatment can be felt.

Even so, the three passages do have a kind of continuity, and, in addition, they are unified by a common tone. There can be no doubt that Montherlant intended this prose to be 'elevated', at least in comparison with the tone of the rest of the chapter. Witness the similes that crowd the passage. In the passage *not* quoted here the flight is likened to a long, undulating ribbon, and this in turn to a flying carpet from the Arabian Nights or to an airborne serpent. And the course they take is like the invisible tracks of ships on the sea, or the paths of the stars. Here we have had the noise of their wings compared to the roar of bicycle tires on a racetrack. Something pulls them toward the south as if they were a compass needle or the wand of a water-finder. Three birds fly by themselves, separated and unconforming, like deep thoughts. Tangier, with her blueish breast, is a wild dove on the shoulder of Africa.

It must be conceded at once that such figures are not the work of a compulsive maker of images. They appeal to the intelligence, not to the sensual imagination. No one has ever seen geese that in any sense looked like 'deep thoughts'. The figure is an incitement to reverie and meditation, whose power lies in its suggestiveness. The undulations in the line of birds *make one think of*, not see, the air serpent or the magic carpet; the same is true of the sea lanes, the compass, and the dowser's hazel. Even the equation of Africa with a woman and Tangiers with an iridescent bird sitting on her shoulder (if indeed this is what Montherlant means his reader to see) requires some effort of our imagination; it surely does not leap spontaneously to the mind's eye.

But it is unlikely that Montherlant is aiming at an effect of spontaneity here. His intention seems, rather, the contrast in tones.

Here is a passage, adjacent to these others, which does not involve the migrating geese: 'Dans le fond de la salle, sa houppelande sur les épaules (il avait toujours froid), son feutre sur la tête (pour se distinguer de ses voisins, en étant aussi rustre qu'eux), il voyait ces grossiers au comptoir, avec leurs cris, leur effrayante santé, leurs panses à planter le couteau dedans, leurs dents tellement vertes que ce n'étaient pas des dentures, c'étaient des jardins' (p. 898).

The contrast between this prose and that in the passage about the geese could hardly be more marked. The use of parentheses to toss in casual explanations is conversational and relaxed. The use of the preposition in the phrase qualifying the fat paunches appears oftener in speech than in writing. The image involved by it, like the one comparing teeth with green gardens, is not meant, surely, to be elegant. The general level of dignity is close to what, in looking at the opening pages of the novel and the description of old Elie de Coëtquidan reading by the light of the shop window, we called the fundamental tone of *Les Célibataires*.

The tonal contrasts, at this important juncture in Montherlant's narrative, occur repeatedly, and the alternation of levels can hardly be unintentional. Yet nothing in the logic of the narrative itself requires it: Léon de Coantré could easily have died without the obbligato concerning the flight of migrant birds. What keeps the elevated passages from being functionless bravura is that, as has already been suggested, they offer Montherlant an additional means of being present in his book and of defining his own relation to his story. But why this controlling need to be present and to define?

Montherlant himself has protested, somewhat wryly, that critics have seen self-portraiture only in those of his characters who have something unpleasant about them.[4] He does not deny that self-portraits are to be found in his works. His complaint is simply that if a character is revealed

---

[4] He returns to this theme repeatedly, especially after 1948, in newspaper articles replying to adverse criticism. See also 'Postface', *Demain il fera jour*, p. 127.

to be a relatively decent sort, the critics dismiss all possibility of a resemblance with the author. We may take his position in the matter to authorize our searching the novels for pictures of himself.

His injunction to fairness applies more pressingly as the works progress. Alban de Bricoule, in *Le Songe*, is a young athlete who becomes a soldier, and, since his creator was a sprinter and football player before becoming an infantryman and being seriously wounded in the First World War, the parallel between artist and model is clear. The central figure of *Les Bestiaires*, also named Alban de Bricoule, is a barely post-adolescent schoolboy who has somehow persuaded his normally conservative and protective family to let him go to Spain and try fighting bulls; his similarity with the Montherlant who attended Sainte-Croix de Neuilly, contrived to spend vacations in Spain, and ultimately got severely gored in the bull ring, is incontestable. It is doubtful if either character would impress most readers as anything but amiable: both are young, and various traits—their egotism, for example—are probably excusable in view of their youth. In any case, Montherlant has acknowledged the element of autobiography in the two novels and thus absolves us of any unfairness in this instance.[5]

Costals, the protagonist of the four novels of the series called *Les Jeunes Filles*, is a less simple case. His misogyny, egotism, and a certain self-complacency may destroy for many readers what others feel to be his interest and charm. Even though Montherlant has defended behavior like that of Costals in other writings, one might hesitate to make the identification: the traits so readily excusable in the young seem less so when they have hardened into a character on the verge of middle age. Furthermore, the author has not acknowledged the relationship.

On the other hand, Jeanne Sandelion seems to speak in a tone of authority in *Montherlant et les femmes* to the effect that the resemblance between Costals's disposition toward women and Montherlant's is in no way coincidental.[6] Her testimony may be taken as grounds for believing that if young Alban de Bricoule is a fictional transposition of the novelist as the latter imagines himself to have been between the ages of fifteen and twenty-five, Costals has something in his personality of an older, more experienced Montherlant.

[5] The acknowledgment is implicit in his having reprinted excerpts from newspaper references to his adventures in the bull ring, as a sort of coda to his novel, pp. 582–3. For a condensed discussion of the general importance of sports to Montherlant, see Cruickshank, pp. 11–21.

[6] *Montherlant et les Femmes*, especially Chapter X, 'Montherlant et le mariage'.

That the habit of putting himself into his books should persist in *Les Célibataires* seems implausible, at least at first glance. Obviously, poor Léon's story is not his author's. He is years older than Montherlant was at the time of writing. Nothing that has been written about Montherlant suggests the monstrous practical ineptitude of Léon's character. This son of very minor nobility, like the rest of his family out of contact with reality, is rejected by a society that has no place for him; he is just not up to coping with life. His withdrawal from the world into the role of combined gardener and handyman in his mother's home ends with her death; when liquidating her estate leaves him destitute he throws himself on the charity of an uncle and is sent off to live in a family property in a deserted corner of Normandy, where we have watched him die. It seems most unlikely that Montherlant would care to reincarnate himself in such a doddering incompetent.

But a kind of identification is still not impossible. Novelist and character come from the same hereditary social class and are in a sense socially fossilized. Léon's plight of extreme social inadaptation is one into which any aristocrat can imagine himself falling. It is not Montherlant's, but with sufficient bad luck it might have been his: there but for the grace of God ... Attentive readers of Montherlant will remember that at the opening of *Les Bestiaires*, young Alban's grandmother bears the family name of Coantré. This suggestion of a family relationship between the autobiographical hero and Léon may not be coincidental.

This is not to say that Léon is a self-portrait projected into the future, that is, a prefiguration of the author in his fifties conceived as if in a bad dream. The suggestion is, quite simply, that author and character have enough in common to form a basis for strong sympathy, so that when the character is hurt the author suffers and is outraged when the character is wronged. This I propose as the explanation of the passage about the geese: out of this strong sympathy for his unfortunate creature comes a strong and very personal emotion which is expressed through the contrast in tones. In other words, Montherlant is present in his story by virture of a stylistic strategy.

Closer inspection of *Les Célibataires* reveals other instances of using tonal variation as a means of intervention in the narrative. For example:

> ... Elle avait connu les hommes d'affaires mal rasés, qui lui parlaient la cigarette à la bouche,—l'indécent galimatias judiciaire, honte d'une nation civilisée,—les notes d'avoués où il y avait des 'droits de corres-

pondance' qui *se montaient* à quarante francs, et des 'frais de papeterie'
à cinquante, tandis que les 'conclusions' et les 'constitutions' ne coû-
taient que vingt sous,—les parents avocats *à qui on tient la jambe sans
bourse délier*, pendant trois ans, mais la quatrième année, mal satisfaits
du faux Sèvres par lequel vous avez prétendu les remercier, *ils vous
laissent en plan* au milieu d'affaires plus inextricables que la forêt de
Bondy,—les 'consultations' qu'on demande aux *nababs de la chicane*,
avec l'espoir qu'ils vous appuieront dans la voie où vous vous êtes
engagée, mais ils vous en dissuadent et cependant on s'enfonce dans
cette voie, par horreur *de tout reprendre de l'alpha* dans une autre,—
les décisions *d'où* dépendent votre fortune en entier, et qu'il faut qu'on
prenne *dans le quart d'heure*, non pas qu'il y ait une nécessité matérielle,
mais simplement parce qu'il ne faut pas retenir longtemps l'avocat-
conseil, qui *n'a pas que vous dans la tête*; enfin elle connut le calvaire que
c'est de n'être pas insolvable, la caverne d'honnêtes gens qu'est le
monde, l'indifférence et l'épouvantable légèreté des hommes aux mains
de qui l'on remet sa fortune, et avec elle sa santé et sa vie, indifférence
et légèreté *qu'on ne peut comparer qu'à celles des médecins*. Tout cela la
dévora vivante (p. 766; my italics).

One recognizes the rich colloquialness and, fully as much, the expressive-
ness of this language. The reflexive pronoun in 'se montaient', for example,
hardly changes the basic meaning of the verb, but adds to it the feeling
that these costs rise by themselves, of their own evil accord. 'A qui on
tient la jambe' is a phrase that might be used about a person on whom one
had a claim, but not that one would use to his face unless one knew him so
well that one would not need say it anyway. 'Sans bourse délier' is a cliché
of the level of dignity of the English 'not a red penny'. To refer to the
'forêt de Bondy' correctly, one should know that there was once a wood,
north of Paris, traditionally frequented by the most dangerous robbers;
possibly all the Frenchmen who use the expression do not remember this,
but they do remember the childhood impression that the 'forêt de Bondy'
would be a good place to avoid. Meanwhile, 'dans le quart d'heure', for
something less concrete like 'tout de suite', 'n'a pas que vous dans la tête'
with its negation of the 'ne . . . que' construction, and 'la dévora vivante',
all belong to the same general category, while the reference to the frivolity
of doctors reflects one of the eternal prejudices of the French mind. Indeed,
to describe this language as extremely colloquial hardly does its colloquialism justice.

But this colloquialism, remarkable as it is, provides only a partial
explanation of the tone. The expressions just listed are also an example of
what may be called dramatic suitability. (For this term, invented *ad hoc*,

there is no defence other than it permits naming a certain harmony between the language used and the character it is used *about*.) The passage describes the harassed life of Léon's mother as she defends what little is left by the debts of her husband and the financial fiasco of Léon's attempt to manufacture photographic enlargers.

Here we contemplate a French social phenomenon, so familiar that the French hardly think of it—or explain it to foreigners. Such women were brought up, a century ago (Madame de Coantré was married in 1869) to marry among the right, solid people, be effective wives and mothers, and to run large households through well-organized domestic staffs; from the world of financial necessities, except as it touched household economy, they were supposed to be sheltered. Their education took place in the home, perhaps supplemented by the convent, and was rigidly designed for the purpose here outlined.

With the decline of their class the protection to which they had been born rapidly evaporated, and women like Madame de Coantré found themselves having to deal with a world alien to their temperaments when not actually beyond their understanding. Hence one reason (we shall shortly find another) for the use of quotation marks around such terms as 'conclusions' and 'constitutions', which are perfectly intelligible words but, for this lady, parts of an alien vocabulary: they belong to a world for which she was not made.

Montherlant's technique of 'represented speech' or 'discours indirect libre' is not exactly like Flaubert's: his use of the imperfect tense is only superficially similar and does not admit the reader into the workings of the subject's mind on specific occasions; it emphasizes continual recurrence. And the shift to the present, part way through the passage, underlines the inexorable certainty that the same events will go on taking place, over and over, so long as she lives. The use of 'on' as subject, further defined by the repetitions of the oblique case, 'vous'—you, whoever you are, but always including the speaker—would seem to contribute to the same effect.

But at the same time, she is in a predicament which is special to women of her kind, and this too is reflected by her language. The expressions we have observed are, noteworthily, clichés, and clichés characteristic of one kind of bringing up, of a mind trained to accept and use a speech in a way characteristic of a mode of life.

Furthermore, Montherlant has contrived to convey here, by the manipulations of his style, his own sympathetic disposition toward his character. He likes this woman and is on her side. Another reason—in addition to the one already adduced—for his using quotation marks around the legal words, is to point up the fact that they are barbarous and in a sense barbaric, a shame to civilization as he asserts in an intervention within the larger, indirect one. As in the passage about Léon and the wild geese, his tonal variation reveals his ultimate sympathies.

The novel abounds in passages where he appears *not* to be in sympathy with his characters. The description of Léon's niece, Mademoiselle de Bauret, at the opening of the second part, the general treatment of Elie de Coëtquidan and of Oncle Gustave, *passim*, are direct and full of an often savage irony. Such interventions are as open and intrusive as the tonal ones are discreet and almost surreptitious. One rapidly forms a suspicion that Montherlant's fixed habit is to intervene directly when he is unfavorably disposed toward a character, but indirectly, through the workings of style, when a character stirs his tenderness.

Eventually we are led by this to a slightly changed understanding of what he says could be an epigraph for his whole life as well as for one of his books: *Aedificabo et destruam*, I shall build up and destroy.[7]

The best possible opportunity to observe the functioning of Montherlant's celebrated 'alternances' (already suggested by the Latin motto), and at the same time to observe the effect of his 'presence' in a novel whose hero we may be sure he identifies himself with, is provided by *Les Bestiaires*. Not only is the hero closely patterned on Montherlant, but also the sport involved is one which the novelist himself dearly loved; and, in addition, the novel is peopled by many Spaniards, like Jesús to whom Alban gives his blooded dog, whom Montherlant admired after the fashion of his masters, Stendhal and Barrès.

The climax of the story comes when the young hero, at last master of both his adversary and his own nerves, goes in for the kill:

Il s'abattit sur la brute comme un faucon, se redressa en titubant, la main portée à son cœur qui l'étranglait.

Il se tint devant elle, et il haletait. Elle était finie maintenant, *la lutte contre l'ange*. Quoi qu'il voulût et quoi qu'il fît, rien ne pouvait plus empêcher qu'il l'eût tué. De la double blessure coulait, avec l'avidité d'une source, le sang générateur et purificateur. La bête chancela de l'arrière-train, tenta de se raidir, enfin croula sur le flanc, *accomplissant sa destinée*. Quelques secondes encore ella cligna des yeux, et on vit sa respiration. Puis ses pattes se tendirent peu à peu, comme un corps qu'on gonflerait à la pompe, tandis que dans cet agrandissement leurs

[7] *Les Services inutiles*, p. 51.

articulations grinçaient, avec le bruit d'un câble de navire qu'on serre sur un treuil. Elle arriva avec emphase à la cime de son spasme, *comme l'homme à la cime* de son plaisir, et, comme lui, elle y resta immobile. *Et son âme divine s'échappa, pleurant ses jeux, et les génisses, et sa chère plaine.* Et l'œil brun et bleuâtre se fixa, grand ouvert sur la nuit.

Alban regardait, dans une horreur sacrée, avec la tension du combat demeurée sur son visage, sauf dans le regard qui s'était éteint. Il savait à présent qu'il l'avait aimé, ce monstre, que toute sa vie s'était portée sur lui à l'instant où elle abandonnait la jeune fille, que tous les troubles des sens ne sont qu'un même trouble, que sa terreur et sa haine n'étaient que des formes de son amour. Ce qu'il attendait de suprême était exaucé enfin, *et sa force tombait comme le vent tombe* (p. 561).

The italics (mine) indicate elements in the text which are particularly relevant to the present purpose. It will not be disputed that two of them are similes. I am proposing the notion that the four others are literary allusions, somewhat vague and distant perhaps, but still recognizable.

'La lutte contre l'ange' is clearly biblical; the only argument against granting its status as allusion is the possibility that Montherlant may be less attentive to the story of Jacob than tempted, as he is so often, by the opportunity to make a pun: the bull's name, *Malage*, is Andalusian vernacular for *Mal ángel*. 'Accomplissant sa destinée' comes straight out of ancient epic, and can be Homeric or Virgilian almost equally well. 'Et son âme divine' again echoes the epic (with a touch of parody in *génisses*) and is more or less reminiscent of *Iliad* XVI. 586–857: 'His soul left his body and flitted down to the house of Hades, mourning its sad fate and bidding farewell to the youth and vigor of its manhood'.[8]

In the case of 'et sa force tombait comme le vent tombe' one may allege a reminiscence of a specific line, *Inferno* V, 142:

e caddi, come corpo morto cade.

The dissimilarities are admittedly obvious: the syntactical force of Dante's preterite, re-enforced for the ear by the shock of the double *d*, is not paralleled by Montherlant's less conclusive imperfect; in Dante's poem it is the poet who falls like a corpse, not the passion in one of the characters; and dropping like a dead weight is not exactly like a decrease in the force of the wind. But on the other hand, falling results in each

---

[8] I owe a special debt to several former colleagues at Columbia University for their advice and criticism when the subject of these allusions was presented in a lecture to the French Graduate Union. Among them were the late Pierre-A. Clamens and the late Margaret Gilman. I should be ungrateful, however, not to take full responsibility for the views expressed here. The reader is entitled to know that some of them have been described as 'possibly misleading' (*FS*, VII, no. 3 [July 1953], 288).

case from a sudden loss of physical strength; both phrases repeat the verb for falling in the present tense after using it in the past; both have the rhythmic feature of the pause, enforced in Dante's line by the comma and in Montherlant's by the natural cadence of the phrase; and, further, Montherlant's willingness to call attention to the repetition of a common verb by placing it under stress needs a better explanation than that he has been extraordinarily careless. His work, *passim*, shows ample familiarity with Italian literature, and, even if it did not, he could hardly not have known the chapter of *La Révolte des anges* in the course of which Anatole France's rebelling angel reports: '. . . je causai une telle frayeur à cet imbécile, qu'il s'en alla hurlant sur le palier et (pour emprunter à Dante Alighieri une forte expression) tomba comme un corps mort tombe.'[9]

In short, there is at least a possibility that these four phrases are allusive, although, of course, nothing short of a direct declaration from Montherlant, contemporaneous with *Les Bestiaires* (1926), could put the point beyond doubt. I have found nothing such. But the case for allusiveness can be strengthened if we can show that allusions would serve a very special purpose at this stage in the development of the novel. This demonstration seems possible.

The direct effect of all four alleged allusions is the same. 'Elle était finie, la lutte contre l'ange' shifts the reader's attention from the two figures on the sand of the bull ring to Jacob and the Angel, and in so doing invites attention to the disproportion in dignity beween the two couples. 'Accomplissant sa destinée' invites comparison of the dead bull with the dead hero of an epic—and again there is disproportion. The simile, 'comme un corps qu'on gonflerait à la pompe', evoking the image of a carcass in the abattoir being inflated with a bellows to loosen the hide for skinning, reiterates that there is nothing particularly heroic about a dead animal. Then the renewed comparison with the dead warrior, 'et son âme divine s'échappa', insists once more on the disparity between bull and hero. In brief, all these figures can be read as disparaging the deed which Alban de Bricoule has just performed.

Showing a similar possibility of disparagement in the two remaining figures requires some digression. The simile in 'à la cime de son spasme, comme l'homme à la cime de son plaisir' serves to recall an earlier passage in which Alban finally imposes his will upon the bull. There the presiding, dominant figure running through the rich visual imagery is the couple. The participants in the fight become the wave sweeping over the rock, the god and his votary, the partners in the sexual act. The fight becomes a

9 *Œuvres complètes* (Champion ed.), XXII, 76.

dance, a caress, a communion, and an act of creation. The man feels an electric fluid pass from him into the beast; he thirsts for still more intimate contact; he experiences his performance as a work of seduction. Image and style move together:

> De nouveau l'étoffe capte cette fureur maniée, la dirige, et sous la muleta sauvage, pleine de sable, de bave, de sang, de déchirures, la bête s'écoule comme une vague, et puis—ha!—se dresse comme la vague, dans le claquement de ses banderilles. Alban accompagne le bond de son ha! comme s'il l'aidait, ainsi qu'il aide son cheval avec un cri quand il est sur l'obstacle, et il rejette le buste en arrière dans le même moment où le taureau dresse le poitrail. C'est une succession de plongées et de soulèvements simultanés de l'homme et de la bête; et le couple, aussi, tantôt ralentit son rythme et tantôt le précipite, tantôt se serre et tantôt se détend. Comme les dieux de l'*Iliade*, le temps et l'espace combattent pour eux et contre eux: une différence de cinq centimètres . . . une différence d'une demi-seconde . . . (p. 559).

In this sample, the idea of domination and the characteristic, frequently erotic images of the couple, that is, the wave metaphor (which recalls the earlier use of a wave breaking over a rock) and the figure of the horse and rider, backed by direct visual images of man and bull raising their bodies in concert, is further re-enforced by a series of parallel binary constructions: 'de plongées/et/de soulèvements', 'de l'homme/et/de la bête', 'tantôt ralentit son rythme/et/tantôt le précipite', 'tantôt se serre/et/tantôt se détend', 'le temps/et/l'espace', 'pour eux/et/contre eux'.

All this careful elaboration of figure and style, with its insistence on erotic parallels with Alban's activity, is renewed in the passage about the actual death of the bull by the final simile: Montherlant concludes his scene by juxtaposing the picture of Alban and the bull with the couple *par excellence*, Paolo and Francesca. Possibly the procedure seems, in the nontechnical sense, a bit baroque, but we have already seen how little the novelist is disposed to avoid startling literary effects. And it will hardly be denied that placing Alban and his dead animal so unexpectedly beside the lovers of the *Inferno* puts the young bullfighter and his victory in their proper perspective. As do the allusions and the simile already accounted for, this allusion also disparages—and with thoroughness.

Nothing so resembles a hollow as a swelling! What Montherlant is doing here is what he was doing in the passage near the end of *Les Célibataires*, but in reverse. This time he moves into the elevated style, momentarily but repeatedly, about a subject which hardly merits elevation: the basic strategy of burlesque. It is well for us to remember our earlier observation, that Montherlant tends to reserve indirect and covert intervention for use on characters he finds sympathetic; otherwise *Les Bestiaires* might make only dubious sense. Why should the novelist be so intent upon belittling the crowning moment of his young hero's life, especially when the hero is, on the whole, both an attractive and an autobiographical character? The answer is the structure of the novel itself.

Alban de Bricoule is a Paris *lycéen* who persuades his mother to let him spend an Easter vacation in Spain fighting bulls. After numerous vicissitudes he gets himself admitted to the Duke de La Cuesta's bull farm near Seville, helps test the bravery of the bull calves, and is invited to appear as matador in a charity fight the Duke stages each Easter. Meanwhile he finds the Duke's daughter attractive, and the young lady declares that the progress of their relationship will depend on Alban's willingness to fight the particularly malevolent beast called Evil Angel. After a humiliatingly inept performance against a first bull, Alban does in fact meet and kill this frightening animal—and then discovers that his interest in the Duke's daughter has died with it. Here the narrative proper closes, although the book continues through a fourteen-page Epilogue.

More important than the plot, of course, is the manner of the telling. Montherlant's position with respect to his material is not entirely unlike that of the narrator in *A la recherche du temps perdu* or in *La Vie de Marianne*: a narrator tells his own story from a vantage of superior understanding, taking the role of an observer of an action in which a much younger figuration of himself is a participant. But there is this difference, that the relationship between the two personae is not explicitly stated. Instead, Montherlant commits himself from the beginning to a narrative optics which could be described, with only slight inaccuracy, as a double point of view. The reader alternates in seeing the action through the eyes of the chief actor and those of the observing narrator.

> Dans la chambre, Alban s'apprête à écrire à sa mère. Il commence: 'Chère maman et amie...' Mais il jette sa plume. *Non, décidément, il n'est pas fait pour la littérature.* Et puis, c'est son lit qui le fascine. *C'est prodigieux à quel point un lit ressemble à un taureau. Les cornes... les jambes... la queue... tout y est.* Alban ferme les volets, *pour qu'on ne le voie pas du dehors,* pousse les meubles contre les murs. Dans une main, une règle. Dans l'autre, sa muleta. *D'évidence, le taureau ne répond plus guère, il faut en finir vite.* Quelques passes, qui malheureusement font voler les objets de toilette. Alban s'encourage d'une voix forte: 'Bueno... bueno...' Puis se profile et comme les braves, sans tourner la tête, il met à mort son édredon (pp. 453–4).

My italics mark the spots in the passage where we see what Alban is doing as he sees it; left in roman is what is seen by the narrator. The tone, of course, remains Montherlant's, but the angle of vision shifts rapidly back and forth.

In the first part of the story, this optics permits an almost Cervantine gaiety. In his enthusiasm, Alban buys a Cordovan-style hat before he leaves Paris, but discovers that in Madrid hats follow the Paris style. He is no sooner in Spain than he sets out to see a bull fight, but learns that there are no fights during Holy Week. He goes for advice to an old friend of his father's, Dr. Diaz, who turns out to be one Spaniard better qualified to talk about philosophy than about tauromachy. In despair he tries to buy a book about bull fighting, but discovers that even the bookshops are closed. And when at long last he does get to a *corrida* he is so seated in the box that the headdresses of the ladies sitting in front of him mask the ring,[10] so that he can see the action only if he stands—in which case he will block the view of his host. In this headlong pursuit of the ideal, Alban is forever bashing his head against obdurate reality. The ideal is what *he* sees; reality is the narrator's province. And as the angle of vision shifts back and forth, the characteristic movement of the story becomes a systole-and-diastole, an alternate rise and fall of emotional tension.

After this first third of the book the episodes become much less hilarious. Irony retires. Before we come to the actual *corrida* the tone becomes so serious that certain themes that have been treated earlier as amusing evidence of Alban's mania, such as the parallel between modern bullfighter and ancient bestiary, are resumed with great gravity. *But the rhythm of alternation between high and low emotional tensions remains.* Instead of the familiar conflict of the ideal versus the real we get alternations of hope and discouragement in the love episodes, and of courage and cowardice with regard to the approaching bull fight. The alternations are also less rapid as the novelist shortens the aesthetic distance. But they do not disappear. The procedure is so consistently followed throughout the book that when emotional tension has been raised to the highest possible pitch, in the climatic episode of the fight with the bull called the Evil Angel, the reader is immediately sure that Montherlant will straightway destroy it.

The boy is in the ring at last, and stumbles through his lamentable performance with the first bull. We suffer with him as he bungles every attempt to do his part cleanly and well, and as the bull stupidly persists in getting back on his feet after he is supposed to be dead. We have no

[10] pp. 404–5. The detail may be taken as further confirmation of the autobiographical nature of this novel: like his creator, Alban is short of body.

opportunity to relax: anxiety for the safety of an amiable hero combines with anxiety for the imperiled artistic enterprise. Then Alban's composure returns in time for him to face the second bull. His eventual victory is ours; we are at his side as, from the first passes of the *muleta*, he dominates the *Malage* and leads the beast through the traditional stages of the ritual of combat. One has the experience of the entirely breathless spectator if not, perhaps, that of the actual participant. In terms of aesthetic distance, the reader is about as close as he can ever hope to be brought to an action.

And now Alban plants his sword between the bull's shoulders and steps back, panting. Remembering the tendency which, as Montherlant himself says, marks his whole life ('aedificabo et destruam'), and being still under the influence of what has been previously established as the master rhythm of the book, we now expect the tension to be destroyed again. And in the next sentence comes the reference to Jacob and the Angel, to be followed directly by quick shots of the dead epic hero (twice), of the animal in the slaughterhouse, and of Paolo and Francesca —all of which, we have said, disparage Alban's accomplishment. The allusions and similarities of this passage, then, function to maintain the essential rhythm of the novel. At the end of the passage tensions have abated, and the spectator, only a moment ago so close to Alban and his actions, has been moved back away from them so far that he now remembers that he is not really a spectator at all but a reader.

Of course, there is no knowing whether Montherlant's allusions were made in full awareness of what he was doing. Nothing guarantees that he was not merely responding to his instinct to let down a tension once it had been brought to a peak. Certainly they are not allusions of the kind a writer goes to a book to look up. But their appositeness in the structure of the novel seems to testify to their real nature.

While the chapter just examined presents the climax of *Les Bestiaires*, it is not the final chapter in the book. Still to be accounted for is the Epilogue. Alban has left Spain and is with his uncle, a cattle-breeder who lives in the Camargue. The sun is about to set. They are on horseback, admiring the herd, and the moment is particularly solemn. Informing the entire Epilogue is the kind of Neo-Mithraism (or perhaps Pseudo-Mithraism) which has turned up repeatedly in the body of the novel and in fact gives it its title: young Alban's *afición* has produced an affinity with the religion of the old Legionaries in him, and his uncle, like himself, is a worshipper of the sun and of bulls.

D

There are now no variations in tone.

Sur la grève déserte battait, toujours à la même place, le grand fleuve
sans source et sans embouchure, la mer grecque et romaine, la mer
ibérique et sarrasine. Le ciel était un rêve suspendu. Le soleil qui
s'enfonçait, posé sur l'horizon avec une forme de casque, tendait un
pont de feux mouvants, une route d'or jusqu'à la grève où deux
hommes restaient immobiles, comme arrêtés à l'entrée de cette route.
Et c'étaient un grand-prêtre et un néophyte solaires, à cheval sur leurs
chevaux blancs (p. 167).

As night comes down, the younger man asks the elder to recite his
poem, 'Le Taureau', and the latter does so. Nothing else happens; this is
the only event in the Epilogue. No irony enters; nothing is permitted to
break the elevated tone set by the prose of the opening lines.

In the first sentence one recognizes binary constructions like those in
the elevated parts of the description of the struggle with the Evil Angel:
without inlet and without outlet, Greek and Roman, Spanish and Saracen,
as well as the repetitions. The treatment of the sky, however hard the
reader may find visualizing a 'suspended dream' ('rêve suspendu') revives
memories of Léon de Coantré's three wild geese flying apart from the rest
of the flock like 'pensées profondes': the expression evokes not an image
but an emotion in the observer. There may be additional solemnity in the
metaphor which turns the sun-track on the water into a road, so solid
looking that one could walk on it into the sun. Meanwhile, the reference
to the Mediterranean as a river takes us back beyond the designations in
old maps to the usage of the Ancients. The paired adjectives insist upon
historical continuity. The helmet shape of the sun cut by the horizon stirs
an association with the Roman legionaries. And the conjunction 'et'
at the beginning of the terminal sentence, entirely pleonastic with respect
to the fundamental meaning, revives the use of the conjunction in biblical
narrative[11] and closes the paragraph with this suggestion of one more link
between past and present.

Doubtless the formality of such prose inserts a distance between reader
and character, but the opposite kind of distance from the one associated

---

[11] For example, I Samuel xxii (King James Version): David therefore departed
thence, and escaped to the cave Abdullam: *and* when his brethren and all his father's
house heard it, they went down thither to him.

And everyone that was in distress, and everyone that was in debt, and everyone
that was discontented, gathered themselves unto him; *and* he became a captain over
them … (Italics mine.)

with comedy. Stylistically, this prose confers a considerable dignity upon the two characters.

Now these characters have something in common with Léon de Coantré. Alban's uncle is regarded by their family as a queer sort because of his devotion to cattle-breeding; had his taste been a fashionable one, they would have understood and approved, but as things stand he is an eccentric in their eyes, and embarrassing to explain socially. In the same way, Alban's parents have had to dismiss his enthusiasm for bulls as an adolescent mania: the sport is simply not fashionable in Paris and thus there is something wrong about those who go in for it. (Montherlant himself had been qualified as a poseur in one of the newspaper reports of his being wounded in a bull ring.) And it is on behalf of these social misfits that Montherlant produces his resources of elevated language.

Léon de Coantré is a fool, and being unable to adapt to his environment he must die, but this does not necessarily ennoble the environment. Alban de Bricoule has been guilty of some truly absurd conduct, but this does not make the behavior of those who laugh at his absurdity more praiseworthy than his. Léon signs his own death warrant, but does so by a gesture which in Montherlant's eyes is one of dignity: he has rejected ultimate humiliation. The gesture is undeniably Quixotic, and strengthens the case of those who insist upon the 'espagnolisme' of Montherlant.[12] What counts is that Montherlant endorses the gesture.

The endorsement is stylistic. Léon will die directly, in this same chapter, and the final pages of the book will dwell on the heartless relief of the surviving characters—now that he no longer looks to them for help and they no longer have to hide him from society. But before he dies, Léon can at least be dignified by one sustained flight of lyric prose—prose which contrasts violently with that of the last pages—just as Alban and the uncle have been justified at the end of *Les Bestiaires* by prose of similar elevation.

If this is the proper reading, a final comment about the celebrated 'alternances' and the motto of 'aedificabo et destruam' is in order. Alternation we have indeed seen to be a dominant in his writing: repeated examples of elevation deflated by the irony of practical common sense. But in the last analysis we must conclude that in both these novels the effect of the alternation is arrested, so to speak, upon a note of elevation: on 'aedificabo' rather than upon 'destruam'.

[12] For a typical example see Ventura Garcia-Calderon, 'L'Espagnolisme de Montherlant', *Cahiers du Sud* (1937), pp. 484-94.

In other words, Montherlant's stance with respect to his characters is not at all the one of constantly ironic detachment so frequently attributed to him. Despite the abundance of explicit intervention in these novels, instances of which may shock a reader who has been trained to infer the novelist's attitudes and is disposed to enjoy subtlety, such direct tactics are not sufficient fully to discharge the energy of the novelist's feelings about his heroes. They are also expressed in the structure of the narratives, and, even more, in the style. Style thus becomes a powerful instrument of authorial intervention.

CHAPTER THREE

Saint-Exupéry:
the Poet as Novelist

In all four of the books which concern students of fiction Saint-Exupéry sets up the same fundamental situation: an aviator is aloft in his plane exposed to danger by the very fact of flight itself, while another man, familiar with all the dangers the first is exposed to, anxiously awaits the outcome of the ordeal. The unnamed speaker waits at Cap Juby for Bernis to fly in with the south-bound mail in *Courrier-Sud*; Rivière waits for Fabien to come through the storm in *Vol de nuit*; Major Alias waits for the return of the flight over Arras in *Pilote de guerre*; the 'vrais naufragés' in *Terre des hommes* discover that the real sufferers in catastrophe are not those who are lost but those whose hope slowly drains away on the shore. In the fictions the pilot dies, whereas in the others he survives to continue his meditations, flight having become an instrument of self-knowledge with which the flyer comes to recognize his personal relationship with the universe.

Otherwise the difference between fiction and ruminative essay is not great. Whichever of the external forms he exploits in the given instance, he exploits it for the orchestration of a limited number of recurrent obsessive themes with seemingly unlimited resources of simile, metaphor, analogy, comparison, and something very like New Testament parable. His genius seems to consist of recognizing in whatever he looks at, or thinks of, the lineaments of something else.

In a symptomatic passage in *Pilote de guerre* he remarks that his plane, high over enemy-held territory, must be noticed quickly by the gunners below because of its vapor trail, which he calls a scarf of white pearl dragging out behind like the train of a bride's gown (p. 298). Since this is only one simile among a number, and not one of those to which he reverts shortly as if intending to give it a thematic significance, the reader's attention is not arrested. Four full chapters—twenty-five pages—further on, however, Saint-Exupéry stops to criticize the figure.

J'ai pu inventer sans dégoût cette image de robe à traîne! Je n'ai pas songé à une robe à traîne, pour la bonne raison que mon propre sillage, je ne l'ai jamais aperçu! De cette carlingue où je suis emboîté comme une pipe dans un étui, il m'est impossible de rien observer en arrière de moi . . . (p. 311).

One could not ask better evidence of a writer's supervising his work, of his awareness of the figures he uses, than provided by this challenge of his own image. His criterion is a kind of authenticity: the bridal gown had no part in the experience of his flight.

Yet he does not suppress the image, and we must conclude that other criteria outweigh the experiential one. What are they?[1] We can only conjecture at this point, and the conjecture will be confirmed only by Saint-Exupéry's treatment of imagery in general. We can say, hypothetically, that he was one of those writers who do not feel their thought to be complete until it has been illustrated. Thus, in *Terre des hommes*: 'Il m'est venu quelques images pour m'expliquer cette vérité', and he goes on to write two frequently admired passages, one about domestic ducks which, although they know nothing but the barnyard, are stirred almost to flight when a flock of wild migrants whistles over them, the other about gazelles which have been born in captivity and show no sign of wildness until the day when they begin refusing to do anything but stand at the fence, peering out toward liberty (pp. 249–50). What captures our attention in all this is the object of the infinitive in the sentence quoted. '*M*'expliquer': the necessity is personal; the explanation is not for the reader so much as for the author himself.

Strictly speaking, it is not correct to call this habit 'thinking in images', even though Saint-Exupéry uses the word 'image'. True images are not always involved. In the figures of the ducks and gazelles, one's imagination 'sees' no more than it sees when any concrete noun is pronounced, that is, the thing named. There is no super-position of one subject upon another, no seeing of two things at once, not even the implication of a similarity with something only obliquely invoked. They operate upon the understanding. Compare 'the kingdom of heaven is like a mustard seed'.

In *Pilote de guerre*, Saint-Exupéry exploits an analogy which juxtaposes an abstraction, humanity, with a concrete object, a cathedral: humanity is more than a mass of people as a cathedral is more than a mass of stones. The figure is first presented early in this book, as the writer dresses for the

[1] For a discussion of Saint-Exupéry's literary preferences and habits see Carlo François, *L'Esthétique d'Antoine de Saint-Exupéry*.

flight to Arras. He has just been saying that during the preflight preparations his mind has been full of resentment at the futility of the mission assigned, coupled with irritation at not finding his flying gloves. Then, in a new paragraph, and with no connective to relate the remark with what has preceded, he adds: 'Je ne vois plus la cathédrale que j'habite' (p. 277). The figure is not identified as such, and is renewed only once (p. 295), in the following pages. It could be read as being one of the purely suggestive metaphors favored by the Symbolists, which could permit the reader to assign any equivalence to 'cathédrale' that struck him as appropriate in the context; for example, one implying that the aviator had lost his vocation to defend his country.

Only at the end of the book, when the reader remembers the figure dimly if at all, does Saint-Exupéry return to it. But now the treatment is extensive and explicit.

> On ne dit rien d'essentiel sur la cathédrale, si l'on ne parle que des pierres. On ne dit rien d'essentiel sur l'Homme, si l'on cherche à le définir par des qualités d'homme (p. 377).
> On meurt pour une maison. Non pour des objets et des murs. On meurt pour une cathédrale. Non pour des pierres. On meurt pour un peuple. Non pour une foule (p. 380).
> La cathédrale peut absorber les pierres, qui y prennent un sens. Mais le tas de pierres n'absorbe rien et, faute d'être en mesure d'absorber, il écrase (p. 382).
> L'arbre est plus fort que les matériaux du sol. Il les draîne à lui. Il les change en arbre. La cathédrale est plus rayonnante que le tas de pierres (p. 382).
> Je crois que le culte du particulier n'entraîne que la mort—car il fonde l'ordre sur la ressemblance. Il confond l'unité de l'être avec l'identité de ses parties. Et il dévaste la cathédrale pour aligner les pierres (p. 383).

In context, the passage comes in climactic position: the flyer's meditation has brought him triumphantly to the point where meaning begins to emerge from the pointlessness of fighting on in defeat. The repetitions of phrasing, the frequent syntactic parallels re-enforce what would already be very powerful affective statement. The figure is elaborated here to complete a book-long meditation. The fact remains that here as elsewhere Saint-Exupéry reveals the importance of analogical figure—whether or not it results in the creation of imagery in the strict sense.

Very often, of course, imagery does indeed result. German pursuit planes appear like a swarm of wasps; evacuating civilians flow along the crowded roads like rivers; the German advance moves along the front fluidly seeking the gap through which it can pass unobstructed (p. 307).[2] But such images do not score, of course, by any virtue of unusualness. They are 'classical' in the sense that they please more by their aptness than by brilliance. They do not, in brief, surprise by fine excess.

This is true of *Pilote de guerre*, but will be no less true of the novel *Vol de nuit*—although in it there are few of the rationalized, parable-like figures and a much heavier concentration of true imagery. What impresses the attentive reader will not be the brilliance of the images but their number, and the way in which they betray the unchanging preoccupations of Saint-Exupéry's imagination.

In *Vol de Nuit*, images proliferate in which what I. A. Richards calls the 'vehicle' is connected with the sea.

The novel opens with a marine image: 'les collines, sous l'avion, creusaient déjà leur *sillage* d'ombre dans l'or du soir' (p. 81). In the next paragraph the pilot knows the approach of evening by the same signs as he would a port (p. 81). He is coming to an immense and blessed anchorage, having crossed a hundred kilometers of open country more uninhabited than the sea (p. 81). Night falls, and each illuminated house is like a lighthouse (p. 83). He sees a farm and with a dipped wing salutes this 'ship' (p. 81). And again the pilot feels his passing into night as an approach to a sheltered anchorage, which this time is qualified as 'slow' and 'beautiful' (p. 83). When he has to light his panel lamps, he feels this same entrance into darkness as a submersion. Air currents raising and dropping the plane are 'ground swells' (p. 84). The light on a humble table is recalled, when it is eighty kilometers behind, as a greeting from an island, over the sea (p. 84).

Even though a number of images appear in this first chapter that have nothing to do with the sea, the marine images are so much more numerous than the others as to suggest already, so early in the book, a stylistic dominant. They continue to abound in the rest of the novel.

The basic metaphor (plane : ship; flying : sailing) is older than powered flight itself. Few would deny it the status of a commonplace. Saint-Exupéry's treatment exhibits the truth of the traditional belief that

---

[2] From the context it would appear that Saint-Exupéry had been impressed by German army doctrines concerning the advantages to be derived from the fluidity of armored troop and tank movements. The example of the appropriation of an image may not be unique in his work.

such material can be saved from staleness by adroit handling; he avoids the fundamental analogy itself in favor of exploiting subsidiary aspects; the identification of evening with port, or air current with ground swell, or lighted farm with sea beacon implies the air-sea transfer referentially but does not state it; the writer is like a composer allowing distant echoes to remind his listener of a major theme.

This strategy remains important throughout the novel. Rivière, the director of the airline, feels that he has to draw his planes out of the darkness onto the shore (p. 85). Peaks of the Andes push through the wind like the bow frames of ships (p. 88). Good flying weather is described as a 'strong following swell' (p. 90). A quick reference to men isolated among the crowd on the street making Rivière think of lighthouse keepers renews the lighthouse image (p. 101). Flyers have to bring themselves through the obstacles of the darkness by blind strength, like swimmers (p. 101). An office lamp creates a beach of light in the surrounding dark (p. 101). As catastrophe approaches, after Fabien's plane has entered the area of bad weather, even the movements of a man in an office evoke the basic image: '... les mouvements de l'homme, que la solitude faisait lent comme un nageur entre deux eaux, revenant de l'ombre vers sa lampe, comme un plongeur remonte, lui paraissait lourd de secrets' (p. 102).

As the novel progresses, even contexts which have little to do with the flight directly produce images of the same general category. Thus, in a flashback chapter in which Fabien wakens to leave his wife and go to the airfield:

> Elle admirait cette poitrine nue, bien carénée, elle pensait à un beau navire.
>
> Il reposait dans ce lit calme, comme dans un port, et, pour que rien n'agitât son sommeil, elle effaçait du doigt ce pli, cette ombre, cette houle, elle apaisait ce lit, comme, d'un doigt divin, la mer (pp. 106–7).

A moment later the husband breathes deeply, like a naked diver about to plunge into the sea (p. 108). And twice, before he has reached the airfield, there are references to the city's being only sea bottom once a plane has left the ground (p. 108). The flow of imagery occasionally slackens, as when, for example, the focus falls upon Inspector Robineau, whose dullness is emphasized by his rarely inspiring an image, but only to resume directly. In the last seventy pages of the novel I count some twenty-five more marine images, some of which are developed at length.[3]

---

[3] See especially the reassemblage of images in Chapter XVI, pp. 124–5.

An abundance of subsidiary image clusters are in one way or another associated with this principal system which equates air with sea and plane with ship. For example, three instances have already been noted where lighted farms have been linked with a sort of beacon or signal. They belong to a persistent series in which light is related to life at sea and to the idea of safety.

From the beginning, light has a strong emotional value. Fabien has just taken off after a ten-minute stop at Saint-Julian during which dusk has become evening and the city's lights have been turned on. Airborne again, the flyer looks back on the city which is no more than a handful of lights, then of stars, and finally, tempting him one last time, a bit of dissolving dust (p. 83).

What this means to a flyer is that his horizon has been lost in the darkness so that he can no longer tell whether he is looking back at something on the ground or at something in the sky; the lights cease to signify safety; his uncertainty becomes part of his separation from men.

The same inability to distinguish between ground lights and stars reappears in *Terre des hommes*: lost in his plane over the North African coast, the anxious aviator, who in this book is Saint-Exupéry undisguised, cannot tell whether what shines ahead is a beacon set to lead him home or a low-hanging star beckoning him on into danger. This leaves no doubt that the image in *Vol de nuit* originates in personal experience and may explain its persistent recurrence in the novel. Lighted villages are like beacons turned toward the water, as we have seen, but they are also identified with constellations (p. 83). In one instance stars are (potentially at least) false runway lights—'balisage divin' (p. 98). Fabien, in his plane, thinks of dawn as a beach of golden sand; if he could do so, he would swim toward the day (p. 114). He flies, instead, toward the false safety of the stars above the storm.

In the context it is not surprising that light, blessed light, the antithesis of the night that must in the end be conquered, should take on religious overtones. Thus we have a reference to 'le sanctuaire d'or des lampes du soir'. But those who are tempted to see Saint-Exupéry as a more or less Catholic mystic find no support in the fact that as Fabien approaches catastrophe in the storms, Saint-Exupéry sets up an equivalence of light not with anything of religious connotation but wealth. What it would mean to the flyer to see a single, earthbound light is translated as: 'Riche d'une lumière d'auberge . . .' and this is juxtaposed with images of his being led on to death by stars which in one case are bait leading a victim into a net and in another become pale magnets to draw him on (p. 124). Then, in a final figure, his fate is summed up: 'Il errait parmi les étoiles accumulées avec la densité d'un trésor . . . Pareils à ces voleurs murés dans la chambre aux trésors dont ils ne sauront plus sortir, ils errent, infiniment riches, mais condamnés' (p. 125).

At this point, light imagery, without ever entirely relinquishing its relationship to the imagery of sea and ship, has perhaps established its own independence. It translates the plight of the victim in terms which are not, after all, those applicable to a sailor lost at sea.

One of the air-sea images mentioned earlier likens the 'entry into night' to a dive (p. 84). Despite the obvious differences between French and English idiom, this use of the noun 'entrée' may arrest the reader because of what it confers upon the word 'nuit'—a quality of being something more solid than mere absence of light. He may also wonder why the simile should turn a motion which must literally be horizontal into a metaphorically vertical one. This is not a simple case of the *dead* metaphor contained in 'plonger'; it involves still another cluster of images related both to the sea (because one dives *into* it) and to light (because one *emerges* from the dark when the dive is finished). Certain psychological implications regularly attach themselves to this imagery. An aviator explains to Rivière why he has turned back in fear from a night flight, saying that he has felt as if he were at the bottom of a great hole, hard to climb out of (p. 109). Several minutes later the figure recurs in Rivière's thought that any seasoned, dependable flyer must at some time have had this feeling of having been at the bottom of this 'dark well' (p. 110). Later, when already in great difficulty, Fabien feels himself in 'such a depth of night that one could not climb out of it' (p. 114). And later still, Rivière, helpless to aid the lost plane, thinks of lacking any way to 'throw them a lifeline in that abyss' (p. 122). Even later than this, he thinks of the features of a landscape as 'rising' into the daylight when night has passed, and just before this he has thought of treasure buried 'in the depths of night as in fabulous seas' (p. 126-7). And when Fabien brings his plane up out of the storm into the clear sky he climbs 'bit by bit, in a spiral, in a well that had opened' (p. 124).

In this attempt to deal with the pioneer flyer's feeling of the night itself—something to be conquered, something with frontiers (p. 81) to be crossed, certain figures are not entirely metaphorical. They continue the one noted earlier which develops the idea that the aviator has lost his horizon. For when night swallows the horizon, horizontal and vertical may easily lose even relative meaning: any direction may be up—or down. A man preparing for night flight may thus be readying to dive in a realer sense than we first assume. We shall see again how thoroughly experiential this imagery is.

Yet, perhaps surprisingly, one discovers that figures evoking struggle or conquest are relatively few and do not always compel attention even when present. Something like conquest is implied in references to night as an unsubordinated country (p. 81), to stormy areas as lands at war (p. 84), to an aviator as a reserve whose formation has been called up to attack (p. 107), or to a storm as an unusual offensive (p. 113). Perhaps it is implied also, more indirectly, in a mention of night as unexplored bush (p. 111). (If this is true, possibly any of Saint-Exupéry's occasional references to experience in Africa should also be counted.) But one is impressed by the characteristic obliqueness and by the way in which mentions of conquest itself, or a synonym, rarely produce a real image. One sees little in such comparisons as 'defect in the armor' for something wrong with an aviator's coverall (p. 108) or in 'first steps of his conquest' applied to a man's strides toward the airfield (p. 109). Conquest of the night (p. 111) is a concept not an image (if it is not pure journalese) and at the end of the story it is not a flyer but the groundling Rivière who is called 'victorious' (p. 136).[4]

Since *Vol de nuit* is purportedly a novel about, precisely, conquest, the question we are simultaneously asking is how seriously should we take the work as an example of the novel form. What we have established up to now is that this is a text most conspicuously marked by its imagery, and that this imagery has been used to express the response of certain characters to the experience of flight into danger. But who, exactly, are the characters and what, exactly, do we know about them?

Of the pilot, Fabien, we know that he has a home and a wife who admires his physique while he sleeps, and that he must fly a plane at night. Of Rivière we know just as little; he is a man with a responsibility to see that the mail is taken through. Beyond this we know almost less about him than we know about Fabien. The other characters are entirely

---

[4] It should be added that the tracing of motifs, as opposed to the collection of images, in *Vol de nuit*, would reveal more of the importance of this theme of conquest. The relative infrequency of images connected with conquest seems to me, at least, to call for some psychological explanation.

incidental. Motives are elementary—the carrying out of obligations contracted for reasons we do not know. Background and atmosphere are nothing more than the circumstances of flight; they are either geographical or aeronautical. We see these people only in relation to the activity that dominates their lives.

What do *they* see? Saint-Exupéry narrates in the third person. The perspective varies, being most often that of Fabien or of Rivière and, less frequently and more briefly, that of Fabien's wife or of Robineau. But whichever one has the point-of-view role the flow of imagery continues, unvarying, no matter whose eye observes the action. Four characters are represented as feeling what is happening, at one time or another, in terms of figure. But the figures invariably are part of one or another of the image-systems we have examined, and none of the four is characterized and distinguished from the others by the images he forms. In other words, what comes to us through the characters is the imagery of Saint-Exupéry.

Furthermore, these are not images evoked by the special nature of the story, or by the particular and perhaps exceptional emotions connected with it. They belong, rather, to the personal stock upon which this writer draws whether he is writing a novel or something else, and, within reason, as much to *Terre des hommes* as to *Vol de nuit*.

In *Terre des hommes* mountains 'rolling in the murk' are like cannon on old men-of-war which have broken their lashings and roll about the deck (p. 142).[5] A farm couple are called keepers of a lighthouse (p. 144). A plane which cannot find fixed reference points by which to navigate is as if on the sea at night (p. 149). Twice a plane is called a 'navire' (pp. 151–2). A peak hidden in a fog becomes potentially explosive, just as a submerged mine brings danger into an entire sea (p. 154). The beach of light image noted in *Vol de nuit* presents itself again. Cap Juby is a 'vaisseau aveugle' (p. 187). An Arab who remembers having lived in the Sahara is said to have smelled the sea (p. 195). Officers sleep on the sand as they would on a raft (p. 196). Camels going to be watered suggest the provisioning of an invisible ship (p. 197). Repeatedly a plane cracked up in the desert evokes shipwreck (pp. 223, 224, 232, etc.).

So many metaphors of this sort suggest a subjacent, haunting analogy between the Sahara and the sea. One is aware of its closeness to cliché: the desert has always been a sea of sand, the camel a ship of the desert. Saint-Exupéry seems to be violating, in this case, the common principle,

[5] Nothing in the text indicates awareness of the reminiscence of Hugo's *Travailleurs de la mer*.

proposed most recently by Stephen Ullmann and Richard A. Sayce,[6] that imagery is most effective when it joins two rather widely separated realms of experience. There is also little doubt that at times—for example, when he continues the shipwreck metaphor just mentioned in a development of the idea that the real shipwrecked ones are not the men in the accident but those who await its outcome—what may have begun as metaphor loses its concreteness and becomes merely the illustration of a thought. Aptness, rather than brilliance and the quality of surprise, would seem to be the dominant trait of such imagery. But this judgment must itself be qualified: if the general theme—what the Germans like to call the *topos*—is hackneyed, Saint-Exupéry's variations on it are very rarely so.

Furthermore, they function regularly to interpret individual, and perhaps unique, experience in commonly familiar language. Few of us have intimate knowledge of the desert and fewer still know anything about flying small airplanes unaided by the radars, lorans, and ground-controlled approaches which today reduce the aircraft to the status of a public carrier. We do have our immemorial knowledge of the dangers of the sea.

There are places, especially in *Terre des hommes*, where these same fundamental, subjacent metaphors—these new treatments of old commonplaces—are even used to translate hallucination. Downed in the desert, half-dead with thirst, plagued by mirages, the pilot is overcome by the feeling of being on a ship.

> Je suis . . . Je suis . . . Je suis embarqué! Je me rendais en Amérique du Sud, je m'étais étendu sur le pont supérieur. La pointe du mât se promenait de long en large, très lentement, parmi les étoiles. Il manque ici un mât, mais je suis embarqué quand même, vers une destination qui ne dépend plus de mes efforts. Des négriers m'ont jeté, lié, sur un navire (p. 234).

(He returns to reality for some pages, and then loses himself in the hallucination again.)

> Ma gorge demeure serrée, c'est mauvais signe, et cependant je me sens mieux. Je me sens calme. Je me sens calme au-delà de toute espérance. Je m'en vais malgré moi en voyage, ligoté sur le pont de mon vaisseau de négriers sous les étoiles . . . (p. 236).

The experience reported here, one on the margins of delirium, is one of image-substitution. The difference between literal and metaphorical has disappeared, and the second term has almost entirely replaced the first as

[6] Sayce, *Style in French Prose*, pp. 62–3; Ullmann, *Style in the French Novel*, pp. 214–15.

representative of reality. One does not doubt the authenticity of the account. Yet the material of the hallucination is the much used material of Saint-Exupéry's commonest metaphor.

Our question about *Vol de nuit* is adequately answered. The imagery that dominates it is not one called up by the subject, mood, or tone of that particular book. It belongs to the general stock upon which Saint-Exupéry regularly draws.

It is true that the passage quoted is not entirely typical. Not every page would confirm its testimony. To expect the frequency of marine imagery to be maintained at such a peak would, indeed, be accusing Saint-Exupéry either of bad artistry or of neurosis. Yet such imagery recurs frequently enough through the book, at least, to attract the attention of an already alert reader.

The same material dominates the passage which is also our first example of the momentary flash of deep perception—the 'epiphany'—which recurs so often in the works of Saint-Exupéry's coevals. The passage appears in the chapter of *Terre des hommes* where Saint-Exupéry's burden is the excellence of the plane as an instrument of man's discovering his true relation to the planet he lives on. More immediately he is meditating on the situation he has been left in by the plane's failure, face to face with the unhuman, brute matter of the universe. It is used as one of the many illustrative apologues which make up the texture of the book.

Echoué une autre fois dans une région de sable épais, j'attendais l'aube. Les collines d'or offraient à la lune leur versant lumineux, et des versants d'ombre montaient jusqu'aux lignes de partages de la lumière. Sur ce chantier désert d'ombre et de lune, régnait une paix de travail suspendu, et aussi un silence de piège, au cœur duquel je m'endormais.

Quand je me réveillai, je ne vis que le bassin du ciel nocturne, car j'étais allongé sur une crête, les bras en croix et face à ce vivier d'étoiles. N'ayant pas compris encore quelles étaient ces profondeurs, je fus pris de vertige, faute d'une racine à quoi me retenir, faute d'un toit, d'une branche d'arbre entre ces profondeurs et moi, déjà délié, livré à la chute comme un plongeur.

Mais je ne tombai point. De la nuque aux talons, je me découvrais noué à la terre. J'éprouvais une sorte d'apaisement à lui abandonner mon poids. La gravitation m'apparaissait souveraine comme l'amour.

Je sentais la terre étayer mes reins, me soutenir, me soulever, me transporter dans l'espace nocturne. Je me découvrais appliqué à l'astre, par une pesée semblable à cette pesée des virages qui vous appliquent au char, je goûtais cet épaulement admirable, cette solidité, cette sécurité, et je devinais, sous mon corps, ce pont courbe de mon navire.

J'avais si bien conscience d'être emporté, que j'eusse entendu sans surprise monter, du fond des terres, la plainte des matériaux qui se réajustent dans l'effort, ce gémissement des vieux voiliers qui prennent leur gîte, ce long cri aigre que font les péniches contrariées. Mais le silence durait dans l'épaisseur des terres. Mais cette pesée se révélait, dans mes épaules, harmonieuse, soutenue, égale pour l'éternité. J'habitais bien cette patrie comme les corps des galériens morts, lestés de plombs, le fond des mers (pp. 176-7)

Here, as in *Vol de nuit*, a man is unable to distinguish between height and depth; he has again lost his horizon; air-water imagery is present when the sky is equated to a 'vivier' and perhaps also in the equation with a basin. Another simile involves a diver. And the earth, on which he is riding as if it were a vehicle, is equated with a ship.

The opening figure, 'échoué'—already a marine image: a man washed up on some coast—gives way to the nature description, with the Wordsworthian personification of hills baring themselves to the moon, and the setting then evokes three metaphors. One of these is structured in the most directly metaphoric statement: 'ce chantier désert'. The other two are attenuated by their structure of noun plus 'de' plus a second noun which is adjectivized by its position, with the metaphoric content located in the adjective: 'paix *de travail suspendu*', 'silence *de piège*'. We also observe the use of the demonstrative 'ce', in the first metaphor, a device which Saint-Exupéry uses very frequently to isolate and point out figurative expressions.

The first sentence of the next paragraph contains two metaphors already mentioned earlier: the 'bassin' is that formed by the night sky, which is also a 'vivier' full not of fish but of stars. The metaphors are explained by the complements, a procedure indispensable to a writer whose metaphors are essential parts of a developing thought. (One could compare that of a poet like Rimbaud, so richly suggestive but so often unspecific, who, if he had talked of the 'bassin' and the 'vivier' as vehicles of a metaphor, would have left the identity of the corresponding tenor to the sympathy or ingenuity of his reader.) They have the effect of exchanging one spatial dimension for another, as already noted: a basin and a fish tank are objects into which one looks from above; the speaker is looking into the sky but has no feeling of looking upward. His disorientation and vertigo in the absence of fixed reference points we have identified with the flyer's losing his horizon. It will be noted that the image of the diver places one of Saint-Exupéry's favourite figures in a position of emphasis, at the end of the sentence, and of climax, at the end of the paragraph.

If the third paragraph contains only an imageless, intellectualized comparison, the fourth submerges us in a sea of imagery. The verbs of the personification—'étayer', 'soutenir', 'soulever', and 'transporter'—should not be read as an example of pathetic fallacy. What they achieve in their progressive, four-stage development is the transformation of the earth from a mere support to a vehicle which, at the end of the paragraph, he identifies as a ship.

Meanwhile, the transitional material connecting the first suggestion of the earth-as-transport and the eventual equation of earth and ship is significant, not only because of the noun in 'je me trouvais appliqué à l'astre' or because of the suggestion of passiveness in 'appliqué', but even more so because it turns out to be ultimately experiential: gravitation is transformed into centrifugal force, and spatial dimensions have again been confused. He is riding something which, to his physical and emotional responses, is like an airplane. And this is what, a moment later, becomes a ship.

The earth-ship metaphor continues, becoming increasingly specific, in the next paragraph. Earlier in the book he has pictured the internal, geologic workings of the earth as strange 'slow digestions' (pp. 174–6). Now the comparison is with the creaks and groans of an old sailing vessel heeled over in the wind, and the strident sounds of the hull of a pinnace under sail. And the passage (as isolated here from the rest of the chapter) ends with still another sea-image: he belongs in this landscape as galley slaves who have been buried at sea belong to the sea's bottom.

So he records his own personal, private affinity with the desert—in language and imagery which vary little from that of *Vol de nuit*.

He was a poet and a sea-haunted one. Was he also a novelist? Not, one would say, any longer than it took him to discover that his poetry did not require the support of a story. He wrote, as is often said, the poetry of flight. It was the poetry of a moment in the infancy of aviation, of undeveloped planes and rudimentary facilities—and as such is now out of date. But it was also the poetry of man discovering his essential nature through unequal conflict with a hostile element, a subject which will go

E

out of date only when man does. And his imagination assimilated the conflict with man's old, perhaps most symbolic enemy—conflict with the sea.

A survey of his imagery does not reveal a novelist. But a poet, even in the 1930's, did not need to be a novelist.

CHAPTER FOUR

Coherence and Incoherence
in Bernanos's *Monsieur Ouine*[1]

Monsieur Ouine is the one Bernanos liked best among his novels and also the one he found most difficult to bring off. Repeatedly he thought it nearly finished, only to discover on re-reading that perfection was still remote. His friends told him his story was obscure, and he needed no one to tell him that it was exasperatingly difficult to write, a 'lugubre urinoir'. It wore him out until he was as irritated as he was exhausted, 'fatigué de toujours pisser contre le même mur'.[2] When he finally got it done, in 1943—he had started writing in 1932 but had put it aside repeatedly for other work—his Brazilian printers turned out a monumentally bad job, full of errors that Bernanos was too impatient to catch in proof, and the first French edition, which came out at the end of World War II, faithfully copied all the defects. These were finally corrected in the edition of 1953, but the fact that so many critics had by then put their admiration for *Monsieur Ouine* on record testifies that for Bernanos the obscurity he struggled against was no obstacle to success.

For the critic *Monsieur Ouine* thus poses a special problem. Why does not the novel's obscurity, which must not be minimized and can hardly be exaggerated, spoil the book for most readers? That these readers are French, and thus products of a literary culture that attributes a special value to clearness, increases the urgency of the problem. Any solution, however partial and hesitantly proposed, should be welcome.

The solution proposed here is that the obscurity is caused by a fundamental incoherence which operates on the level of rational discourse, which is offset by a countervailing and coherent system of imagery such

---

[1] This chapter enlarges upon a lecture originally given at the University of Leeds, February 1962.

[2] Letter (to Henri Massis?), written from La Bayorre, May 1934: quoted in *Bernanos par lui-même*, p. 167.

as can make for aesthetic satisfaction—but on a level not of rational discourse but of poetry. This pattern of coherence and incoherence is characteristic of Bernanos's writing in general and turns up as frequently in his so-called polemic essays as in his novels.

One of the former, *Les Grands Cimetières sous la lune*, provides an example that has the merit of revealing the nature of the pattern in a relatively brief passage:

> ... Toute vocation est un appel—*vocatus*—et tout appel veut être transmis. Ceux que j'appelle ne sont évidemment pas nombreux. Ils ne changeront rien aux affaires de ce monde. Mais c'est pour eux, c'est pour eux que je suis né.
>
>   *   *   *
>
> Compagnons inconnus, vieux frères, nous arriverons ensemble, un jour, aux portes du royaume de Dieu. Troupe fourbue, troupe harassée, blanche de la poussière de nos routes, chers visages durs dont je n'ai pas su essuyer la sueur, regards qui ont vu le bien et le mal, rempli leur tâche, assumé la vie et la mort, ô regards qui ne se sont jamais rendus! Ainsi vous retrouverai-je, vieux frères. Tels que mon enfance vous a rêvés. Car j'étais parti à votre rencontre, j'accourais vers vous. Au premier détour j'aurais vu rougir les feux de vos éternels bivouacs. Mon enfance n'appartenait qu'à vous. Peut-être un certain jour, un jour que je sais, ai-je été digne de prendre la tête de votre troupe inflexible. Dieu veuille que je ne revoie jamais les chemins où j'ai perdu vos traces, à l'heure où l'adolescence étend ses ombres, où le suc de la mort, le long des veines, vient se mêler au sang du cœur! Chemins du pays d'Artois, à l'extrême automne, fauves et odorants comme des bêtes, sentiers pourrissants sous la pluie de Novembre, grandes chevauchées de nuages, eaux mortes ... J'arrivais, je poussais la grille, j'approchais du feu mes bottes rougies par l'averse. L'aube venait bien avant que fussent rentrés dans le silence de l'âme, dans ses profonds repaires, les personnages fabuleux encore à peine formés, embryons sans membres. Mouchette et Donissan, Cénabre, Chantal, et vous, vous seul de mes créatures dont j'ai cru parfois distinguer le visage, mais à qui je n'ai pas osé donner de nom—cher curé d'un Ambricourt imaginaire ...[3]

Bernanos has been explaining how he has overcome his feeling of the futility of all such enterprises and undertaken writing what will be *Les Grands Cimetières*; and the question *why* has been inextricable from a related question *for whom*. He has already invoked this audience: 'J'hésite

[3] Palatine-Plon ed., pp. 12–13. Page references of quotations of *Les Grands Cimetières*, hereafter incorporated in the text, are to this edition.

à franchir le premier pas, le premier pas vers vous, ô visages voilés! Car le premier pas franchi, je sais que je ne m'arrêterai plus, que j'irai, vaille que vaille, jusqu'au bout de ma tâche, à travers des jours et des jours, si pareils entre eux que je ne les compte pas, qu'ils sont comme tranchés de ma vie' (p. 11).

In passing we note that he has used one of his favorite rhetorical devices, anaphoric repetition ('le premier pas, le premier pas vers vous') in which the second element enlarges and explains the first, and which so often appears in his prose when the emotional tensions begin to rise. And he has also used one of his favorite *topoi*, the figure in which something requiring special effort is compared to a forced march; here it is the effort of writing, but later it will be assimilated to the labor required merely to live.

But meanwhile, exactly who are these 'visages voilés' of whom he is saying that his beginning to write will be a first step toward joining them? He answers the question in the first lines of the passage used here to illustrate the characteristic pattern of coherence and incoherence. They are the select few to whom he is transmitting the call he has himself received, too few to change the ways of the world but the few for whom, even so, he was born. Here again the anophora ('c'est pour vous, c'est pour vous que je suis né') marks intensity of emotion. And now, emotion sweeping him along, he has moved into a prosopopoeia, turning away from his present reader to address these imaginary figures. After the break in the page marked by the three asterisks he resumes this figure and elaborates it.

And here he also revives his commonplace of the forced march, which is now that of fatigue-worn, dusty veterans, hard-faced and sweaty, who have never surrendered. But are these the 'visages voilés' whom, earlier, he has spoken of joining? It develops presently that he is addressing the imaginary companions of his childhood who have since peopled his novels; they are the heroes and heroines: Mouchette and Donissan from *Sous le soleil de Satan*, Chantal de Clergerie and Cénabre from *L'Imposture* and *La Joie*, and the nameless priest whose story is the *Journal d'un curé de campagne*. This is what we mean by incoherence: without the least warning he has shifted from addressing the people *for whom* he writes and is addressing those *about whom* he has written. For how can the fatigued troop of veterans be identified with the readers for whom he is writing *Les Grands Cimetières*? There must, obviously, be some connection in Bernanos's mind, but a link is missing here in his book.[4]

[4] The passage presents even further difficulties. How literally should we take what Bernanos says? One of the primary sources of the character of Chantal was the

The lines that follow the illustration, and that bring to an end what must be thought of as his Preface even though he does not call it one, do nothing to relieve our perplexity, for in them the creatures of his imagination are forgotten and he turns to address his present readers: '. . . . et c'est cela qui vous fait prêter l'oreille, compagnons dispersés à travers le monde, qui par hasard ou par ennui avez ouvert un jour mes livres' (p. 13). Surely these are not the people who are *in* his 'livres'. Are they to be identified with the 'visages voilés'? We simply cannot say.

Thus, on the level of literal discourse, the level of prose intended to convey ideas, Bernanos is incoherent. Essential pieces of information have been omitted.

And yet, on another level, we do know what he means or, perhaps more accurately, what he meant to mean. Each time he mentions his audience, and no matter what he says its members are, the *topos* of the forced march reappears. We have already seen it juxtaposed with the 'visages voilés', and it inhered in the image of the 'troupe fourbue'. Bernanos renews it shortly thereafter in the reference to the fires of eternal bivouacs. Two sentences below this reference he is thinking of the day when he may have been worthy of taking command of the inflexible troop. And finally, in the closing lines of the Preface, which follow our illustration, he returns to the figure once more: 'Mais le plus mort des morts est le petit garçon que je fus. Et pourtant, l'heure venue, c'est lui qui reprendra sa place à la tête de ma vie, rassemblera mes pauvres années jusqu'à la dernière, et comme un jeune chef ses vétérans, ralliant la troupe en désordre, entrera le premier dans la Maison du Père' (p. 13).

If this were poetry we were working on instead of prose, there would

spiritual biography of Sainte-Thérèse de Jésus, whose *Novissima verba* was printed only in 1926. There may be grounds for sharing Von Balthasar's opinion that Bernanos may have read the *Manuscrits autobiographiques*, published in 1896. But is it likely that he read them at the age when he was tramping the roads of Artois?

Similar doubts arise regarding the character of Cénabre. It has never been a secret that an important prototype of this intellectual priest was the ex-Jesuit Henri Bremond, whose *Histoire du sentiment religieux* may have displeased Bernanos. But Bremond's work was written after the First World War, and its author can hardly have come to Bernanos's attention at the time in question. Michel Estève's notes in the Pléiade edition throw no light on this matter.

An adolescent imagination already crowded by characters later to appear in novels may be commoner among gifted individuals than one would at first suspect, though evidence is rare. It seems wiser, on the whole, not to hold Bernanos to the letter of exactness in all this, and to underscore what he says about memberless embryos and the lack of faces. We may read him as saying that as a youth he imagined creatures whom he still loves.

be no question: this *topos* of the forced march would strike the reader as a dominant. The writer persisting in a task that he has not wanted to undertake, the veterans (real or imagined) of the dusty road, the years of the writer's own life, and so forth, are bound together by the same presiding image. What Bernanos takes to be his audience are people like himself, including those in his novels, toward whom he can feel a kind of fraternity because they, like him, are inflexible, indomitable, and like him determined to push along until the end on the way they have chosen. The figure of the forced march, in other words, corresponds to the emotion underlying the passage and the Preface as a whole.

It seems to be the force and intensity of emotion that disrupts the coherence of the passage taken as a piece of rational discourse. Exclamations replace the declarative sentences that are the norm in the opening paragraphs of the Preface, and a number of sentences are left uncompleted by any verb. The second sentence suggests emotional turbulence by its disturbed internal structure: the repetition at its beginning, the apposition of a singular, 'troupe', with a plural, 'visages', and the apposition following it of 'regards' with 'visages' form a progression from total forms to faces and from faces to eyes that suggests an ordered movement toward closer and closer focus, but at the same time opens a series of figures to be catalogued only under the heading of catachresis: only by stretching metonymy severely can 'regards' fulfill a task, assume life and death, or refuse to surrender. If such a sentence does not disquiet the reader, the probable reason is that he is distracted by the intensity of the emotion and does not feel the syntactical and rhetorical discontinuity.

In the concatenation of nominal phrases (with qualifiers) that begin with the reference to the 'chemins du pays d'Artois', emotion again introduces discontinuity. How should one understand its relation to the exclamation that precedes it? If the 'chemins' are the same in both it is possible to read the sentence as if the roads he does not want to see again because of some youthful error are identical with the roads from which he would return, after his long tramps, to muse over the eventual population of his novels. But this makes sense only if the order of events has been distorted, making him say that for a time he walked the roads with these fantasies and then, *later*, lost them. If such a reading seems unlikely, it is only because of the guiding power of the coherent imagery.

Such is the persistent pattern in Bernanos's writing that is proposed here as the secret of *Monsieur Ouine*.

Bernanos himself spoke of *Monsieur Ouine* as a 'roman onirique',[5] and the description is not entirely inaccurate: one alert critic has even treated all the novels as if they belonged to the sub-category of dream literature.[6] The events in *Monsieur Ouine* seem frequently as disconnected as those in dreams and almost as gratuitous. And in one episode at least the protagonist seems to be asleep: the only way to explain how Philippe can hold his final conversation with Ouine, two hours after the latter has died, is by assuming that the boy has dropped off to sleep after emptying his wine bottle.

But it must be admitted that many dreams are more coherent than this novel, and the judgment of the friends who warned Bernanos of his obscurity stands confirmed: *Monsieur Ouine* is undoubtedly the Bernanos novel that offers the stiffest challenge to readers who insist on understanding what they read. Even the most attentive has trouble finding out what happens.

We never do learn who killed the little *valet de ferme*, so that from one point of view this novel can be thought of as a mystery story whose author has forgotten to give us the solution. We do not know where the demented *maire* went, whether to kill himself or merely to wander away, after writing 'adieu' with his finger in the dust of the rectory; and are not much better informed on subjects such as whether Ginette meant to harm Philippe when her horse nearly ran him down, or whether Philippe really saw, or only thought he saw, Ouine leave the house on the night of the *valet's* murder. How Ginette contrived the physical and mental decline of her husband, Anthelme, is also a mystery. So is the relationship between Philippe's mother and her companion, the English girl who is simply called Miss. It is not even clear whether Philippe's father, who is referred to repeatedly in the course of the story but never seen, is dead or just permanently absent.

Confusion as to *what* has happened is frequently confounded by our not knowing *to whom*. Many of the characters are called by more than one name, but we learn this only gradually. Bernanos does not, for example, make clear that Madame de Néréis is also Ginette, is known to some as Jambe-de-laine, and is the person referred to toward the end of the book as Fanny. Such identifications the reader must ferret out for himself; his disorientation is assured unless he does so.

As an added source of difficulty, there is also the question *why*. Why should Ginette want to hurt Philippe? Why should Philippe try to strangle

[5] Letter written from Barbecena, 15 November, 1943, quoted in *Bernanos par lui-même*, p. 168.

[6] Henri Debluë, *Les Romans de Georges Bernanos ou le défi du rêve*.

Miss? Why should old Vandomme tell his poacher son-in-law that the game is up and he must kill himself before the police come when the old man knows perfectly well that the younger one can not have drowned the *valet*? Two of the major characters, Ginette and the *maire*, are undoubtedly insane, so that what they do may not be susceptible to rational explanation, but the other characters are presumably of sound mind and yet their motives are often equally obscure.

The matter of motivation can be overdone, of course.[7] Any 'oneiric' novel—for that matter, any novel intended to produce heavy atmospheric effects—is likely to suppress the kind of information that brings daylight with it. But even so the whole role of the central figure in *Monsieur Ouine* is, for many readers, not so much mysterious as opaque. There should be some connection, one would naturally think, between Ouine's presence in the village and the horrid series of disasters that take place: the murder of the *valet*, the murder of Ginette by the villagers, the suicides of Eugène and Hélène, Ginette's attempt to kill Philippe, the latter's attempt to murder Miss, the suicide of the insane *maire* (if indeed suicide was his fate and if I am right in assuming that Ginette and Philippe intended to do what they did). Yet we learn nothing more relevant to this connection

[7] The motivation of the characters has always puzzled many well-equipped readers of Bernanos. For example, Rayner Heppenstall ('The Priest as Scapegoat', *Partisan Review*, Sept.-Oct. 1946, pp. 448–57), while praising the novelist for his 'profound judgment of motive', professes not to see why the baleful Russian chauffeur in *La Joie* should kill the heroine after seeing her saying her prayers, or why Cénabre in *L'Imposture* should be brought to violence and the brink of suicide by intellectual pride, or what the suicide of Mouchette means to Abbé Donissan in *Sous le soleil de Satan*. His own explanation is that in such figures Bernanos revives the primitive institution of the scapegoat, the sacrificial victim who assumes the accumulated sins and guilts of the community. Heppenstall does not, of course, claim that Bernanos had anything of the sort in mind. He is only showing how, so to speak, the behavior of such characters would be described by someone like Sir James Frazer. But the very cogent fact remains that the motives Bernanos obviously thought he had attributed to his characters have failed entirely to get through to the critic.

Part of the difficulty is doubtless theological. A critic who does not believe in the literal presence of evil in the world, and wants no part of its personification in Satan, is unlikely to accept the explanation of the conduct of certain humans as a product of Satan's works. He can hardly choose not to treat their stories as allegory. It is not clear how widely Heppenstall had read in Bernanos at the time, but it seems quite possible that if he had known more of the non-fictional writings, and seen how literally and un-allegorically Bernanos took 'le Mal', he would have understood the nature of his own perplexity.

Heppenstall would surely have been even more perplexed by *Monsieur Ouine*, where the role of the central figure is even more mysterious than in the earlier novels.

than that where Ouine is, evil has moved in also. And this explanation seems peculiarly inadequate because this retired teacher of languages does not strike us as especially wicked; he merely seems fatigued and ill.

It is only when we have read the other books of Bernanos that we realize that the mere fact of Ouine's being at ease in this literally God-forsaken parish identifies him. Any mind but his active, restless, sceptical and fundamentally sterile one would suffer in such a place; he is un-anguished and serene. As we shall hear him say, the bad smells of rot do not disturb him, but we do not know what he means until we learn that this is the stench of the modern world, and this lesson is not easily available in the novel named for him. We get it, rather, from reading Bernanos's other novels and even such polemical essays as *La Grande Peur des bien-pensants*. This is equivalent to saying that to know any one of Bernanos's books thoroughly one must have read the complete works. The requirement may seem a heavy one to impose even on the most well-disposed reader.

In any event, even the most experienced reader of Bernanos finds the obscurity of *Monsieur Ouine* a sufficient challenge to his attention and understanding. Of the usual *who, what, why, where,* and *when,* only the last two elements are likely to be set forth openly in a given episode, and sometimes not even they. A master criminal sits quietly observing crimes he does not even appear to will, while people kill, die, and go mad in a disjointed nightmare of violence.

An image system capable of offsetting all this, in the way the image of the forced march offsets the incoherence of the Preface to *Les Grands Cimetières*, must of necessity be extensive and, perhaps, obsessive at once.

The most cursory reading of *Monsieur Ouine* reveals an extraordinary number of analogical figures, and there can be no doubt that Bernanos intended them to be in it, since five times in the course of the novel his awareness of them is directly expressed. For example, he introduces one figure as follows: 'Comment ne pas l'imaginer sous les espèces d'un animal familier? ... Entre elle et la vie, le rongeur industrieux multiplie ses digues, fouille, creuse, déblaie, surveille jour et nuit le niveau de l'eau perfide' (p. 1351). In another place, it occurs to Steeny that the English girl's head is triangular like a snake's, and he imagines her starting to hiss (p. 1443). In a third, a character, distressed by the variety of the images of misfortune which have crowded his mind, finds that they have fused into a single elementary one, the image of an obstacle (p. 1461).

As a general rule, the images are charged with more than one function:

they contribute to the creation of atmosphere and at the same time serve one of the recognized techniques of narrative. For example, characteriza-tion: this is one of those novels in which the point of view passes frequently from one character to another, so that the individual's way of seeing or feeling his world becomes an index of what he is. When, for example, old Vandomme thinks that all that is left him by his misfortune is to endure, the thought comes to his mind as 'durer comme un arbre'; in a more active mind this might not be an image at all, but in the context of what we know about him, it seems likely that he *sees* some similarity between himself and the old trees he lives among—he is the kind of man who would see it.

But there is also reason to suspect that a number of the characters may be drawn, in whole or in part, from the novelist's own vision of himself. To go on using Vandomme as example, he has much in common with the Bernanos whose children's misfortunes caused him so much concern and who in his later years reduced all his ambitions to one: to endure. The village priest of Fenouille echoes Bernanos's feeling of great helplessness in the presence of the evil of the modern world. The crazy *maire* of the village has a mental condition not entirely unlike the crises of anxiety for which the novelist repeatedly underwent treatment. The boy Philippe is as in love with open roads as was the young Bernanos we have seen pictured in the Preface of *Les Grands Cimetières*. Even M. Ouine has some of Bernanos's obsession with himself as a child—'le petit garçon que je fus'—and the feeling that, in comparison with childhood, all adult life is a derogation. Consequently, the same images which are used to characterize may, from another point of view, be seen also as the material of a very personal poem: the private view of a life which has become a nightmare.

We are thus excluding several functions of the imagery from our present consideration in order to fix attention on one. Our excuse for doing so is the importance of this particular function in determining the novel's effect upon the reader.

The images that recur most often have to do with the following subjects: water, mud, animals, insects, decay, stenches, cancer and kindred illnesses, and bareness. These, except bareness, have very common associations with each other in most human imaginations: water is frequented by animals, breeds insects, forms mud and causes decay; mud and decay encourage insect life; decay causes stench; such ills as cancer and diabetic gangrene frequently stink and are suggestive of rot and so on. These connect the image-system with the physical background of the story:

this novel may be a bad dream, but the landscape of the dream is not a dream landscape but a very real one that Bernanos knew from having lived in it and that has a verifiable geography. The action is set near enough Boulogne for a character to drop in there on casual business, and near enough Poperinghe for even a poor man to be able to transport bodies there for burial. The region is damp; the clay of the soil turns to dust under hot sun, but the rest of the time—the major part—it turns to slippery and adhesive mud. The first evening of the story the weather is clear, but thereafter either rain is falling, or has just fallen, or is about to. The landscape is saturated and sodden.

Water plays a constant role in the literal story. After the *valet de ferme* has been strangled, his body is thrown in a torrent that in its turbulence looks like beer (p. 1393). On his way to tell Eugène that the end has come, Vandomme walks over a black and saturated earth that exudes something like ink (p. 1434). Eugène and Hélène go off to take their own lives with water hissing around their feet (p. 1474). On the last evening of his life, Ouine is suffering from the damp that rises at sundown to torture his tubercular lungs (p. 1545).

We have already noted an image in which a water animal industriously maintains the level of a sheet of 'perfidious water'; the water in question is equated with the barrier of detached gentleness which Philippe's mother holds up between herself and the rest of the world (p. 1351 f.). (We shall return to this image later because there is an animal in it.) In another which links water with an internal state, Steeny-Philippe's consciousness, just after he has found himself choking the governess, becomes like a punctured cistern that thenceforward gives only a muddy water, loaded with anxiety (p. 1451). Ouine, returning from talking with the priest, sits down beside a stream whose water has been dirtied by a film of soapsuds (p. 1470). And the poor priest likens the sin and crime that surrounds him to an ordure which should be liquefied in sewers and swept away by subterranean rivers (p. 1487).

Not unexpectedly, given the situation, a feeling of spiritual danger is frequently associated with the water-images. Philippe, sitting in the silence of the sick man's room, feels the magic of Ouine's presence as being like a 'caress of water' on his forehead, breast, and palms (p. 1365). The priest watches the *maire* cower insanely in a corner and thinks of the last, still-lighted porthole of a ship sinking in the rain on a dark night (p. 1517). Ginette makes gestures like those of an exhausted swimmer (p. 1416), and the priest, in another desperate moment, unwittingly throws up his arms like a swimmer giving up the struggle (p. 1487).

Water is almost never introduced in a pleasant association. It goes with morbid mental states, unhealthiness, filth, death, and disaster. But this is water alone: mud will be much more relevant yet to the situation of Fenouille.

Mud determines the essential sadness of the landscape. From the first mention, it appears always as unhealthy. Ouine speaks of having had to treat his stone floor with chlorine to get the centennial dirt out of the cracks, and remarks that the mud, freed by the acid, bubbles out as if from numerous tiny wounds (p. 1362). It is he, also, who points to its symbolic meaning, which is again in his mind when he refers to the stirring of evil instincts in the village under the stress of crime as agitating the sad sheets of mud (p. 1465). And while we are not sure that a reference, some pages later, to the little, muddy village holds a symbolic content, there can be no doubt about the meaning of 'barbotait' (p. 1483) as stating the equivalence of mud and crime.

Mud is in turn linked with excrement—as in the priest's reference to ordure and sewers (p. 1487)—and this association obsesses the *curé* as he plunges into the funeral harangue which has the unsought effect of turning the people of Fenouille toward the final and most horrid murder. He sees, and almost touches, mounds of excrement, these sheets of mud (p. 1488).

Thus when the horror reaches its climax the identification is so fully established, the equation so complete, that mud becomes an autonomous symbol, independent of structured metaphor. When the priest advances toward the open grave, slips, falls, and fouls his surplice in the mud, we have no need to ask the meaning (p. 1493). And no more need we ask it when Ginette de Néréis, also at the grave, faces the crowd who are about to maul her, and receives a handful of mud on her bosom (p. 1500): she will be no more the victim of the wrath of these people than of their sin and everything else that mud has come to stand for.

In such a way, two principal elements of the background of the novel acquire significance extending far beyond the literal. Other image clusters will also contribute to the accretion of meanings.

Water and mud are associated constantly with offensive smells. On the morning when the body of the *valet* is taken to the *mairie*, a stale odor of stagnant water rises so strongly from his clothing that the bystanders blink (p. 1403). The *maire*, whose awareness of his own guilt and foulness is summed up in his hyper-acute (as well as erectile) nose, is plagued by smells in the air which to him bring horrid proof that in the midst of life we are in corruption. 'Un air plus riche, plus dense, chargé d'odeurs qui glissent les unes sur les autres, où se pénètre sans se confondre jusqu'au cœur du jour quand la force de midi les étale en une seule nappe épaisse, toute bouillonnante sous le soleil comme ces grasses eaux, pleines de bulles' (p. 1395). (One cannot help observing how frequently, in such imagery, the same vocabulary appears. 'Glisser', 'nappe', and various words for bubbling recur constantly.)

The other character in the story who is most conscious of smells, and finds them unpleasant, is M. Ouine. It is he, significantly, who directly associates evil stench with evil, and who adds that it is one he does not fear (p. 1467). In addition, it is also he who draws attention to the smell of diabetic gangrene at the deathbed of Ginette's husband, Anthelme (p. 1366).

Ouine is also the one most aware of disease and death; he makes a number of the images in conversation. And other speakers link him with these subjects. Ouine, himself, refers to pity as an itching of all the wounds of the soul (p. 1364), and in another passage remarks that pity has as much chance of working in the village as a surgeon would of working in a sheet of pus (p. 1464). (Again the word 'nappe'!) In another place we learn that he is, himself, full of pus (p. 1530). His tuberculosis is at one juncture termed a smoldering fire but in another a kind of rot (p. 1470); and as death approaches his lungs finish rotting away (p. 1529).

But the decay characteristic of him, and with which he may have infected the village, is present in other minds, also. The tortured *maire*, in the last glimmer of his sanity, wonders what thoughts occur to the dead 'underground, all eaten up, really rotten' (p. 1518). And his wife becomes convinced that the difference between Fenouille today and Fenouille in former times is that the old men have begun to rot (p. 1511). Old Vandomme, whose one intent was to endure in his misfortune 'like a tree', reminds people at the *valet*'s funeral of a tree, but one that has decayed (p. 1482).

Both the *mairesse* and the *curé* attach to the motif of poison the somewhat kindred motif of rot. A poison must be in the air, says the lady, causing the decay of the old (p. 1511), and the priest declares that the village is not only defenceless against poisons but that the people now can distill their own within themselves out of any material whatsoever, as a diabetic secretes sugar from every source (p. 1492). In another context— talking with the doctor—the priest comes perilously close to agreeing with an earlier remark of Ouine's. The latter had declared that sympathy and compassion meant not suffering-with, but rather rotting-with

(p. 1464), and the priest cries out that suffering is a 'poisoned thorn in the heart of man' (p. 1525).

This universe of water and mud, crime and despair, illness and poison and rot, Bernanos populates with a remarkable amount of subhuman life: animal, reptile, bird, and insect. It slinks and snarls, crawls and swarms. In losing its spiritual life, Fenouille appears to have lost its humanity, also.

We have already seen the aggressively patient mildness of Philippe's mother compared to a small animal that labors to protect the water level of a sort of polder. Before we have finished with it, we know that this little beast is a rodent, repairs his own dams and dikes, steers with his tail as he swims (p. 1532). A bit later the woman's heart itself is assimilated with the animal by a choice of adjectives (p. 1352), and a few lines further on the animal metamorphoses into a spider spinning its web.

Other images effect the same transfer between human and subhuman more rapidly because they are less fully developed. Thus Ginette compares herself to a white-headed spider, makes Philippe think of a gigantic bird, and moves her head like a hunted animal (p. 1357). Ouine compares himself to a marine jelly on the ocean floor (p. 1368), and Philippe later recalls the image (p. 1373). The boy twice thinks of his house as a cage; in one of these images his mother and Miss are pretty beasts and the latter needs to be muzzled like a ferret (p. 1385). Dr. Malépine likens Ginette to a raven smelling death (p. 1401) and also calls her house, disconcertingly, a nest of lies and ... frogs (p. 1404). The *maire* watches the doctor like an animal worriedly watching its master (p. 1405). The total effect is to confine us in a world of animals. The reader is never long away from Bernanos's menagerie.

Contexts in which insects are invoked are extremely varied. The *maire*'s incipient madness is referred to as a flyblown wound (p. 1395). Ouine explains that he feels as if wrapped in some mysteriously protective substance that moves about with him wherever he goes, and at the same time is like the cocoon of a silkworm. After Ginette overturns her wagon, it lies with its shiny belly turned upward, like an insect's (p. 1411). The woodsman who witnesses the episode says that Ginette, herself, looks like an insect and Philippe agrees: she is like some disgusting thing with antennae, mandibles, and claws (p. 1416). Vandomme feels his own thoughts go round in circles, like a great fly (p. 1455), and Ouine describes the moral condition of Ginette's house by saying that it is full of dead lies, efforts, and struggles which have been crushed by accident like so many insects.

The beasts in some of the animal images are innocent or pitiable. Confronted by the doctor and the *maire*, Ginette looks from one to the other like an innocent little creature (p. 1403). Her sly, inexorably patient eye is that of a captive animal (p. 1406). As she crawls away from her over-turned cart, the movements of her shoulders and her dragging legs remind Philippe of his old spaniel with its broken back (p. 1411). The image of the small animal in a trap is one of those Bernanos elaborates at length and the poacher condemned to die for the crime he has not committed evokes a complex metaphor in which he is likened to one of his own victims (pp. 1456-7).

More often than not, however, the animals in the metaphors are stupid, dangerous, or cruel. Thus the men at the *valet*'s funeral snort like cattle and huddle together like a herd attacked by wolves (p. 1483). Twice they are likened to something naked that writhes around the coffin (pp. 1484-5). After the funeral the crowd takes on the character of a predatory animal (p. 1459), and shortly afterward becomes a cat letting its victim try to escape (p. 1501).

In brief, almost every character in the novel is at some time compared to an animal. Ouine is a sleek old tomcat, fat, shiny, and velvet-pawed. Ginette, in addition to being the animals, birds, and insects already reported, is an old she-wolf. Philippe is equated with a captious pony and with a young cat glutted with cream (pp. 1448, 1453). Vandomme twitches his shoulders like a horse plagued by flies (p. 1430). The poacher, Eugène, is like an animal hunted or trapped (pp. 1453 ff.). The *maire*'s wife speaks of her husband as an old cat who has become a mouse (p. 1439). In fact, the only major figure to escape identification with some lower form of life is the priest—who is also the only one to have escaped corruption by the evil that stalks Fenouille.

Not all the animal images are connected with crime and what the Catholic church condemns as sin. Some, for example those attached to Vandomme, clearly arise from the author's affection for his character. Others have to be understood (as were certain cryptic references in the Preface of *Les Grands Cimetières*) in terms of Bernanos's disposition toward the world in general and of a theological interpretation of modern history which we have come to know not so much from any one book as from habitual reading of the composite expression available only through the complete works. The plight of many individuals is not of their own making: the responsibility for their sins, crimes, suicides, and murders lies upon the world they live in. Thus in this novel the spiritual death of the parish has cut the source of the life of individuals. They have been turned into dangerous, hunted beasts, but they are also the *enfants humiliés*.

Even so there is no denying that, to judge by the total evidence of the imagery, Bernanos imagines these people as beyond the reach of Christian redemption. He evokes a universe of crawling, snarling, writhing things— 'saletés' is Philippe's eloquent word—inhabiting the muck and damp of a world that has literally gone to the Devil. They belong to the infamous menagerie of our vices. As the *curé*, who like all of Bernanos's good priests is both enemy and victim of the modern ethos, tells the doctor, who is the almost official apostle of the modern, if this village or many another were set afire, out would come scuttling varieties of beasts whose very names have long been forgotten.

This brings us to the point where we must ask what his imagery, and his treatment of it, shows us about Bernanos as novelist—as well as inquire about its roles in this particular novel.

No doubt the use he makes of the image in many instances is the one any skilful novelist would make. *Monsieur Ouine* being one of those novels which exploit multiple points of view, the reader sees the action through the eyes of Philippe, the *curé*, the *maire*, Vandomme, Hélène, to say nothing of the brief glimpses of how things look to other characters and of the numerous passages which can, logically, be only the interventions of the author himself. It has already been noted that numerous images characterize the people to whom they occur; we should add that they also reveal motivation. It is Philippe, for example, who so often sees the similarity of another character with something subhuman, and the fact of his doing so may well be a symptom of his revolt against his surroundings, which in turn is what attaches him to M. Ouine. Similarly, in the case of Vandomme, images that characterize him also perform the additional function. His mind is full of thoughts of death and of the dead. 'Les morts accourent de toutes parts, serrés autant qu'un vol de corneilles ... On a beau les chasser cent et cent fois, ils reviennent encore—pis que des rats' (p. 1430). It is the image, as much at least as the thought itself, that obsesses him. A bit later: 'Sacrés fantômes! ... Les voilà qui le cernent de leur vol noir, sacrées corneilles' (p. 1432). Tone and syntax identify these as occurring within the old man's mind, so that we know that his obsession with the dead is behind his wanting to endure and determines his rigid, automatic conduct on the day of the funeral.

This functioning of the imagery may be an adequate explanation of there being so little that is original in the material from which the images are made. Mud and water, stench and illness, decay and poison have a long history in the literature of human weakness. They are likely to be the furniture of any Inferno, beginning with Dante's. *Hamlet* is full of pus and corruption. So is the poetry of Baudelaire. But these materials are also

F

those which are within the experience of the characters, as familiar in the Artois as in Dante's Hell. Bernanos is using them to turn the physical background—the 'setting'—of his novel into a moral universe, thus imparting to the surroundings a moral implication, making them a metaphor for moral and spiritual horror.

Meanwhile Bernanos seems to achieve special atmospheric effects by varying the concentration of imagery in different parts of the story. The water and mud images, for example, occur in every section, and the association with the moral correlatives is established very early, but incidence increases as the story approaches the moment of Ginette's murder. Whether this concentration functions to increase the reader's ominous feeling that something horrible is about to happen should perhaps be left to be decided by each individual who reads the book. Our inability to describe such a feeling without resorting to further tropes—our own— warns that an unusual degree of private response and perhaps of arbitrariness is involved here. But if the response were shared by a considerable number of sensitive readers, would it not be fair to say that something like a thickening of atmosphere has been made to occur by an increase in the frequency of mud and water images?

Coherence, as a literary concept, seems always to involve causation. If the events do not seem to 'flow' one out of the other, the second growing out of the first and the third out of the second, the narrative itself does not cohere. If the behavior of a character is represented as gratuitous and unmotivated, if we do not learn why he acts as he does, again we speak of incoherence. No one who has read *Monsieur Ouine* doubts that the book is in some degree incoherent in both these ways.

One very real advantage of using an unoriginal imagery of the kind *Monsieur Ouine* offers is precisely that it is traditional—and can be made to mitigate incoherence. If we do not always know why some of the characters do what they do, at least we know *what they look like* as they do it and the imagery translates the look in terms as familiar to us as to them. This is an evil world they live in, and the imagery never lets the reader forget the fact. Bernanos first gave this novel the title of *La Paroisse morte*, and the images, in their totality, are not long in reducing the inherent metaphor of this title to the literal fact of death. Where God is not, the human rapidly gives way to the unhuman and the subhuman, and to the filth in which these breed.

Cursory inspection also reveals that the basic motifs of this imagery do not belong exclusively to *Monsieur Ouine*.[8] Like Saint-Exupéry's, the images remain the same, to a very large extent, though the stories change. (When the locale of a novel changes as it does in the case of *Un Crime*, which is set in the hill country of Grenoble instead of the flatlands of the Artois region, the mud and water go with it.) *Le Journal d'un curé de campagne* is, in many respects, as different from *Monsieur Ouine* as possible: narration is in the first person, the unvarying point of view is entrusted to the hero; it uses the 'journal' form, with a hero-narrator who, like his creator, spurns being an 'écrivain'. Yet the mud and water, animals, crawling things, stenches, sickness, corruption, pus, and rot are all there.

Imagery thus becomes a key to Bernanos's view of the world and of life, as well as a guide in the reading of his novels. And here we remind ourselves that how he feels the world he lives in is as well set forth in his polemic books, like *La Grande Peur des bien-pensants*, as in his novels. And again it comes to us, as in the case of the Preface of *Les Grands Cimetières*, that the only way to understand any one of his books fully is to come to it with a knowledge of all the others. His coherence is in the totality of what he wrote. We read him for this total view, and feeling, of life—as we would a poet.

We have said the same about Saint-Exupéry.

We shall say it, also, about André Malraux.

[8] The statement is confirmed by Miss Susan Keane, whose doctoral dissertation, *An Index of Bernanos's Imagery*, is in preparation at Harvard.

CHAPTER FIVE

Malraux and the Poem of the Walnuts[1]

Les Noyers de l'Altenburg occupies a special position among Malraux's works: written in 1941, in the interval between his release from prison after the French defeat and the beginning of his activity in the Resistance, it bridges the gap between his fictions and his long essays on the nature of art. According to his Foreword, he had written it as part of a longer work, to be called *La Lutte avec l'ange*, of which the rest—in what state of completion we do not know—fell into the hands of the Gestapo. Originally published only 'for readers interested in what might have been', and thus in a sense abandoned, the book was one Malraux found difficult to give up completely. As late as 1953 an article by his one-time translator, Haakon M. Chevalier, reported that *La Lutte avec l'ange* could be expected to appear eventually, in a new form and completed; it is clear that Mr. Chevalier was writing not merely with the approval of Malraux but also with the latter's active collaboration.[2] Yet, twenty-five years after the old one, we still do not have the new text and a resumption of the work seems highly unlikely.

Not all critics feel that *Les Noyers* was a failure. Professor R. W. B. Lewis, for example, one of the few interested in Malraux's novels as novels, finds that this one 'succeeds' perhaps better than several of the others.[3] Malraux appears to have done his book considerable disservice by persisting in treating it as a fragment which, however interesting, must somehow be considered marginal, and on the whole one must prefer Mr. Lewis's judgment to the author's: *Les Noyers* does not read like a fragment; it has a beginning, a middle, and an end, and can be treated as

---

[1] Some of the ideas developed here were suggested more briefly in my *Malraux and the Tragic Imagination*.

[2] Haakon M. Chevalier, 'André Malraux: The Legend and the Man', *MLQ*, XIV, no. 2 (June 1953), 199–208. A number of the points made in this review-article were made, some months earlier, in a letter from Malraux to me, and some of the information given in Mr. Chevalier's text, regarding Malraux's plans, could only have been furnished by the novelist himself.

[3] Richard W. B. Lewis, *The Picaresque Saint*, pp. 284–8.

an aesthetic whole. In addition to its interesting 'external' structure it possesses an extremely dense and rich 'internal' one.

The central element in this internal structure, to which everything else in the book is sooner or later related, is the account of the moment of deep perception the hero experiences at the end of a long afternoon's discussion among international intellectuals assembled at an old, disaffected, Alsatian priory called the Altenburg.

> La plénitude des arbres séculaires émanait de leur masse, mais l'effort par quoi sortait de leurs énormes troncs les branches tordues, l'épanouissement en feuilles sombres de ce bois, si vieux et si lourd qu'il semblait s'enfoncer dans la terre et non s'en arracher, imposaient à la fois l'idée d'une volonté et d'une métamorphose sans fin. Entre eux les collines dévalaient jusqu'au Rhin; ils encadraient la cathédrale de Strasbourg très loin dans le crépuscule heureux, comme tant d'autres troncs encadraient d'autres cathédrales dans les champs d'Occident. Et cette tour dressée dans son oraison d'amputé, toute la patience et le travail humains développés en vagues de vignes jusqu'au fleuve n'étaient qu'un décor du soir autour de la séculaire pousée du bois vivant, des deux jets drus et noueux qui arrachaient les forces de la terre pour les déployer en ramures. Le soleil très bas poussait leur ombre jusqu'à l'autre côté de la vallée, comme deux épais rayons. Mon père pensait aux deux saints, à l'Atlante; le bois convulsé de ces noyers, au lieu de supporter le fardeau du monde, s'épanouissait dans une vie éternelle en leurs feuilles vernies et leurs noix presque mûres, en toute leur masse solennelle au-dessus du large anneau de jeunes pousses et des noix mortes de l'hiver. 'Les civilisations ou l'animal, comme les statues ou les bûches . . .' Entre les statues et les bûches, il y avait les arbres, et leur destin obscur comme celui de la vie. Et l'Atlante, et la face du Saint-Marc ravagée de ferveur gothique s'y perdaient comme la culture, comme l'esprit, comme tout ce que mon père venait d'entendre— ensevelis dans l'ombre de cette statue indulgente que se sculptaient à elles-mêmes les forces de la terre, et que le soleil au ras des collines étendait sur l'angoisse des hommes jusqu'à l'horizon.[4]

The narrator's father, Vincent Berger, has just heard a categorical denial of the possibility of defining Man as continuously identifiable with

---

[4] pp. 105–6. For works which are not included in the Pléiade edition of Malraux's fictions, I have used the Skira edition of 1943, in preference to later French editions, because the paper is more durable and the edition thus more likely to be available to the reader. The texts do not vary.

himself. If allowed to stand, the argument would make any 'Idea of Man' untenable. In reply to a question whether there exists a datum on which the notion of Man can be based, the ethnologist Möllberg (who has been identified as Leo Frobenius)[5] has returned an irrefutable negative: cultures may change, he says, but they do not communicate one with another—a culture ignorant of the relation between sexual intercourse and birth has no bridge to one informed by the idea of paternity; potlach culture is forever walled off from one that has the concept of exchange; one where the status of the king depends on conjunctions of sun and moon is shut off from one dominated by the feeling of destiny; one with no idea of the soul is entirely different in mental structure from one that conceives of a soul capable of surviving the body. The Greek, Möllberg cries passionately, has no more in common with Gothic Man, living as the latter did in an eternal present, than Gothic Man has with the Modern, who lives in a sense of history. This is the Spenglerian lesson Möllberg has learned from his years of exploration and study in Africa. As another participant puts it, this makes the issue, the absurdity or non-absurdity of the world.

The 'absurd' has had but one meaning for Malraux ever since he first broached the idea in *La Tentation de l'Occident*: absence of meaning. And meaning here is an exact synonym for 'value'; what lacks one lacks the other. Möllberg himself is made to say:

> Si les structures mentales disparaissent sans retour comme le plésio-saure, si les civilisations ne sont bonnes à se succéder que pour jeter l'homme au tonneau sans fond d'une implacable métamorphose, peu importe que les hommes se transmettent pour quelques siècles leurs concepts et leurs techniques; car l'homme est un hasard, et, pour l'essentiel, le monde est fait d'oubli (p. 99).

Although Malraux's interpreters have been curiously reticent about saying so, this view puts the whole structure of Malraux's own thought in peril. If Man is an illusion, then so is human destiny, man's fate, 'la condition humaine'. But Vincent Berger's refutation of Möllberg has been in the making since the start of the Colloquy.

On the wall of the meeting room are three sculptures: one a ship's figurehead which is an effigy of the Titan, Atlante, one a gothic figure of Saint Mark, and the third another gothic saint. All three are carved of the native walnut wood. The Altenburg Priory stands in the midst of the Holy Forest, where walnuts have been growing since the Middle Ages.

---

[5] By Claude-Edmonde Magny in 'Malraux le fascinateur', *Esprit*, 16ᵉ année, no. 149 (Oct. 1948), 513–34.

From time to time, the kind of woodsmen who have harvested these trees for centuries pass beneath the windows as the talk proceeds, and the heavy fall of logs from wagons in the neighboring square occasionally interrupts the speakers. Between Möllberg and the woodsmen outside there is, at one moment, something almost approaching a dialogue.

Il parlait maintenant avec passion: dehors des hommes chargeaient des troncs semblables à ceux que mon grand-père avait pendant quarante ans fait empiler devant la mairie de Reichbach, semblables à ceux qu'empilaient les bûcherons de la Sainte-Forêt au moyen-âge . . . (p. 98).

The wood enters the discussion as a key metaphor when Berger asks whether there cannot exist, beneath his varying manifestations in different cultures, a 'fundamental man'. This Möllberg denies: fundamental man is a myth created by intellectuals thinking about peasants. Möllberg asserts that Man exists only by virtue of what he thinks and believes; without thought and belief—culture—there is no such thing as Man at all. Here he points to the walnut carvings; these gothic sculptures and the ancient figurehead may be of the same wood but there is no fundamental walnut—there are only chunks of wood.[6]

Time runs out, the Colloquy suspends for tea, and Berger steps outside into the fresh air of a sweet evening. He wanders up the hill from the Priory to a point where a valley opens out, falling away toward Strasbourg and the Rhine.

Malraux has prepared the setting with great care and no visible concern about falling into the pathetic fallacy. A summer rain had been falling at the beginning of the Colloquy and had just ceased as Möllberg began to speak, with the first sunshine glistening on the drops that streaked the windowpanes and backlighting the head of the speaker. Later, as the weather cleared, the sun had seemed to coat the glass with copper. And now that Berger has left the building, the scene before him is freshly washed.

[Les champs] s'étendaient derrière le prieuré entre deux masses de forêt, tachés des étoiles de chicorée sauvage du même bleu que le ciel du soir—un ciel maintenant aussi transparent que celui des hautes altitudes, où dérivaient des nuages éphémères. Tout ce qui montait de la terre reposait dans un calme rayonnant, baignait dans le poudroiement des débuts de crépuscule; les feuilles brillaient encore d'un éclat verni frémissant des derniers courants frais nés de l'herbe et des ronces

[6] p. 102: 'Mais sous ces formes il n'y a pas le noyer fondamental, il y a des bûches'.

... Le soleil se couchait, allumant les pommes rouges des pommiers. Il avait atteint les grands arbres: sapins déjà pleins de nuit, une goutte encore transparente à l'extrémité de chaque aiguille, tilleuls tout bruissants de moineaux; les plus beaux étaient deux noyers; il se souvint des statues de la bibliothèque (pp. 104–5).

Such nature description is rare in Malraux's writing, and even here he is less concerned with the looks of the external world than with his hero's response to it. From the dominant color, blue, above and below, we move to the *effect* of the sky, its transparency, defined by a comparison; the adjective attached to the clouds affirms not color or shape but impermanence—an impression. The verbs of the next sentence, 'reposait', and 'baignait', are almost metaphors and, like the parallel prepositional phrases, leave the reader with no objective fact upon which his mind can fasten; a 'calme rayonnant' is quite probably a moment of twilit peace during which one is aware of the sunlight as forming rays, but a 'poudroiement' can be explained only by saying that one may at times *feel* the purplish light of early evening as a sort of dust. One must emphasize the word 'feel' since, patently, no evening haze is there to shut off the vista which is the subject of the paragraph following. Here, as everywhere in the passage, we are primarily aware of the effect of light on the eye and sensitivity of the beholder. This is equally true of the sentence in which the slanted light of sunset lights up the presumably already red apples in the orchard.

Veteran Malraux readers will testify to remembering only one other place in the novels where the reader, if not necessarily the character involved, is so aware of the beauty of the world about him. This is the passage in *La Condition humaine* where old Gisors, the father of the now dead Kyo, watches the sky as his mind dwells upon the emptiness of the world after the death of his son. That moment, like this one, is an instance of abnormally intense perception.[7]

There, as here, emphasis falls upon the relation between the scene and the beholder's mood. One observes, in the present case, that Malraux does not permit Vincent Berger to be completely conscious of the scene before him. In the quotation above, suspension point-ellipses have been used to replace nondescriptive elements, so that the impressionistic nature of the visual material can be fully apparent. With these elements replaced in the context, the extent of Berger's distractedness comes through. Thus:

A Kaboul, à Konia, rêvait mon père, il n'eût été parlé que de Dieu ... Combien d'interrogations étrangères avaient été poussées avec la

---

[7] Pléiade ed., p. 415: 'Gisors avait vu la fuite des animaux vers les sources, à la tombée de la nuit', etc.

même passion, sous les voûtes mêmes de ce prieuré. [Le soleil se couchait, allumant les pommes rouges des pommiers.] Vaine pensée, vergers aux inépuisables renaissances, que toujours la même angoisse éclaire comme un même soleil! Pensée de jadis, pensée d'Asie, pensée de ce jour d'été pluvieux et ensoleillé, si accidentelle et si insolite,—comme la race blanche dans le soir à Marseille, comme la race des hommes derrière la fenêtre de la chambre mortuaire, le bouleversant et banal mystère de la vie dans le jour inquiet de l'aube (p. 105).

The ellipsis here is part of Malraux's text; the square brackets which enclose the sentence already included in the earlier quotation have been inserted to indicate the second interruption in Berger's meditation as his awareness returns for a moment to the outside world. These interruptions are characteristic. The mental life of Malraux's characters rarely follows the logical progressions of coherent discourse.

From his stylistic behavior one gathers that the key to the meditation lies in the long sentence beginning with the anaphora: "Pensée de jadis, pensée d'Asie . . .' But what, exactly, is the thought in question? It is one of a former time—and we know that earlier Vincent Berger has crossed the whole of southern Asia; it may be accidental in the sense of having been evoked by the very special circumstances, and unusual for more or less the same reason. It is also, in the sentence just above, qualified as vain and futile. From general experience with Malraux's texts we know that he is likely to express emotional tension by using anaphorae, parallel constructions, incomplete and ejaculatory sentences. But what, once again, is the actual thought that requires this array of special procedures?

One sees three possibilities: first, the thought that in Asia all discussion would have to be theocentric; second, the thought of all the discussions, presumably not theocentric, that have taken place in these (European) surroundings; third, the thought that a great amount of mental energy has been expended here, first and last, for nothing. Studying the syntax does not help greatly to choose among the three. It is the general sense of the passage and, beyond this, of the entire chapter, that prompts accepting the third: these orchards have witnessed the eternal futility of thought that has revealed only the anxiety of powerful minds, the anguish that brings them back again and again to these same inscrutable subjects. Our hesitation in choosing is a measure of Malraux's incoherence.

The general sense of the passage includes, of course, the series of references with which the key sentence ends. Each looks back to an earlier event in the story. Each event has already been treated at length, and each is characterized by the fact that its significance has not been completely clear either to the reader or to the character undergoing the experience.

Vincent Berger's return to Marseille, after his failure as emissary of Enver Pacha to the far-flung, loosely allied Pan-Turkish tribes, had culminated in a moment when he became conscious of re-entering time and resumed contact with Europe after his six years in Asia. He had come through Customs at the end of the day and taken a room at the Old Port; and now, on a blue evening, like the later one at the Altenburg, he watched the crowd hurry past him. Most of them were women, and style had changed during his absence. Shops, windows, street throngs, women —especially women, so different from those of the Orient, and unveiled —left him with a feeling of having awakened from a long sleep. He was reminded of something he had read in a newspaper: a murderer had been quoted as having said that, while the victim of the crime means nothing, the fact of having killed changes and renews even the most simple things, 'the streets, for instance . . . even the dogs'.[8] This feeling of seeing everything as if for the first time, with an absolutely fresh and undistracted eye, Vincent Berger recognizes as identical with the one he is experiencing now, here outside the Priory.

The second moment of perception had taken place when Berger, now returned to Reichbach in Alsace, was shown the room where his father, Dietrich, had committed suicide. Vincent and his uncle Walter had been asking each other the meaning of the suicide itself, and of the father's request that he be buried in the Catholic church. With his mind caught up in the whole incomprehensible mystery of the human adventure, Vincent saw, through the window, the people of the little town passing back and forth, and realized that he was looking into the secret of life.

> Et de la simple présence des gens qui passaient là, hâtifs dans le soleil matinal, semblables et différents comme des feuilles, paraissait sourdre un secret qui ne venait pas seulement de la mort encore embusquée dans son dos, un secret qui était bien moins celui de la mort que celui de la vie—un secret qui n'eût pas été moins poignant si l'homme eût été immortel (p. 69).

He had then recognized his feeling as the same one he had known at Marseille, but more intense.

[8] Skira ed., p. 58: 'Les journaux français étaient pleins du procès des anarchistes qu'on appelait alors "les bandits en auto"; l'un d'eux avait répondu aux questions des médecins: "L'individu tué n'a aucune importance! Mais après, il arrive une chose inattendue: tout est changé, les choses les plus simples, les rues par exemple, les chiens . . .'

The third in this succession of epiphanies is the one taking place when, after the Colloquy, Vincent Berger finds himself facing the perspective of the cathedral of Strasbourg framed by the massive walnut trees. There will be three others before the story is finished, but this one is the novel's center; the others comment upon and confirm the intuition it embodies. The entire novel is constructed upon it.

Marshaled here as if in a sort of final testimony are various symbols familiar from the earlier novels. At Marseille for example, a whistle of a steamer intrudes upon the moment of special perception, just as the same sound comes to the ears of T'chen, Kyo, and the others at crises in *La Condition humaine*.[9] The hands which speak so eloquently of humanity under extreme tension in *Le Temps du mépris* again compel attention. (Walter Berger, for example, has the hands of a woodsman of Reichbach.) And insects reassume their familiar symbolic role.

Early in the Colloquy, Möllberg asserts that his search among primitive races for the origins of man reveals not some primordial brute, or ape, but 'a kind of ant'. So far back as research can go, he says, one finds cities where life was absolutely regulated by moon and planets. (It is here that he talks about kings whose status follows the changes of the moon.) Such a civilization, he says, is mindless and lives in 'absolute fatality': the king is king only in the way the queen of a termite colony is queen. He sums up by making the metaphor explicit: nothing is better than a prolonged study of termites for making up one's mind about man.

Three academic studies of insect symbolism in Malraux[10] leave no need to explore the ant-termite symbol here. As early as *La Voie royale* the novelist was using it to evoke the subhuman and the inhuman. It retains both meanings in *Les Noyers*. But a second use of insect symbolism now emerges. As Vincent Berger has stood over the bed where Dietrich Berger's body has been found, and pondered all the inscrutabilities of the suicide, a lone ant, oblivious to the presence of the human, has crawled

[9] Whereas the visual qualities of Malraux's imagination have been studied repeatedly, I know of only one attempt to date to assess the importance of sounds in his work, G. O. Rees, 'Sound and Silence in Malraux's Novels', *French Review*, XXXII, no. 3 (Jan. 1959), 223–30. The prevalence of klaxons, steamer sirens, factory whistles, and such would seem to merit further investigation.

[10] My 'Notes on Malraux's Symbols', *RR*, XLII, no. 4 (Dec. 1951), 274–82; René Girard, 'Le Règne animal dans les romans de Malraux', *French Review*, XXVI, no. 4 (Feb. 1953), 261–7. G. O. Rees, 'Animal Imagery in the Novels of Malraux', *FS*, IX, no. 2 (1955), 129–42.

the length of the sheet, from the foot of the bed to the bolster, and straight on over the revolver Dietrich had taken to bed with him in case his overdose of veronal did not work. And here we remember that in *Le Royaume farfelu*, the army which has marched through the desert to attack an enemy city is frustrated by the attack of a swarm of scorpions, and that in *La Voie royale* the insects crawling over the walls of the empty temples threaten to frustrate Claude Vannec's purpose of detaching and collecting the sculptures he has come from Europe to find.[11] In this second usage of the symbol overtones of the equation of insect and non-human are of course not absent, but the idea of frustration is clearly more immediate. When the ant moves along the bedsheet, we are sure that Vincent Berger's effort to understand his father's action will be thwarted. One may justifiably take Malraux's revival of these old symbols, in pages which lead up to the ramified symbol of the walnuts, as a warning to be awake to the full content of the latter.

In addition to the revival of symbols, he also restates several of the themes which are woven in the fabric of his earlier novels. Adventure—in Malraux's almost metaphysical sense—has been the first, and eventually defeated, aim of the hero of the *Noyers*: we are even told, as we were of Perken and Ferral, that he too has wanted 'to leave a scar on the map'. The words 'space', 'time', and 'death' appear with their customary frequency.[12] Each of the principal speakers at the Colloquy is associated with his private kind of frivolity (the making of tiny grotesque figures, for example) which furnishes him, like Clappique, momentary relief from the almost intolerable burden of the human condition.[13] The familiar expressions about 'the absurd', 'human dignity', 'humiliation', and other similar themes recur at important points in the dialogue, as do such words as 'destiny' and 'fatality'.

Such a mobilization of symbol, theme, and motif confers special

---

[11] Until Malraux authorizes a collection of his early writings, the most accessible version of *Le Royaume farfelu* will be found in the volume of the Skira edition entitled *La Tentation de l'occident*. *La Voie royale* (like *Le Temps du mépris*) is omitted from the Pléiade edition.

[12] With respect to the frequency of such thematically important words and phrases in Malraux, I have had the advantage of using the unpublished Harvard doctoral dissertation of Ralph Tarica, *Imagery in the Novels of André Malraux: An index with commentary*.

[13] In view of Malraux's interest in the mythomania of Clappique and in the latter's baroque taste for assuming multiple roles and disguises, it may be important that in *Les Noyers* Vincent Berger advises his son to reduce to a minimum 'la part de comédie', p. 40.

importance upon the central symbol of the walnut trees for which they prepare the way, and the more so because it is a remobilization. The moment of unusually deep perception will see Vincent Berger's intuitive recognition of the new symbol and of its relation to these other symbols and themes.

Is it mere coincidence that two of the most powerful books to come out of the defeat of 1940 invoke exactly the same presiding symbols? We have already seen Saint-Exupéry equate a cathedral with humanity, and oppose it to the pile of stones equated with mere masses of people. Noteworthily, he also associates the cathedral with trees, and together the objects stand for a kind of human continuity. Evidence is plentiful of the two writers having been sharply aware of each other's work.[14] All question of 'influence' aside, it must be granted that the conjunction of the tree and the building enduring out of the past would be a natural one for two such writers to have thought of independently of each other at such a moment of history. But the evolution of the tree symbolism in recent French fiction suggests further social and metaphysical considerations.

Trees have abounded in the symbolic patterns of the French fiction of the last fifty years or so, and frequently have symbolized some sort of human continuity: the wood of La Morinière in *L'Immoraliste*, the groves of Saint-Saturnin in Jean Schlumberger's novel, the pines that in the novels of Mauriac are forever waiting to burst into flame. But the meaning of the symbol varies with the kind of continuity. In all these instances they are uniformly associated with a family fortune, not to be differentiated radically from such things as the family business of Mann's *Buddenbrooks* or the estates where the trees grow. They may represent whatever a character revolts against in his need to assert his own individuality, as in *L'Immoraliste*, or what he defends almost with his life, like the heroine of Jacques de Lacretelle's *Hauts-Ponts* whose identity becomes inseparable from that of the property. Thus the symbol is ambivalent in a sense... But its purport, even so, is always to be determined within the *Weltanschauung* of the middle class.

In contrast, Malraux's walnut trees are symbols of the continuity of a metaphysical concept, Man himself, the legitimate possessor of a destiny. And the symbol does not, as in the novels mentioned above, incite to action. Vincent Berger will not do something because he has seen the walnuts; he will simply feel something, and what he feels he will assimilate

---

[14] The extent of this awareness will eventually be apparent from a comparison of the work of Dr. Tarica with a dissertation by Mr. David Pauling, now in preparation, on the imagery of Saint-Exupéry.

to the trees themselves. This measures how far Malraux's last fiction has moved out of the ways of the novel, and how close it has moved to those of poetry.

Readers old enough to recall in any detail the silent cinema may remember the Emil Jannings film *Variety* in which the hero has been confined in prison and is again set free at the very end. In the last sequence, the prisoner moves down a central corridor toward the world outside, and as he approaches them the greater exterior gates swing open outwards. There, framed against a darkened sky in which are wisps of cloud, a giant poplar waves slowly and gracefully in the wind. Undoubtedly some laconic caption was used to drive home the point—after so many years one does not quite remember, but the common practice would have required it— but the caption would have been entirely superfluous: opening gates and swaying tree could mean only Liberty.

We can hardly fail to notice that Vincent Berger's 'epiphany' here is similarly cinematographic—as, for that matter, are the other notable ones in Malraux's novels: the exit of Katow in *La Condition Humaine* and the descent of the wounded plane crew to Valdelinares in *L'Espoir*. Malraux, himself, exploited all the possibilities of the latter in the film he directed; and the late James Agee, a more professionally adept worker in the medium, did a script of the death scenes of Kyo and Katow which was never actually 'turned' in a film but which exists in print.[15] The essential difference between the device as used in the Jannings film and as it is used here is one of complexity. What is symbolized by the trees requires a considerable elaboration.

Language assumes a double function here. There is an element of objective description: Malraux must show what any eye, not just Berger's, would have seen. But, at the same time, what is happening within Berger's mind is even more important. In the beginning sentence of the paragraph both functions are being performed simultaneously and at times by the same word. In 'la plénitude des arbres séculaires', for example, 'plénitude' is objectively descriptive, since anyone who saw the trees could verify their fullness, but 'séculaires', while it may be read as meaning merely that the trees are very old, means far more than this to Berger because it revives what we know to be his feelings about time. And the word 'effort', still in the same sentence, is entirely the interpretation of Berger's response to the gnarled and twisted look of the trees: he feels them possessing a sentient life of their own, and even a will.

---

[15] *Films*, II, no. 1 (Nov. 1939), 51–61. Interrupted almost immediately by the onset of the war, publication was never resumed.

A tendency toward animism marks the whole passage. The walnuts exert effort, manifest will, and wrest strength from the ground. The use of reflexive verbs creates a feeling of greater activeness: 's'enfoncer', 's'en arracher', 's'épanouissait', 'se sculptaient'. 'Poussée', by association, shares this quality. Life is in the trees because present in Vincent Berger's sensibility.

So, as we have noted, is time. Both the trees and the surging life suggested in 'poussée' are 'séculaires'. Their metamorphosis is 'without end', and their life 'eternal'. Such adjectives tell us, not how the trees would look to us, but how they *did* look to Malraux's hero.

The combination of descriptive and interpretive functions explains the association of certain nouns with adjectives that at first surprise the reader. In 'crépuscule heureux', 'crépuscule' means what it would mean to anyone, but it is 'heureux' only because of Berger's mood. The case of 'statue indulgente' is similar, except that here the situation is more complex: before we can ask how a statue can be indulgent we have to learn how two walnut trees can become a statue. The answer lies, of course, in the fact that a statue motif has already been prominent in the whole episode: Möllberg has used the other walnut sculptures to deny something; this one is being used to affirm the opposite. The new statue presents itself spontaneously, by a kind of animism: the trees *sculpture themselves*. And thus the statue, existing on the level of metaphor by its own will, can be qualified as indulgent. The expression condenses a wide spread of emotions: Vincent Berger needed this confirmation of the error in Möllberg's view. The ellipsis involved in juxtaposing the ideas of statue and indulgence can consequently be bridged, but it must be observed that the effort furnished by the reader is not inconsiderable. More important, the effort is of the same order as the one required of him by Malraux's technique of inserting in his novels the word-pictures that contradict the prudential logic of the stories themselves. His art is fundamentally elliptical and discontinuous, in the structure of his fictions and in the detailed strategies of his prose.

Malraux's procedure is poetic also in his reduction of the total source of Berger's emotion to one which can be effectively dealt with in a single symbol. Berger has left the Colloquy, remember, in a state of extreme mental tension because of a very general proposition: that cultures do not intercommunicate and that thus no valid foundation exists for the 'notion de l'homme'. For the major part of the symbol he picks up, of course, the metaphor which Möllberg has formulated: the wood of the statues is 'fundamental' man, while the statues made of it are the contrasting cultures. But, except for one passing reference to the Atlante statue, the only culture which figures specifically in this epiphany is the Gothic, figured not only by the fervor in the expression of the 'ravaged' face of Saint Mark but also in the cathedral framed there by the old trees.

Close readers of the *Psychologie de l'art* and of *Les Voix du silence* are already aware of how much attention Malraux was to pay, later, to the distinction between Romanesque and Gothic. His principal thesis about the nature of art—which has been vigorously challenged by many professional art students—being that a style expresses the spirit of the culture which produces it, he protests at length that Gothic is in no way perfected Romanesque, or an 'improvement' upon it, and that the squat stylizations of the Romanesque do not lead to the overlengthened ones of the Gothic. He feels, it would seem, that the situation is paradigmatic: if the argument holds in the case of the Gothic it will hold generally. This idea also pervades the opening pages of the *Noyers*, set in another cathedral (Chartres), where he is obsessed by the faces of the men about him. From the very beginning of the war, he says, they have seemed more gothic than modern, and in the prison camp, especially with their beards grown out, they look less like modern prisoners than like men of the Middle Ages. This sets the major theme of the work: if Modern Man and Gothic Man, under the accidents of time, can be shown to be made of the same fundamental stuff, then the thesis of separate and discrete cultures which are forever cut off from each other must collapse. And in that case, Man can be said to have a destiny, his hope and his fate will not be simply two more delusions among all the others, and Malraux's sense of the human tragedy will be preserved.

In the *Noyers*, no proof is possible: its material is intuition, not rational logic. Proof—or the attempt to prove—will come later, in the books on art. But the intuition is no less complete. 'Entre les statues et les bûches, il y avait les arbres, et leur destin obscur comme celui de la vie'. And, the passage continues, everything else is swallowed up by this and buried in the shadows of the indulgent statue of the enormous trees.

One recognizes in this passage the other stylistic habits Malraux falls into when his prose expresses deep emotion: the preference for abstract nouns as subjects of main verbs—for example, 'plénitude', 'effort', 'épanouissement', in the first sentence—and the tendency to modify the subject extensively with modifiers that serve to concretize it; the use of parallel constructions in building periodically toward the climax, and the frequent use of parallel prepositional phrases to slow the sentence toward the end. And so often, he repeats especially important words: 'arracher', 'épanouir-épanouissement', 'séculaire', 'encadrait-encadraient', 'forces de la terre', 'statue'. His vocabulary is the one he reverts to whenever human destiny is his subject: 'arracher', 'volonté', 'métamorphose', 'force', 'angoisse'—words characteristic of an imagination that conceives the whole history of humanity as action, will, and conquest. A student with the perceptiveness and active intuitions of a Leo Spitzer might use a passage where such words appear as the point of departure for an investigation of Malraux according to the doctrine of the 'philological circle'; here it is enough to identify the passage as characteristic of Malraux in moments of extreme elevation.

There are two additional moments of epiphany in *Les Noyers*.

One is in the episode when Vincent Berger, now in German uniform on the Eastern Front—he is Alsatian and this is in 1914–1918—watches the first German gas attack. It has been studied in every serious discussion of Malraux to date and needs no extensive scrutiny here; quotation suffices.

Berger has seen the wave of gas, followed by the wave of infantry. He has seen the soldiers turn back, each rescuing a gassed enemy instead of pressing on to clear the trench. He has joined them, helped carry one of the victims, and is poisoned by the gas in his turn. He stumbles along, his mind fogged by pain and intoxication, but the significance of what has happened does not escape him:

> . . . La pitié? pensa-t-il confusément, comme lorsqu'il avait vu revenir les compagnies; il s'agissait d'un élan bien autrement profond, où l'angoisse et la fraternité se rejoignaient inextricablement, d'un élan venu de très loin dans le temps—comme si la nappe des gaz n'eût abandonné, au lieu de ces Russes, que des cadavres amis d'hommes du quaternaire . . . Jusqu'au ciel miroitant et bleu, le coteau montait avec son odeur retrouvée d'arbres, l'odeur des buis et des sapins qui ruissellent sous l'averse. *Tout à coup le souvenir de l'Altenburg traversa l'obsession de mon père: il était en face de vastes bouquets de noyers* (p. 163: my italics).

A final epiphany, somewhat less explicit but related to these others in its implications, comes in the last section of the book when the narrator, whose World War II tank has just spent the night in a tank trap under enemy guns, comes on a peasant couple, too old to go away, waiting in their village for the holocaust to 'wear itself out'. The phrase is almost identical with the one used by the captured soldier at the beginning of the book.[16]

---

[16] Skira ed., p. 195. 'Qu'est-ce qu'on pourrait donc faire? Vous, vous êtes jeunes; quand on est vieux, on a plus que d'l'usure'. Compare p. 23. 'Moi. j'attends que ça s'use . . . —Quoi? —Tout . . .'

G

A quarter of a century after the publication of the *Noyers* we still do not know what Malraux intended *La Lutte avec l'ange* to be. Unless some document comes to light—or, perhaps even less likely, unless Malraux himself explains what was to be the relation of *Les Noyers* to the rest— speculation is vain. We may suspect what we will: the novel itself seems to lead into nothing, and it is hard to imagine a continued accumulation of these epiphanies. (What one *may* imagine, of course, is the juxtaposition of the *Noyers* with a longer and less discontinuous narration which would serve as an implicit commentary on the epiphanies. Why they should need a commentary, however, is less clear.) The ultimate significance of the *Noyers* may be contained in the simple fact that Malraux did not feel the need to resume work on *La Lutte avec l'ange*. It could be that the part we have completes a sort of cycle in his development.

In the Introduction of *Le Temps du mépris*, he had denied that this story was a novel in the ordinary sense. It was, in his view, reduced to two major elements: a man, and his feeling of life;[17] what he calls 'individual antagonisms', which may be what E. M. Forster tags as 'personal relations', do not have a place in it. The Nazis who figure in the book are almost unseen, and the comrades who rescue him are designated only by their role, for example, the Aviator.

What else is *Les Noyers* than another story of one man and his feeling of life? A reasonably solid case can be constructed for the reading that sees *La Condition humaine* and *L'Espoir* as assembling groups of such isolated individuals, each unable to communicate with his fellows, each essentially alone with his sense of destiny. Kyo Gisors is unable to recognize his own voice on the phonograph record; T'chen is never lonelier than when forming part of the human chain that lowers a grenade thrower over the edge of a roof.

Seen in such a context, *Les Noyers de l'Altenburg* would be the book in which, even more than in *Le Temps du mépris*, Malraux eliminates all intrusive action, leaving only what will bring his hero to the moments when the intuited meaning of life presents itself entirely uncontaminated. And this time, more than ever before, his protagonist is the surrogate of the author.

The events in Vincent Berger's career, including an intellectual formation, years of absence in the Orient, participation in violent political action, return to intellectual life in Europe, and a second experience of violence, follow the pattern of Malraux's own career and not that of the suburban businessman who was Malraux's father. Malraux's inattention

[17] Skira ed., p. 16.

to fictional plausibility—did Vincent Berger die of the gas, and if he did so, how was the account of the attack included in Vincent's sheaf of notes on his Encounters with Man?—leads to the suspicion that the father is in the story only to permit Malraux to contemplate his own experience from a certain psychic distance. The figure of the father may also have offered the additional advantage of allowing the use of an elevated prose which might not have seemed appropriate to a first-person narrator.

Even if not entirely rectilinear, the development from a novel like *La Condition humaine* to one dominated by epiphanies seems very natural. It seems hardly less so that after the *Noyers* the next step should be the discarding of characters and the pretext of fiction altogether. As is so often pointed out, the essays that were to become *Les Voix du silence* formed a poem as well as a treatise. It is clear that the poet of *Les Voix* had already emerged in *Les Noyers*.

CHAPTER SIX

First-Person Narration

Despite all that has been said about there having been no noteworthy development in the technique of French fiction between 1925 and 1950, one change did indeed take place: the personal 'récit', or Northrop Frye's 'confessional mode', regained much of its old popularity. Céline's *Voyage au bout de la nuit* and *Mort à crédit*, Bernanos's *Journal d'un curé de campagne*, Sartre's *Nausée* and all three major fictions of Camus are first-person narratives (or variants on the first-person mode) in which the narrator is also the central actor.

Not that there was anything new, of itself, in returning to a mode of fiction which had already given the French *Adolphe*, *Volupté*, *Le Lys dans la vallée*, *Dominique*, and *L'Immoraliste*. But now, in the 1930's and 1940's, when a group of very distinguished novelists turn to it at once, each imposes on himself a set of inhibiting conditions. Each uses a narrator whose character will not permit him to raise his voice and at the same time remain plausible. Not one permits his protagonist to think of himself as heroic. And only one, Camus's Jean-Baptiste Clamence, can be suspected of considering himself even interesting. Such men would be most unlikely to assume an elevated tone without stepping 'out of character'. And yet several of them—most but not all—arrive at one of the peaks of perception which we have been calling 'epiphany'. Off hand, one would think that epiphany and elevated language went together.

Bernanos in Le Journal d'un curé de campagne[1]

We have already noted that Georges Bernanos was approaching forty when he wrote *Sous le soleil de Satan*, and explained[2] that he had to wait so long to turn novelist because he was simply 'not ready' earlier. Not ready for what?

This much is clear: he can not have been waiting for his technique to

---

[1] Some of the material used here first appeared in 'Georges Bernanos and his priest-hero', *YFS*, no. 12 (1953), 54–61.

[2] See the introductory paragraphs of *Les Grands Cimetières sous la lune*, quoted here p. 46. Actually, Bernanos exaggerates his age: his first novel was finished when he was thirty-eight not forty, and he had written shorter fiction even earlier.

ripen, or he would have waited longer. Bernanos was to learn by doing: by common consent, his first novel, a portrait-novel in the form of a fictional biography, is as clumsy as its awkward priest-hero. The reader follows Abbé Donissan through the two essential chapters of his life: the one in which he meets and overcomes Satan, and the one in which he attempts, and fails to produce, a miracle. His character does not develop during the course of the story. In the first part he is young, discouraged, and inept, a conundrum to himself and a problem to his superiors; in the second he is an older but hardly a different—and certainly not wiser—man. The reader perceives only dimly the causal relation between the two parts, and the resulting incoherence is augmented by a similar failure to establish a relationship between the main action and the lengthy, pathetic story of the girl Mouchette, which forms the prologue. Mouchette is seduced by the neighboring squire, murders him, bears his child, and eventually commits suicide. Her life touches Donissan's only once, when, on the end of the night on which he has met the devil, Donissan also meets the unfortunate girl, tries to give her a counsel of salvation, sends her home where she cuts her throat with her father's razor, and then bears her bleeding body in his arms to the church—to everyone's great scandal. The structural difficulty is that this meeting takes place not in the prologue but at the end of the first part of the principal action. The reader is never sure of what is going on—and even less of *why*.

We see Donissan only from the outside, and in a sense this perspective is appropriate, for the man is a saint in the eyes of his creator and the book is fictional hagiography. Too much specific information about Donissan's motives would strip him of the mystery which must surround the holy life, and in addition the average reader is hardly qualified to share, through the adoption of an internal point of view, in seeing life as a saint must see it. We do hear the advice poor Donissan's superiors give him, and Bernanos does explain, in more or less independent, interpolated essays, the nature of the spiritual life and of the supernatural forces at work. But the psychological information these provide is adequate only to leave us in a position like that of the reader of *The Sound and Fury* before his discovery that Faulkner's tale is literally told by an idiot.

What Bernanos meant by not being 'ready' was that years had had to pass before he could see the figure of his holy innocent of a priest clearly enough to permit writing even a structurally incoherent book. He had, we know,[3] been contemplating his hero for a long time, perhaps so long

---

[3] In addition to the introduction to *Les Grands Cimetières*, see *Bernanos par lui-même*, p. 176.

that the creation threatened to overpower and take command of his creator. It was only when at last he solved the problem of a structure suited to the material that haunted him that he wrote what many critics—the outstanding exception being the late Albert Béguin—consider his master-piece.[4]

Meanwhile, the presence of another priest-hero (in many respects the same one) is partly responsible for disrupting the structure of Bernanos's second novel. This time he had intended a long tale of a 'bad' priest and had had no doubts of his ability to bring it off once he got his 'mauvais prêtre' on his feet.[5] But by the end of the first of the four parts of *L'Imposture*, the portrait of this character is nearly completed; we have seen him driven almost to the verge of insanity by his own lack of faith; and Berna-nos seems at something of a loss to know what to do with his creation. The second part—a picture of a group of the kind of *bien-pensants* Bernanos particularly detested—and the third part, taken up with the 'bad priest' Cénabre's encounter with a mythomaniac beggar, have relatively little to do with developing the original and startling figure portrayed in part one. Bernanos has taken the occasion to make some people who revolt him look especially odious, and he has dramatized the meeting of a man pathologically unable to tell the truth with one who has denied the Truth; he has hardly advanced his story, and, as in *Sous le soleil de Satan*, the relation between the parts has again been left obscure.

And suddenly, in the fourth part, the book acquires a new hero: the very simple little parish priest whom Cénabre called in on his night of crisis, informed of his (Cénabre's) lack of faith, insulted, and in a final fury knocked down. Abbé Chevance has never done well as a priest; his spiritual earnestness and naiveté have scandalized his charges and embar-rassed his superiors. He is far from having the intelligence to understand what has gone on in the mind of the learned and sophisticated Cénabre, but he has been spectacularly successful as the confessor and director of other, very simple people, a 'housemaids' confessor', and now at the very end of his life has been given a chance to organize a parish of his own in a very poor section of Paris. He never builds the parish. His health is failing him as this fourth part of the novel opens, and much of this part is taken up by a delirious inner monologue, in which he imagines that he is

---

[4] *Bernanos par lui-même*, p. 79.

[5] Letter to Henri Massis, written from Saint-Jean-de-Luz, August 1926, quoted in both *Georges Bernanos, essais et témoignages* (p. 42) and *Bernanos par lui-même* (p. 160).

crossing Paris to bring spiritual help to the unfortunate Cénabre. He does not actually do so, but he does succeed in taking over the entire last part of the story.

That Bernanos intended him to be a character very like Abbé Donissan is clear from a letter which identifies both priests with a historical model. 'This morning I went to see the rectory at Ars. Nothing in that place disappointed me. I saw the books of Abbé Donissan and the rabat of Abbé Chevance'.[6]

Much has been written on Bernanos's ideas about Divine Grace; but we learn still more from studying the figures who, in his purview, are its likeliest recipients. Chevance, Donissan, and St. Jean Viannet, the Curé d'Ars, are the type of whom France makes her saints in these days when intellectual capacity is so rarely sanctified.

Take away their yearning for salvation and such men would have many traits in common with characters like Céline's little Bardamu, in *Voyage au bout de la nuit*, the various weaklings, like Jean Peyrouère, who populate the novels of Mauriac . . . and Dostoevski's Underground Man. They are born inept and somehow defeated, mediocre in intelligence, clumsy in dealing with their fellow men, and perpetual victims of the world around them. Particularly blessed, for Bernanos, are these men whose mental furniture is so scanty that their success in winning souls can be attributed to nothing other than the grace of God.

Chevance dies at the end of *L'Imposture* and can hardly be said to dominate *La Joie*, but he figures in this novel indirectly, even so. For Cénabre, who is prominent in it, can not be absolutely sure that his belief is a secret. He had told Chevance of it; Chevance had been the confessor of the girl Chantal; and Chantal, now the heroine of *La Joie*, had heard Chevance babbling on his death bed. Concern about what Chevance *may* have said motivates Cénabre's hostility toward Chantal and gives Chevance a certain status in *La Joie*.

Some measure of the fascination this kind of character exercised upon Bernanos is furnished by its having found its way even into his detective story, *Un Crime*. The supposed *curé* of Mégère is a woman who has murdered the real *curé*, disguised herself, and assumed his village role. To succeed in this imposture she must put on the character of a typical Bernanosian priest with all his essential traits: clumsiness in his common contacts with the parish, general social awkwardness, apprehension lest he displease his superiors, awareness of the danger of putting an end to

---

[6] Undated letter, probably July 1927, written from Bagnères de Bigorre. So far as I know it is unpublished. I have seen the autograph.

his priestly career almost before it has begun, the possession of some secret which makes him especially uncomfortable. Now the vicissitudes of *Un Crime* and *Un Mauvais Rêve* have been amply studied[7] and their impoverished author's inability to write a piece of potboiling trash, even when he most wanted to, makes a touching chapter in his biography. We would doubtless be wrong to overload his characterization of the priest, in this case, with special significance. But it is still true that, even here, when Bernanos needed a priest in a story his imagination automatically reached out to the kind that had already become familiar to the readers of his novels. For whatever it is worth, we have here further evidence of what seems almost an obsession.

Monsieur Ouine offers even further testimony. Bernanos had already sketched out in the writer Guérou, of *L'Imposture*, a character committed to evil and intent on exercising a completely baneful influence. Ouine must be taken as an attempt at a full-length characterization of the same sort. But the novel in which he appears is one with a welter of subsidiary characters and a remarkably complicated action.

One would suppose that there were already matter enough here for one, or even several, novels.

Yet we know that very early in the writing of this story of a 'dead parish' Bernanos had the intention of inserting the figure of still another of his heroic priests. And it is this hapless *curé* of Fenouille whose funeral sermon over the murdered shepherd helps bring about the mob-killing of the mad woman. His character is the combination of zeal, discouragement, naiveté, and ineptness which we have long since come to recognize as typical. It is as if Bernanos could not imagine a fictional situation in which such a figure did not enter. His presence here contributed one more to the total of distractions[8] which prevented Bernanos's finishing *Monsieur Ouine* for so many years.

The novelist became so taken, once again, by his creation that he put aside *Monsieur Ouine* to write his *Journal d'un curé de campagne*. Abbé Pézeril's study of the text of *Monsieur Ouine*[9] shows that Bernanos had reached the point in his narrative where the *curé* of Fenouille finds the semi-naked and almost completely insane mayor of the town hiding in his rectory, when he put down the novel he had been struggling with

[7] By A. Béguin in his edition of *Un Mauvais Rêve*. The substance of his work is repeated in the Pléiade ed.

[8] See letters quoted in *Bernanos par lui-même*, pp. 165–8 and the notes on the novel in the Pléiade ed., pp. 1854–8.

[9] Daniel Pézeril, *Bulletin des amis de Georges Bernanos*, nos. 35–6 (April 1960), 1–4.

for years to begin one which he would complete in a matter of months. This change opened the remarkable 'second period of fecundity' which saw Bernanos carrying along almost simultaneously three major books. In the absence of conclusive documents, we can only speculate about what caused this sudden release of creative powers; we note only that it surely came when, and *perhaps* because, he had discovered a way to satisfy himself with his handling of the haunting priest-hero.

Just before the break in the manuscript of *Monsieur Ouine* the young *curé* is walking back to his rectory from the center of the town, alone and deep in thought.

> ... Un autre que lui, bientôt ... Qu'importe! Il n'avait jamais été ici qu'un passant et la vieille église le repoussait sans colère comme le rejetait ce village dont il pouvait apercevoir les toits, car église et village n'en faisait qu'un. Aussi longtemps que l'antique citadelle dresserait ici sa tour, aussi longtemps que le clocher lancerait dans l'espace son cri d'appel, elle serait du parti de la paroisse, elle serait du parti de gens d'en face. Ils pourraient bien la profaner, l'abattre, elle leur appartiendrait jusqu'au bout, jusqu'à la dernière pierre elle ne les renierait jamais. Oui, couchée dans l'herbe, elle offrirait encore aux traîtres, aux parjures, ses beaux flancs éventrés—leurs petits viendraient jouer dans les ruines. Faute de mieux la vieille Mère les protégerait de la pluie et du soleil. Oh! sans doute, elle l'avait accueilli lui-même avec douceur, mais c'était comme un hôte provisoire. Quoi qu'il arrivât, elle ne le protégerait pas contre eux, eux, ses fils. Et, dès qu'il aurait quitté Fenouille, elle—la paroisse—elle ne le connaîtrait plus (p. 1514).

How should one label this prose? Clearly, what is reported here is the thought in the mind of the young priest. Just as clearly, the marks of direct discourse—quotation and attribution—are absent. The tense and mood system of the verbs, with the imperfect as the commanding tense and the conditional for happenings projected by the *curé*'s imagination, are characteristic of *discours indirect libre*, situating us somewhere in the mid-region between directly reported thought and interior monologue.

But does even an educated Frenchman think in the imperfect of the subjunctive? Is it plausible for him to think of the old church as 'l'antique citadelle'? Would one expect the anaphorae: 'aussi longtemps que ... aussi longtemps que', 'elle serait du parti ... elle serait du parti'? Or the chiasmus: 'elle leur appartiendrait jusqu'au bout, jusqu'à la dernière pierre elle ne les renierait jamais'? Would his mind produce the re-enforcing appositives; 'profaner, l'abattre,' 'aux traîtres, aux parjures'? Or the metaphor of 'les beaux flancs éventrés'? To raise these questions at all is to answer them.

By long habit, Bernanos regularly characterizes by their speech mannerisms only figures of secondary importance, and he never (I think) so characterizes a priest. Even Abbé Donissan, the most completely rural of the whole gallery, is not permitted to fall into the speech-ways of the peasant, for example, even though an imaginative reader may feel that the poor man's inarticulateness often arises from his not speaking the language in which he is addressed. It is thus not unusual for us not to be able to identify the characteristic speech of the *curé* of Fenouille.

But we hardly need do so. The rhetoric of the passage of 'represented speech' we have been contemplating is not of the kind a man uses when he has no listener. It belongs to another level of appropriateness. How effectively the style sets up a distance between character and reader in this instance is immediately apparent from comparison with a famous passage in which such distancing is not felt.

The old farmer Rouault is watching Emma Bovary drive away with her new husband.

> Lorsqu'il eut fait cent pas environ, il s'arrêta, et, comme il vit la carriole s'éloignant, dont les roues tournaient dans la poussière, il poussa un gros soupir. Puis il se rappela ses noces, son temps d'autrefois, la première grossesse de sa femme; il était bien joyeux, lui aussi, le jour qu'il l'avait emmenée de chez son père dans sa maison, quand il la portait en croupe en trottant sur la neige; car on était aux environs de Noël et la campagne était toute blanche, elle le tenait par un bras...[10]

This is, of course, a classic example of what Flaubert meant by getting 'into the skin' of a character and it is plainly different, in effect, from Bernanos's device. Indirect discourse, as Bernanos uses it, does indeed bring about a change of point of view, as it does in Flaubert: the reader is being shown, not told, about the working of the hero's mind; but a veil of style still hangs between us and any feeling of participation. We remain spectators.

One can see how such a procedure would suit Bernanos in the literary circumstances. In the Roman Catholic view a saint is not completely like the rest of us. Even though the details of his physical and emotional life are remarkably similar to our own, some mystery must remain; we must be made to understand his experience without feeling that we share it.

[10] Edition du Centenaire, pp. 30–1.

A kind of indirect discourse, free in a sense but conducted somewhat as if the character were *writing rather than speaking*, could be immensely useful for his purpose.

And what does the diary form achieve if not this same general effect: the point of view of the central character, the feeling in the reader of seeing life as this character sees it, and yet from a different distance— appropriate to a man who is not a saint—imposed by an awareness of style? We do not, of course, know for a fact that a realization of this was what made Bernanos put aside *Monsieur Ouine* and write his *Journal d'un curé de campagne*. But we do know that it would have given him a sufficient motive to do so.

However it may have been, the new procedure made it inevitable that the character of his priest-hero should evolve still further. 'Further', in this situation, is the proper word, for although the priest-heroes of these novels owe their existence to Bernanos's preoccupation with a certain kind of priest, differences manifest themselves. The *curé* of Fenouille may be as inept, as capable of causing scandal, as much a nuisance to his superiors as was Donissan in *Sous le soleil*, but Donissan was, above all else, inarticulate—and the *curé* of Fenouille contrives in his way to be extremely eloquent. Similarly, Chevance is characterized by his extra- ordinary capacity for mental confusion—whereas the *curé* of Fenouille sees, with soul-searing clarity, the import of what has happened and the meaning of what he has done. The *curé d'Ambricourt* develops one step further: he can write.

He is aware that keeping a diary is an unpriestly activity, often prompted by worldly vanity; he is awake to the dangers of 'literature' and wants to be an 'écrivain' as little as Bernanos himself. Yet the story is that early readers did indeed mistake the novel for the actual diary of an actual priest dying of a very real cancer. The misapprehension may not testify to the perceptiveness of readers who fell into the trap; it does say something important about the quality of the writing.

There was also a further consequence of the change of form: Bernanos had placed himself in a position such that he could not describe the death of his hero. The final agony regularly occupied in his novels the place reserved for epiphany by several of our other novelists. But a first person narrator is in an awkward situation such as need not be discussed in detail here. In place of a chapter on 'la sainte agonie' the novelist has the *curé d'Ambricourt* leave a legacy of three words: 'Tout est grâce.' For readers of Bernanos's religious disposition at least, each is left to imagine an epiphany of his own.

Céline[11]

An important study by Leo Spitzer stresses the point that the language of Céline's novels is often closer to spoken than to written French.[12] Spitzer notes, in particular, a prevalence of sentences of the general type: 'je ne sais pas moi ce qu'il t'a dit à toi le type.' ('Moi' returns to and re-enforces the original subject, while 'à toi', repeating the indirect object of 'dit', heightens the contrast between the first and second persons and suggests that 'il' may not have told the same story, and 'le type', closing the sentence, brings the focus of interest—the man whom all this is really about—back into the center. This is, of course, an accurate representation of the way certain Frenchman talk: it avoids complex syntax by repetitions which clarify through distributing emphasis.

Such sentences are particularly frequent in the reported speech of Céline's characters. 'Elle en a grand besoin la race française, vu qu'elle n'existe pas! que j'ai répondu moi . . .' (p. 11.) But they are also plentiful in straight, first-person narration: 'Je me pensais aussi (derrière un arbre) que j'aurais bien voulu le voir ici moi, le Déroulède dont on m'avait tant parlé, m'expliquer comment il faisait, lui, quand il prenait une balle dans le bidon!' (p. 16). The frequency cannot fail to characterize the speaker, identifying him with a certain level of society and suggesting a certain level of education.

Actually, this practice is only one among several that mark Céline's language as being not the written but the spoken tongue.

> Moi d'abord la campagne, faut que je le dise tout de suite, je n'ai jamais pu la sentir, je l'ai toujours trouvée triste, avec ses bourbiers qui n'en finissent pas, ses maisons où les gens n'y sont jamais et ces chemins qui ne vont nulle part. Mais quand on y ajoute la guerre en plus, c'est à pas y tenir. Le vent s'était levé, brutal, de chaque côté des talus, les peupliers mêlaient leurs rafales de feuilles aux petits bruits secs qui venaient de là-bas sur nous. Ces soldats inconnus nous rataient sans cesse, mais tout en nous entourant de mille morts, on s'en trouvait comme habillés. Je n'osais plus remuer (p. 16).

As so often happens in conversation, the speaker has begun to talk before his sentence has organized itself. He first emits three seemingly unrelated ideas ('moi', 'd'abord', 'la campagne'); next he inserts a parenthesis; then he begins to think consecutively in a sentence that could stand

---

[11] Material in this section originally appeared in 'Céline's Quest for Love', *Accent*, II, no. 2 (Winter 1942), 79–84.

[12] 'Une habitude de style (le rappel) chez M. Céline', *FM*, 3ᵉ année, no. 3 (June 1935), 193–209.

by itself ('je n'ai jamais pu la sentir') but that is actually followed by another ('je l'ai toujours trouvée triste'). This last is presented as unrelated to the previous one, but we are allowed to assume that a change in intonation may do the work of an omitted causal conjunction. Finally the thought opens out into three exactly parallel descriptive explanations, introduced by 'avec' instead of a causal such as 'à cause de', and the images of mud, empty houses, and aimless roads. Also conversational are the absence of a pronoun subject for 'faut', the suppression of the negative particle before 'ai', the pleonastic 'en' before 'finissent', the still more clearly pleonastic 'y' before 'sont', the 'y' before 'ajoute' that *may* refer all the way back to 'campagne' but more probably encompasses everything that has been said up to this point. There is a similar conversational quality in expressions like 'c'est à pas y tenir', and 'on s'en trouvait comme habillés' and these are again marked as spoken, rather than written, by another suppression of 'ne' and the use of the indefinite subject 'on' which has been made definite by the plural of the past participle, 'habillés'.

But for all the abundance of conversational forms, this same paragraph also contains the sentence: 'Le vent s'était levé, brutal,' and so forth, which does not suggest speech. To judge by its balanced construction and the concluding fall ('qui venaient/de là-bas/sur nous'), it results from the exercise of perceptible literary taste.

Thus a new question arises: how pervasive is the use of the spoken language and what role does it play in the total economy of the work? For instances of reversion to the literary tongue are by no means rare in it. For example:

Il existe pour le pauvre en ce monde deux grandes manières de *crever*, soit par l'indifférence absolue de vos semblables en temps de paix, ou par la passion homicide des mêmes en la guerre venue. S'ils se mettent à penser à vous, c'est à votre torture qu'ils songent *les autres et rien qu'à ça*. On ne les intéresse que saignants, les *salauds*! Princhard à cet égard avait bien eu raison. Dans l'imminence de l'abattoir, on ne spécule plus beaucoup sur les choses de son avenir, on ne pense guère qu'à aimer pendant les jours qui vous restent puisque c'est le seul moyen d'oublier son corps un peu, qu'on va vous écorcher bientôt du haut en bas (p. 82).

Except for the italicized words (the italics are mine), a small question as to the use of the possessive pronoun in 'son corps', and an even smaller one regarding the position of 'un peu', this is the written language. Another, more formal author might have used 'votre' instead of 'son' and placed 'un peu' between verb and noun, but this difference is hardly decisive. The italicized sentences are, of course, indisputably conversational, but one may suspect them of being part of a self-conscious literary strategy: they appear just after such relatively formal expressions as 'indifférence absolue' and 'passion homicide' and their function may be that of counteracting the formality.

Now Céline has been praised both for having created an 'antistyle'—something like M. Roland Barthes's 'zero degree of writing'—and for his accomplishments as a stylist.[13] The judgment that attributes him the mastery of 'antistyle' is incomplete, on the face of it, and his measure as stylist has been taken from his Rabelaisian, perhaps Joycean, gift for inventing words; and again the judgment is incomplete. What we have been observing suggests, rather, a literary intention of contrasting 'antistyle' with a style which is noteworthily elevated, or, in other words, a calculated mixture of contrasted nonliterary and highly literary language.

Inspection shows a range of tones comparable to Montherlant's. For example:

> L'immense éventail de verdure du parc se déploie au-dessus des grilles. Ces arbres ont la douce ampleur et la force des grands rêves. Seulement des arbres, je m'en méfiais aussi depuis que j'étais passé par leurs embuscades. Un mort derrière chaque arbre. La grande allée montait entre deux rangées roses vers les fontaines. A côté du kiosque la veille dame aux sodas semblait lentement rassembler toutes les ombres du soir autour de sa jupe. Plus loin dans les chemins de côté flottaient les grands cubes et rectangles tendus de toiles sombres, les baraques d'une fête que la guerre avait surprise là, et comblée soudain de silence (p. 59).

Such figures as 'éventail de verdure', 'ampleur et force des grands rêves', 'rassembler toutes les ombres du soir', and verbs like 'se déploie', 'montait', and 'comblée', belong to the vocabulary of traditional description. But the third and fourth sentences remind us that we are still listening to the first-person narrator: 'Des arbres, je m'en méfiais' is an example of his favorite syntax; so is the verbless, almost exclamatory sentence following. The only conclusion possible is that this hero, Bardamu, is capable both of the vulgar syntax that Spitzer identifies (and the vulgar, when not obscene, vocabulary that goes with it) and of the kind of expression which

---

[13] For example, Albert Paraz, *Le Gala des vaches*, pp. 160–1, believes him second only to Rabelais in inventing neologisms. Several he quotes, however, such as 'migrer' and 'blablabla', are mere borrowings from English.

would be characteristic of a literate and even poetically sensitive individual.

That this individual should shift so abruptly from one tone to another provides an insight into his character. The speech he uses is a matter of choice. He *prefers* to use a proletarian syntax, just as he *prefers*, so often, to describe life in language that may be called Villonesque.

Read in the reverse order from that of their publication, *Mort à crédit* and *Voyage au bout de la nuit* tell a story (which follows their creator's own at many points) of an unfortunate child who grows into an equally unfortunate man. The boy, Ferdinand, is both physically and mentally *le merdeux*, haunted by his inability to keep himself clean. He also furnishes, near the beginning of his story, a case of sex-linked hysteria which would have interested Krafft-Ebing deeply. His childhood experiences are of poverty, gratuitous cruelty, and nastiness. Everything he touches—his parents' business, the preparatory school he is sent to in England, all the schemes of his friend the wild inventor Courtial—crumbles as soon as he approaches it. Most of the people around him are mad; his father has obsessions; Courtial's only contact with reality is established when he commits suicide. As he grows up, Ferdinand is himself the victim of nightmarish mental illness. He is constantly frustrated, and his symbolic response to frustration is masturbation; it is his childhood response to beauty, also, whether beauty is represented by an attractive woman who lives up the alley or, more generally, by anything attractive, anywhere. This subject returns like a leitmotif through both novels. Death is the only dependable rule: Grandmother Caroline, who is good to Ferdinand, dies of pneumonia; Norah, the kindly wife of the English school principal, drowns herself; Courtial does himself in with a shotgun.

In *Voyage au bout de la nuit*, Bardamu insists repeatedly that he does not have 'la tête solide'. He goes mad a first time under the stress of war and again after he has been ill in Africa. He crosses the ocean to America in such delirium that he thinks his ship is a Spanish galleon. When he finds a measure of calm and repose, at the end of the story, he finds it in the job of attendant in an insane asylum.

It would be a major misreading to call him—or Céline—an escapist. If any lesson at all is to be learned from *Voyage au bout de la nuit* and *Mort à crédit*, it is precisely that there is no escape. The more this unhappy little man tries to run away from human beastliness and his own wretchedness, the clearer it is that these cannot be left behind. And eventually he stops running.

This is the classic formula of the 'homme traqué'. The fugitive protagonist belongs with such characters as the priest in Graham Greene's *Labyrin-*

thine Ways (*The Power and the Glory*) and Faulkner's Joe Christmas. Like them he finally sees the futility of flight and doubles back to face his pursuers.[14]

Céline's (or his hero's) frequent recourse to the rhythms, syntax, and vocabulary of common speech thus reflects his fundamental feeling about his experience of life. As a doctor he hates medicine, 'cette merde'. He also hates literature. One assumes that life is worth preserving, the other that it is worth writing about.

> La grande défaite, en tout, c'est d'oublier, et surtout ce qui vous a fait crever, et de crever sans comprendre jamais jusqu'à quel point les hommes sont vaches. Quand on sera au bord du trou, faudra pas faire les malins nous autres, mais faudra pas oublier non plus, faudra raconter tout sans changer un mot, de ce qu'on a vu de plus vicieux chez les hommes et puis poser sa chique et puis descendre. Ça suffit comme boulot pour une vie toute entière (p. 27).

And yet Céline practised both medicine and literature. And yet his protagonist gives in, on occasion, to using words with art.

Doubtless we should take the prose in which Céline is writing 'as if talking' as establishing a fundamental tone from which the other, more elevated tones are departures. If so, it is obligatory to notice the similarity with Camus's *L'Etranger*; in the latter novel a basic tone reflects the protagonist's disposition toward life. A decade before *L'Etranger*, Céline has already adopted the device of avoiding the kind of conjunction which links the parts of a sentence as if imposing a kind of logic upon experience. Purely copulative conjunctions commit nobody. 'We went up the hill and sat down' introduces two facts but no relationship between them such as purpose or cause. Current criticism identifies the practice with an attitude toward experience which is not that of Céline's hero, but the practice is Céline's, even so.

The latter contrives to express inherent discontinuity even in punctuation. In *Voyage* suspension points are already often used instead of periods, with the obvious purpose of indicating a stop of a special kind: they occur in dialogue for the most part and connote a marked lack of connection between what has just been said and what will come next. Six years later, such ellipses are all through the text of *Mort à crédit*. They throw into even stronger contrast those passages in which con-

---

[14] For a recent and very searching discussion of the fugitive hero, see Richard W. B. Lewis, *The Picaresque Saint*, pp. 220–4. Much of what Professor Lewis says about Graham Greene might be equally well said of Céline.

versational syntax is markedly absent and in which discontinuity of expression (and perhaps of vision) do prevail.

If Céline achieved something unique in the way of first-person narration it is not merely because he invented something called an 'antistyle'. Indeed, as soon as the 'antistyle' is used in a sort of counterpoint with something else, we are right to regard his achievement as stylistic. Through style he characterizes, diagnoses, transmits a view of life.

Jean Giono in 'Un de Baumugnes'

The notion that Céline was the first to cast a novel in 'spoken' rather than in 'written' prose would hold little water even if this were an accurately complete description of his novels. Giono's *Un de Baumugnes* had been published in 1929. The narrator is not the central figure, to be sure, but he is a participant in the action as well as a witness of it; we see what happens from his point of view; and we hear the story in his words.

The advantages of this formula for Giono are not so apparent as those their variations of the first-person form offered Bernanos and Céline. The latter's story is autobiographical at least in the degree that the events —war, education, travels, and so forth—follow the outline of what was roughly Céline's own experience. And Bernanos, even though his first-person narrator hero is far from being an autobiographical figure, was writing about a character type that was, as he makes clear, a part of his own biography, and an obsessive one. Giono, on the other hand, does not seem to have felt any special personal involvement with either his narrator or his hero, and by adopting the restricted point of view of the narrating character, and the restraints imposed by the need of this man's speaking his natural language, appears to have submitted himself voluntarily to a severe discipline. Given the date of this novel, early in Giono's career, the most likely explanation of his adopting the form may be that he was still experimenting.

As always in the early novels of Giono the central figure, the Man from Baumugnes himself, is one of those semi-mythic creatures like Panturle in *Regain* and Bobi in *Que ma joie demeure*, in many ways unlike other men, and seen from the outside. But in this instance the formula is varied by the use of the interposed, narrating character who stands between the action and the reader.

Here is his voice:

> Le patron, quand on le regardait d'un peu près, ç'a n'avait pas l'air d'un mauvais homme. Sous sa grande barbe noire, tout emmêlée, on

H

voyait le dessin de sa figure, encore à beaux traits; ses yeux, quoique
charbonneux et à feux, comme des ailes de guêpe, avaient, par longs
moments, des fils de regards doux comme de l'eau douce et pleins de
bonnes paroles; mais, dame, le menton disait: 'ce que je veux, je le veux'.
    Dans ces affaires j'ai vite fait, moi, de me mettre au courant et dans le
bon courant. Je travaille et je ferme le bec. On pense: 'celui-là, c'est un
d'attaque, pas besoin de le surveiller', ça me laisse de bonnes heures
pour après.[15]

The order of the first sentence—with the pseudo-temporal but actually
circumstantial clause following the subject as a parenthesis—the use of 'ç'
as a personal subject, the placement of 'mauvais' before its noun, the
use of 'on' twice in the sense of 'I, as would anyone else', hardly require
comment. The voice is telling, not writing, its story. The speaker's
character, his peasant shrewdness, are summed up in phrases like: 'je
travaille et je ferme le bec'.

The impression we gather from this passage will be confirmed constantly as we read.

Yet at the same time this man is speaking not only as an itinerant
farm laborer but also as a character in a novel by Jean Giono—and the two
qualities interfere somewhat with each other. He is speaking in French,
for one thing, rather than in Provençal patois.[16] And, for another, his
story is studded with the analogical figures which are Giono's signature:
'yeux comme des ailes de guêpe', 'regards doux comme de l'eau douce'.
Equally characteristic of the author is the anthropomorphic animism of
which we get a suggestion in his attributing speech to the man's chin:
things having no special life of their own will be brought alive and en-
dowed with human characteristics.

Certain departures from the norm of Giono's work have been forced
upon the novelist, however, by his use of the first-person narrator. As
Professor Ullmann has remarked,[17] the material of metaphor, everywhere
in Giono, is taken from areas within the experience of the characters:
that is, objects are regularly compared with other objects that are familiar
to the characters in daily life. The observation is exact, but there may even
so be a chance that it applies to some of Giono's novels more completely
than to others—to this one, for example, more than to *Regain*. For while
most of the metaphor in *Regain* exploits objects from the hill-dwelling

    [15] *Une de Baumugnes*, Grasset ed., p. 66.
    [16] See A. V. Roche, 'Les Provençalismes et la question du régionalisme dans
l'œuvre de Jean Giono', *PMLA*, LXIII, no. 4 (Dec. 1948), 1322–43.
    [17] *Style in the French Novel*, p. 224.

life of farmers, a certain share of it is marine and nautical: the heath itself rolls like the sea; Gédémus's knife-sharpening machine pitches about like a ship; clouds rising in the spring sky also evoke images of ships.[18] The absence of similar excursions out of the novel's locale in *Un de Baumugnes* may be a sign of Giono's awareness of the need to keep his narrator 'in character'.

The explanation seems even more plausible with respect to the structuring of images. In *Regain* Giono does not hesitate to introduce an analogical image on one page, return to and develop it on a second, and revive it with a further reference on a third.[19] Such behavior in a first-person narrator would almost inevitably persuade the reader that this peasant was being inordinately attentive to his own literary effects.

It may even be that the speaker is somewhat less dedicated to the making of metaphors than is Giono himself. The uncertain business of counting images is particularly complicated when the metaphors are Giono's: we have trouble telling which ones are meant to be such and which, although images to us, are 'dead' and 'fossilized' by long use in the local idiom; and it is so often hard, if not impossible, to know where one metaphor stops and another begins. Even so, the most cursory inspection of the texts of *Regain* and *Un de Baumugnes* leaves little doubt: the reader is far more aware of the presence of imagery in the third-person narrative than in the other; there is more of it and it is more obtrusive.

However much the early Giono may at times seem caught in the grip of a neurosis that makes him see everything as if it were something else, study reveals important differences in the use of metaphor from novel to novel. In *Que ma joie demeure*, for example, metaphors play descriptive and characterizing roles, and in addition have a function in the structure itself. What makes Bobi, the hero, a prophet promising salvation to the people among whom he suddenly appears is his capacity to perceive analogy where they see only literal fact. He starts his career among them by showing a ploughman that the constellation Orion looks like the flower of a wild carrot,[20] and the story of his reviving the neighborhood is one of their learning to see metaphors where he does; their new 'joie' is to see poetry where previously they have seen only prose.

[18] Grasset ed., p. 75: 'Le vent souffle à travers les montants de bois de la machine à aiguiser comme à travers la mâture d'une barque', and p. 233: 'L'escadre des nuages a largué les amarres . . . On a vu bouillonner le ciel sous la poupe du dernier nuage.'

[19] For example, Grasset ed., pp. 115–17, where the Gaudissart Brook becomes angry, crouches, purrs in its nest, stretches, blinks its eyes, stretches again and finally leaps.

[20] Grasset ed., p. 20.

A complete study of Giono's gradual discovery of the *literary* uses of his gift for analogical figure would be a most interesting supplement to those already available on him. It might confirm the view already implicit in Pierre Robert's *Jean Giono et les techniques du roman*,[21] that Giono is much less the instinctive genius, much more the shrewd and calculating craftsman than he has sometimes seemed. Such evidence as we have now suggests strongly that Giono is no more exempt than other recent novelists from what looks more and more like a rule of modern literary behavior: to use a first-person narrator is to accept a marked restriction, which, however put, can finally be reduced to saying that he must not sound literary.

The emphasis, in this formulation, must be placed upon the word 'sound'. It is, after all, the narrating figure and not the novelist who must avoid the taint of literature. Giono, like Céline and Bernanos, transposes into a lower key when he turns to narration in the first person. But the convention of speech, like the convention of diary-keeping, is still, first and most of all, a convention. And it is one which imposes, as we have seen, an additional stylistic obligation upon the novelist.

Sartre in 'La Nausée'[22]

Sartre's choice of a narrator in *La Nausée* cannot have been difficult. The modifications taking place in Antoine Roquentin, subsequent to his discovery of his own superfluity and irrelevance, and of the meaning of the 'absurd', *are* the story. By their nature such modifications are perceptible to the subject alone. Another character would be limited to seeing such changes in conduct as the modifications brought about. These are few. The action takes place inside Roquentin, and only he is aware of it.

This in itself imposes certain necessities upon the novelist. His principal character must be reasonably articulate and adept in self-analysis; he must be capable of reflectiveness; he must be engaged in some occupation which leaves him a certain amount of leisure. It is also convenient that he should be a man of letters in his way: the biography of an eighteenth-century adventurer named Rollebon may never be finished, but his preoccupation with it makes natural his keeping the journal which would seem to be another of the imposed necessities. The choice of a form is narrowed by the

<hr>

[21] See my review, *RR*, LVI, no. 1 (Feb. 1965), 77–8.

[22] Some of the material in this section appeared originally in 'The Prolapsed World of Jean-Paul Sartre', *Accent*, VII, no. 1 (April 1946), 2–13.

adoption of first-person narrative to letters, journal, or pseudo-talk—and two of these three are precluded by the character's retiring personality and his being so thoroughly alone in the world.

Sartre's hero is a negligible little specimen of preatomic man with a small but sufficient income, red hair, and a homely face, old enough to have acquired a considerable experience and a marked distaste for life. In several ways he reminds the reader of the helpless hero of *A vau-l'eau*, whose inability to struggle against the current of life finally reduces his activity to a desperate and unavailing attempt to find a restaurant that will not ruin his digestion. Sartre's man is perhaps less reconciled to unhappiness: at least he has loved once, although not very successfully, and is looking forward to a reunion with the same woman which may prove him still capable of love. Meanwhile, the insipid mediocrity of his existence is revealed by the way he has adopted, as an interim substitute, an entirely glandular relationship with the proprietress of his favorite café, who interrupts her bedside prattle about the retail liquor business to express the hope that he 'won't mind if she keeps her stockings on'. We come to know about his past because he is eternally raking it up in his mind, comparing it with the present, questioning its value. And we know what he looks like because he contemplates himself in the glass, examines himself in disquieting detail—and is deeply displeased by what he sees.

What may seem, in this last peculiarity, to be a symptom of an especially morbid state is really the first step on the path along which Roquentin is moving toward one of those moments of perception which is not unlike what, as they occur in other writers, can be called 'epiphany.' Other manifestations have followed it. He has been terribly lonely and envies people who move about in groups because 'you have to be several men together to bear existence', and he wonders whether it is a lack of friends which makes him feel so naked. Lately he has had moments when he has been absolutely afraid to look at his beer glass on the café table and has been unable at such times even to turn his head. He has also been unable to indulge a somewhat anomalous pleasure in picking up pieces of waste paper, clean or dirty, which he has previously been fishing out of the gutter: lately something inexplicable has made him withhold his hand. But what has bothered him even more has been another sudden inhibition which has prevented his throwing a pebble in some water, for in this instance he has felt the psychic paralysis pass up his arm as though it had started from the underside of the pebble.

Once before in his life he has experienced a nameless upheaval of his instincts, which then precipitated his decision—for which he has never been able to think up a satisfactorily rational explanation—to give up a life of travel for one of scholarly retirement in the French coastal city where he now is, and he wonders if once more his emotions are preparing to upset his entire way of life.

This is Roquentin's situation as the story opens. Suspecting that he will get worse, he has started a journal into which he plans to pour his observations on his own condition, for the purpose of bringing the circumstances out into the open. His difficulty will be that his fundamental malaise lies so deep that he can hardly describe it with words: it is preeminently subvocal. Much effort must be expended in the mere verbalizing of it. There is no pre-established vocabulary upon which to draw. His recurrent attempts at verbalization, as his case progresses, together with the incidents which cause or grow out of these affective states, form the core of the novel.

By the time we have reached page thirty-four, Roquentin's disgust with living, the nausea for which the book is named, is upon him. A first attack is brought by sexual disappointment, when the café proprietress misses their rendezvous because of some errands in town. Subsequently, when the crises have become habitual, less and less will be required to push him over the edge of ordinary consciousness into his private slough of despond: a boresome conversation, the failure of someone to appear at the expected time, the sight of a decrepit or otherwise disfavored individual, and finally anything at all that stimulates his awareness of the one small fact that he is alive. Let him become aware of his existence, and almost nothing can bring him out of the torpid state into which he quickly passes. He gains occasional relief from listening to jazz records.

The nature of his seizure can be described as one of overwhelmingly acute awareness and sensitivity, plus the ability to see the world without the benefit of intervening preconceptions. For illustration: we speak frequently of seeing things with a special kind of eye—the 'painter's eye', the 'reporter's eye', or the 'dramatist's', or the 'doctor's', or the 'moralist's'; individuals build up the habit of looking at the exterior world through the film of their personal preoccupations. In other words, they have built up habitual (and probably salutary) prejudices which affect their reception of stimuli.

Whatever psychological truth lies beneath this metaphor at all must be applicable in some degree to everyone. But suppose that through some accident to his nervous system, one of us should shed these prejudices and see the world not with a poet's or soldier's or ice-man's eye, but with an eye *tout court*. Would he not have to report somewhat as Roquentin reports his sensations when standing, during a moment of such crisis in a public park, that Existence had suddenly removed its veil and lost its character as abstract category, becoming the dough out of which all things were made; that the diversity and individuality of things was only an appearance, a sort of varnish over them which melted off, leaving only masses without shape, soft and disorderly, nude with a frightening and obscene nudity? (I am, of course, paraphrasing Roquentin here.) This sounds as if the 'buzzing, booming nothing' which psychologists tell us is the content of a baby's consciousness has suddenly become about all that an adult and experienced mind can identify outside itself. In any event, for Roquentin there exists only himself and, exterior to himself, a sort of multimorphous paste. It may seem that Sartre's character has contrived to have a particularly violent nightmare with his eyes open.[23]

Readers who come to *La Nausée* with at least a cursory familiarity with the principal doctrines of Sartre's Existentialism will see the similarity between Roquentin's condition and what the Existentialists know as *anxiété*, and perceive, at least as metaphor, the connection between this kind of vision and the concepts of 'lucidity' and 'good faith'. But Sartre was not in a situation to expect this kind of collaborative reading when he wrote his book, and we are obliged to deprive him of any such benefit when studying *La Nausée* as a novel.

The nauseated response to awareness of his own being is, of course, what the novel is written to convey and the theme which the novelist must orchestrate at the expense of considerable effort. Unconditioned vision, the 'unprejudiced vision' described just above, can perhaps be thought of as a subtheme: it is, in any case, fundamental: feel this way about life and you see it in this way.

On the page where Sartre makes Roquentin invite the humanity around him to see itself and the surrounding world as he does, the world simply flies apart as the ordinary relationships between things break down. A man out walking sees coming toward him from the other side of the street a red rag, blown along by the wind, which turns out to be a quarter of rotted meat, dust-spotted and dragging along the gutter spasmodically spouting blood. A mother examines what at first seems to be a pimple on her child's cheek, sees the flesh swell, split, open up, and a third eye appear. Others feel their clothing suddenly develop a life of its own. One man feels something scratching in his mouth and learns from the mirror that his tongue has become an enormous earwig, a part of himself which he has to tear out with his hands. The page continues:

[23] Gallimard ed., pp. 161–3. Subsequent page references incorporated in the text are to this edition.

… Et celui qui se sera endormi dans son bon lit, dans sa douce chambre chaude se réveillera tout nu sur un sol bleuâtre, dans une forêt de verges bruissantes, dressées rouges et blanches vers le ciel comme les cheminées de Jouxtebouville, avec de grosses couilles à demi sorties de terre, velues et bulbeuses, comme des oignons. Et des oiseaux voletteront autour de ces verges et les picoreront de leurs becs et les feront saigner. Du sperme coulera lentement, doucement, de ces blessures, du sperme mêlé de sang, vitreux et tiède avec de petites bulles (p. 200).

And some lines lower, after detailing a few similar horrors, he adds: 'Je m'adosserai à un mur et je leur crierai au passage: "Qu'avez-vous fait de votre science? Qu'avez-vous fait de votre humanisme? Où est votre dignité de roseau pensant?" ' (p. 200).

Two aspects of the page strike us immediately: the violence of the vision and the fact that so little in it is unfamiliar. The obscene forest and the figures flying about it was not new to Vergil and was old stuff to Dante. Pascal's thinking reed has served its time. The crawling, bloodspurting meat, the third eye, the living garment, the earwig, are the material of a certain kind of twentieth-century painting. Whatever else is to be said about it, such prose is surely rich in allusiveness.

Here once more we are confronted by the paradox of so much recent first-person narration: Roquentin scorns literature; a recent attempt to re-read *Eugénie Grandet* has been a failure; Maurice Barrès has been the subject of a peculiarly ridiculous dream in which the great writer has had his bottom spanked to the rhythm of derisive music. And Roquentin has made it a discipline to avoid being 'literary' in his journal: 'Je n'ai pas besoin de faire de phrases. J'écris pour tirer au clair certaines circonstances. Se méfier de la littérature. Il faut écrire au courant de la plume; sans chercher les mots'. (p. 77).

Yet few novels reveal a greater awareness of literature than does this one, so aware in fact that some of the evidence is almost too obvious to mention. For example, the reference to Pascal. I doubt that there would be much profit in insisting on what may be a chance association of the thinking reed with the rustling phalli of the passage quoted, but more specific implications should not escape: his insistence falls on the matter of human dignity. Pascal puts the hope of man in the fact that while he *is* a reed, the feeblest thing in nature, he is also a reed that thinks; he also points out that the human mind, that magnificent creation, can be rendered unserviceable by the buzzing of a fly. Roquentin would add that the feat of the fly can hardly be called stupendous. In his last years, Pascal lived with the hallucination of a great pit yawning beside him. Roquentin accepts the pit and rejects Pascal. Other, similar rejections are impressively numerous.

He spurns the central core of the teaching of André Gide. What happens to Roquentin might even be read as a specific and formal reply to Gide—even though the latter's name is not mentioned. For Gide was an apostle of a kind of self-culture through experience, of personal growth through exposure to the possibility of having things happen to you, in short of adventure. But Roquentin, who has been everywhere from London to Saigon, until references to his past sound like a somewhat comic version of a Cook's advertisement, has come to the conclusion that experience exists only as a word. The lover of adventure in the story is the pitifully unattractive creature whom Roquentin thinks of as the *Autodidacte*, who in seven years of educating himself at the public library has gotten through the Encyclopedia as far as 'L'. When this unfortunate, who would give his soul to have any adventure at all ('lose one's purse, miss a train, spend a night in jail'), tries to buttonhole Roquentin on the subject, the latter sends him away delighted with a pocketful of postcard views from here and there, and the thought that travel is adventurous as well as broadening. For Roquentin, adventure is no more than an attitude toward experience: the claptrap of moving about the world, love affairs with harlots, street fights ... Gradually you replace the thing that has happened to you by a word, and after a while you have the word and nothing besides; his memories seem to him like coins in the devil's purse, because when you open it there is nothing but dead leaves. Significantly, the *Autodidacte* comes to a bad end: just before the end of the story a schoolboy tempts him into making a homosexual gesture. For it he is beaten by the librarian and thrown out of the library. All his Gidian thirst for knowledge and openness to influence (the Encyclopedia), respect for experience and love of adventure exit from the story with him.

Nor could Roquentin long tolerate the atmosphere of the world of André Malraux. Twice in Malraux's novels characters whom the author has no intention of making comic—one is Klein in *Les Conquérants*—declare that it is difficult simply to be a man. Sartre puts the same words in the mouth of his silly *Autodidacte*:

> Il est vrai que tous les hommes ont droit à notre admiration. C'est difficile, très difficile d'être un homme ... (p. 153).
> Vous êtes trop modeste, monsieur. Pour supporter votre condition, la condition humaine, vous avez besoin, comme tout le monde, de beaucoup de courage. Monsieur, l'instant qui vient peut être celui de

votre mort, vous le savez et vous pouvez sourire: voyons! n'est-ce pas admirable? Dans la plus insignifiante de vos actions, ajoute-t-il avec aigreur, il y a une immensité d'héroisme (p. 154).

In the interval indicated by the first ellipsis above, Roquentin has answered that he has never found being human particularly difficult, and one must admit that however great Sartre's debt to Malraux may have been, it does not include the revelation of a particularly tragic world.

In addition, he manages rather thoroughly to do away with the basic assumptions which underlie the work of Proust. One does not relive the past, Roquentin declares, because it is definitively dead. Nor is there anything meaningful in the 'écoulement' of time. And privileged moments simply do not exist. By privileged moments Sartre does not mean all that Proust means in *Le Temps retrouvé*. It is Anny, Roquentin's one-time mistress, who in earlier days has specialized in creating (though not by involuntary memory) brief periods of complete euphoria which she refers to as 'moments privilégiés'. She realizes, in middle life, that these do not have any real meaning. It is the term she uses, of course, which distantly invokes the figure of Proust.[24]

For someone who aspires to avoiding the 'literary' in his writing, Roquentin would seem so aware of literature as to be in danger of a certain corruption of his own style. And indeed he does not escape it. The 'degré zéro' writing which is typical of most of the book gives way to more sophisticated techniques whenever he falls into his crises of morbidly acute awareness—or what it seems perfectly fair to call his anxiety states.

One excellent example of this transformation is the passage already mentioned in which the piece of meat crawls bleeding down the gutter toward the hypothetical man whose eye has just been stripped of its protective prejudices. We have already remarked that such visions are not uncommon in some contemporary painting. Working with words on paper, instead of charcoal or paint, the technique consists of juxtaposing image elements which are perfectly plausible to the imagination, but make the reason recoil because such a juxtaposition would be possible only if the world with which we are in contact began to disintegrate. Underlying this are two procedures which have frequently been attributed to the Surrealists, although they can hardly be considered to hold a monopoly: one, the projection of metaphor into the plane of action; the other, a kind of metamorphosis of images. These two procedures are closely related.

[24] The 'revolt against literature' is, of course, not exclusively French. See Ernest Hemingway, *Green Hills of Africa*.

For example:

Je vois une vieille dame qui sort craintivement de la galerie en arcades et qui regarde Impétraz d'un air fin et obstiné. Elle s'enhardit soudain, elle traverse la cour de toute la vitesse de ses *pattes* et s'arrête un moment devant la statue en remuant ses *mandibules*. Puis elle se sauve, *noire* sur le pavé rose, et disparaît dans une *lézarde* du mur (p. 44; my italics).

The fundamental image here imposes the figure of an insect upon that of an old woman. But the interest is less in the somewhat banal figure itself than in the way the figure is developed. The use of *pattes* for feet being quite common, we reach the end of the first step, as she scuttles across the court, only with the feeling that we are looking at something which is not entirely human. In a second step, the movement of her mandibles (instead of human jaws) makes the identification specific: she is at least *like* an insect. But when next she crosses the court again she is just something black against the pink background, and finally she disappears into a crack in the wall as no human but only an insect could do. So far as the imagination is concerned she has metamorphosed from one form of life into another.

Meanwhile, seen from another point of view, this same analogical figure is an example of metaphor turned into action. The woman is not merely compared with an insect—she becomes one. In the first process, comparison, the burden is upon the intellect: the thought is that she is *like* an insect. In the second, she *is* one; we are rather near the borders of hallucination.

Such strategies Sartre reserves for the moments of great mental tension in Roquentin's story.

Je vois ma main qui s'épanouit sur la table. Elle vit—c'est moi. Elle s'ouvre, mes doigts se déploient et pointent. Elle est sur le dos. Elle me montre son ventre gras. Elle a l'air d'une bête à la renverse. Les doigts, ce sont les pattes. Je m'amuse à les faire remuer, très vite, comme les pattes d'un crabe qui est tombé sur le dos. Le crabe est mort: les pattes se recroquevillent, se ramènent sur le ventre de ma main. Je vois les ongles, la seule chose de moi qui ne vit pas. Et encore. Ma main se retourne, s'étale à plat ventre, elle m'offre à présent son dos. Un dos argenté, un peu brillant—on dirait un poisson, s'il n'y avait pas ces poils rouges à la naissance des phalanges. Je sens ma main. C'est moi, ces deux bêtes qui s'agitent au bout de mes bras. Ma main gratte une de ses pattes, avec l'ongle d'une autre patte . . . (pp. 127–8).

It is hard to remember, reading this, that the subject is the simple physical act of opening a hand, wriggling the fingers momentarily, closing it again, and then scratching one hand with the other. For the length of three sentences what we are watching is clearly a hand. Then in the fourth comes the ambiguity: the hand is on its back. The next sentence chooses between the possibilities: the opposite of back is taken to be belly, not palm. In turn the sentence following rejects the metamorphosis: the hand is *like* some small beastie, turned belly-up. The fingers are *like* claws, can be wriggled *like* the claws of a crab turned over on its back. At last, the identity of the 'vehicle' of the metaphor is recognized. But now, as the fingers close, the crab dies; the legs fold in upon themselves, come back over the belly; but this is not a crab's belly but the 'belly' of a hand.[25]

Such a passage stands out in contrast with the prose that has preceded it. There has been one earlier place where it has been revealed that under mental stress, Roquentin feels the presence of objects so strongly as to be almost hallucinated by them, and it is marked by the use of striking metaphor. But after it, the habit of the diarist has been to restrain the tendency of seeing analogies and to attenuate the statement of those he sees. He prefers to introduce them with phrases like 'c'était comme qui dirait' or by using 'en' before the noun ('s'aller perdre en mille ruisseaux'), by appositive position with 'ce' (une 'borne . . . ce phare blanc') or by the linking of two nouns with 'de' ('sa voix de rainette'). This practice remains the dominant one through most of the book. But where his anxiety closes in upon him, when mental tension mounts, and when he approaches his moments of perceiving the true nature of reality, metaphors multiply and become conspicuous. At the same time feelings are con-cretized ('Oh, le long serpentin, le sentiment d'exister'); thoughts are felt as physical things ('Les pensées . . . je les sens naître derrière ma tête'). And the style of Roquentin's journal rapidly turns into something not unlike a stream of consciousness. 'Les maisons. Je marche entre les maisons, je suis entre les maisons, tout droit sur le pavé; le pavé sous mes pieds existe, les maisons se referment sur moi, comme l'eau se referme sur moi sur le papier en montagne de cygne, je suis' (p. 130).

Such a style fits uncomfortably in a journal—and in the cool mood of critical analysis one wonders whether the keeper of a journal would be disposed, or able, to write in this way, as well as whether a man who had had such an experience would be in any shape to record it at all. On the subject of his strange 'epiphany' Roquentin has turned on the floods of modern literary technique.

[25] For a very complete treatment of the crab image in Sartre's work, see **Marie-Denise Boros**, 'La Métaphore du crabe dans l'œuvre littéraire de Jean-Paul Sartre', *PMLA*, LXXXI, no. 4 (Oct. 1966), 446–50.

Simone de Beauvoir has told in her autobiography about Sartre's controlled experiment upon himself with hallucinants, and it has already been pointed out that some of the vision-stuff which haunted his memory afterwards finally found its way into his fiction.[26] Nothing could seem more likely, but it is fair to ask in turn where the material for the hallucinations came *from*. The lower orders of life have had considerable prominence in no little French literature, from Malraux to Mauriac. (See, for for example, the role of insects in the former's *Voie royale*.) One is disposed to ask whether when Sartre's crab, spider, and earwig imagery found its way into his writing it did not merely return to the source from which it came—literature. And, more particularly, whether Sartre does not owe some of his image-material, as well as his techniques of metaphor, to the Surrealists. Such questions are speculative, but the speculation may not be entirely empty.

Meanwhile, what is not speculative at all is the conclusion that in Sartre we have one more case of what would appear to be the rule in recent first-person narration. The first-person participant narrator has a character; short of making him a writer by trade, the novelist inevitably runs into a problem of keeping him in character and at the same time allowing him to use the literary resources the telling of his story demands. Since the story is almost invariably (the exception is Giono) the character's attainment of a new and intense awareness of his own situation in the universe, these demands are likely to be heavy. Thus the novelist's success would seem, at least in the cases we have been studying, to depend on his being able to give the character access to the resources without overwhelming the reader with a feeling of psychological impossibility.

No writer was to face this dilemma more persistently than did Albert Camus.

Albert Camus in 'L'Etranger'[27]

Critics, most noteworthily John Cruickshank,[28] have long been aware of the native exuberance in Albert Camus's style—and of the novelist's

---

[26] See *La Force de l'âge*, p. 216, and Ullmann's discussion in *Language and Style*, pp. 186–8.

[27] Material in this section regarding the concentration of images in *L'Etranger* appeared first as 'Camus: Image, Influence, and Sensibility', *YFS*, II (1950), 91–100.

[28] *Albert Camus and the Literature of Revolt*, pp. 142–88. These two chapters remain among the most perceptive and at the same time sanest discussions of Camus as writer.

ability to discipline it when necessary. Those who speak of his achievement as 'classical', in the French sense, probably have in mind, more than the elegance associated with the concept, a manifest power to control and restrain. They mean by 'classicism' what Valéry means when he says that it regularly implies an antecedent romanticism.[29]

Whatever the value of views like Valéry's for illumining the categories of literary history, the light they throw on Camus is precious: they draw attention both to the 'snaffle and the bit' and to 'the bloody 'orse', to the combined presence of Dionysus and Apollo everywhere in his work. Restraint can only be measured by the size of the force held in check. Hence the usefulness, for the present discussion, of the little collection of poetic essays, *Noces*, published five years before *L'Etranger* and intended, according to the prefatory note to the second edition, to be *essays* in the literal meaning of the term. Hampered by no requirements beyond those of self-expression, his lyricism comes out in an unabashed, incessant flow of metaphor. (The numbers in the text are to facilitate subsequent reference):

Dans cette splendeur aride, nous avons erré toute la journée. Peu à peu le vent, à peine senti au début de l'après-midi, semblait grandir avec les heures et remplir tout le paysage (1). Il soufflait (2) depuis une trouée entre les montagnes, loin vers l'est, accourait (3) du fond de l'horizon et venait bondir (4) en cascades (5) parmi les pierres et le soleil. Sans arrêt, il sifflait à travers les ruines, tournait dans un cirque de pierres et de terre (6), baignait (7) les amas de blocs grêlés (8), entourait chaque colonne de son souffle (9), et venait se répandre en cris incessants (10) sur le forum qui s'ouvrait dans le ciel. Je me sentais claquer au vent comme une mâture (11). Creusé par le milieu (12), les yeux brûlés, les lèvres craquantes, ma peau se desséchait jusqu'à ne plus être mienne. Par elle, auparavant, je déchiffrais l'écriture du monde (13). Il y traçait les signes de sa tendresse ou de sa colère (14) la réchauffant de son souffle d'été (15) ou la mordant de ses dents de givre (16). Mais si longuement frotté du vent (17), secoué depuis plus d'une heure, étourdi de résistance, je perdais conscience du dessin que traçait mon corps (18). Comme le galet verni par les marées (19), j'étais poli par le vent, usé jusqu'à l'âme (20). J'étais un peu de cette force selon laquelle je flottais, puis beaucoup, puis elle enfin (21), confondant les battements de mon sang et les grands coups sonores de ce cœur partout présent de la nature (22). Le vent me façonnait à l'image de l'ardente nudité qui m'entourait (23). Et sa fugitive étreinte (24)

---

[29] 'Variété', *Œuvres* (Pléiade ed.) I, 604.

me donnait, pierre parmi les pierres (25), la solitude d'une colonne ou d'un olivier (26) dans le ciel d'été.

Ce bain violent de soleil et de vent (27) épuisait toutes mes forces de vie. A peine en moi ce battement d'ailes (28) qui affleure, cette vie qui se plaint, cette faible révolte de l'esprit. Bientôt, répandu aux quatre coins du monde, oublieux, oublié de moi-même, je suis ce vent (29) et dans le vent, ces colonnes et cet arc (30), ces dalles qui sentent chaud et ces montagnes pâles autour de la ville déserte.[30]

The presence of the figures inserted in this text is not meant to lead the reader to conclude that it contains thirty metaphors, no more and no fewer. Who can be sure that 'soufflait' (2) is metaphorical? (If it is so, the reason has to be that the influence of the verbs which follow operate upon its character, like an electric current magnetizing a particle in its 'field'.) How decide whether 'la réchauffant . . . ou la mordant . . .'. (15) and (16), are two metaphors or one? And are we right in seeing metaphor in (29) and (30), which insist that his identification with the wind and the landscape are not metaphoric but literal facts? The numbers merely testify that at least thirty times in one passage a question about figurative language arises and thus justify our calling the style luxuriant. And so, perhaps, does the very uncertainty of the counting, since doubts rarely disturb us in texts where metaphor does not proliferate.

Two of the grammatical mechanisms for creating metaphor have been in frequent use in French descriptive prose since, at least, Chateaubriand's descriptions of Niagara Falls. One is the device of animating something in nature by the use of verbs like 'accourait' (3) and 'bondir' (4). The other consists of constructing an adverb in the form of 'en' plus a noun—an adverb which contains an image such as 'en cascades' (5) or 'en cris incessants' (10). Experienced readers will also identify these procedures, especially the first, as favorites of Jean Giono.

Additional reminiscences of Giono abound in the passage. Camus uses his device of metamorphosing one image into another: in (4) he has the wind 'bondir' and the reader responds with the image of an animal, but immediately, in (5), 'en cascades' turns the animal image into one of a stream. He multiplies (11–15) images in which a natural force—here the wind—affects both the inanimate landscape and the human figure in it. And he prolongs a metaphor, or series of metaphors, beyond the point where it loses the power of surprise.

The material of some of his metaphors is also similar to that of Giono's. The 'mâture' image (11) recalls the one in *Regain* which makes Gédémus's

[30] 'Le Vent à Djemila', *Noces*, pp. 31–2.

knife-grinder behave like ship's-rigging in the wind. The speaker's equating himself with a column, and tree, (26) echoes metaphors Giono uses to describe his hero Panturle. The shouting wind evokes a memory of the wind that clamors across the moor near Aubignane. The 'great heart of nature' image (22) condenses the elaborate figure about drums and heart-beat which dominates the banquet scene in *Que ma joie demeure*.[31] All in all, of the thirty instances in the passage where figurative language catches the attention, more than half bring to mind similar pieces of literary behavior in Giono.

Relatively little was said about the influence of Giono on Camus, even at the moment when the search for his sources was most active. The publication of *L'Etranger* sent off the hunt in full cry. Meursault was variously reported as shaped upon the models of Billy Budd, Julien Sorel, and Frank Chambers, the hero of *The Postman Always Rings Twice*. Prototypes for the trial were found in Malraux's *Conquérants*, Kafka, and *The Brothers Karamazov*. Encouraged by Camus's own remark that he had sought a model in 'le roman américain', everyone found abundant evidence that he had learned from Faulkner how to shuffle his time table, and from Hemingway the trick of catching those immediate sensations which are invariably characterized as the 'real, brute stuff of reality'. For a space it had been open season and hunting was good.

Then Camus published *La Peste* and the horns were stilled. Quarry was scarce and uninteresting: what excitement in discovering that Camus must have read *Moby-Dick*? And, in any case, Camus's discussions of his own readings made such discoveries far too easy.

Doubtless Camus would sooner or later have talked about Giono if the latter's influence had seemed important to him. I find no conclusive evidence that he was even aware of it. In spite of the reminiscences, we recognize the essentially personal quality, its uniqueness, in the strange ambivalence which couples an ecstatic love of life with an obsessive brooding over death, not only in this passage and this essay but throughout all of *Noces*. The world is beautiful and outside it there is no salvation; the great good of living is simply in not being dead; yet, in the midst of life death is always at hand, the ultimate vile ignominy. This ambivalence provides the essential movement in the passage quoted, as we progress through the lavish metaphors dealing with the wind's behavior and then with its effect upon the human: from the affirmation of the individual's great sensual pleasure in the touch of wind and sun on epidermis it moves

[31] *Que ma joie demeure*, pp. 154–91.

us to the point where individuality becomes submerged and its private existence is lost in nature (26–30). This by itself would put Camus's personal seal on the passage. In addition, there is also the translation of the feeling of felicity into one of bathing (7, 19, 20, 27), which should remind one of the ritual importance of swimming not only in the novels but also as an aspect of the emblematic 'invincible summer'.

Thus, in spite of the influences perceptible—one might also talk of those of the neo-pagan Gide of the *Nourritures*, as of Nietzsche, Malraux, and perhaps Unamuno—*Noces* is ample evidence of Camus's need to express an intense temperament. Like most of the others discussed in these chapters, he is primarily a poet.

In the context of a discussion of Camus's style, the now often mentioned proliferation of metaphor at the end of the First Part of *L'Etranger* is probably much less significant than the simple fact that, until 1949, nobody had (I believe) studied it. By that year Camus's place as a novelist was well established, and *L'Etranger* an abundantly studied book. It stands to reason that if the concentration of metaphors had not occasioned comment, it was because they did not obtrude from the fabric of the work.[32]

Up to the moment in the story when Meursault turns away from the beach steps and walks off across the sand toward the place where he will shoot the Arab, Camus has used a total of some fifteen metaphors—to allow for differences in counting let it be perhaps twenty. But now, in the single episode of the shooting, he uses no fewer than twenty-five.

To quote the passage entire would be too long. As listed here, the metaphors are in order but, necessarily, out of context:

'La tête retentissante de soleil'; 'la chaleur . . . pluie aveuglante', 'la mer haletait'; 'je sentais mon front se gonfler sous le soleil'; 'toute cette chaleur s'appuyait sur moi'; 'et s'opposait à mon progrès'; 'son grand souffle chaud'; 'à chaque épée de lumière'; 'rocher entouré d'un halo aveuglant'; 'son image dansait devant mes yeux, dans l'air en-

[32] More recently comment has become almost overwhelmingly abundant, so that some outstanding work is threatened with being lost in the welter. One such is Ignace Feuerlicht, 'Camus's *L'Etranger* Reconsidered', *PMLA*, LXXVIII, no. 5 (Dec. 1963), 606–21. Partisans of image counting may be distressed that he disagrees with Carl A. Viggiani ('Camus's *l'Etranger*', *PMLA*, LXXII, no. 5 [Dec. 1956], 865–87) as to the exact total, and that both disagree with the count reported here. I take it that the three of us are persuaded, however, that exact numbers matter less than relative density in various parts of the story.

I

flammé'; 'la journée . . . avait jeté l'ancre'; 'un océan de métal bouillant';
'une plage vibrante de soleil'; '[la plage] se pressait derrière moi':
'la lumière a giclé sur l'acier'; 'la sueur . . . un voile tiède et épais';
'ce rideau de larmes et de sel'; 'les cymbales du soleil'; 'le glaive
éclatant jailli du couteau'; 'cette épée brûlante rongeait mes cils et
fouillait mes yeux douloureux'; 'la mer a charrié un souffle épais et
ardent'; 'le ciel s'ouvrait sur toute son étendue pour laisser pleuvoir du
feu'; 'j'ai touché le ventre poli de la crosse'; 'j'ai secoué la sueur et le
soleil'; 'et c'était comme quatre coups brefs que je frappais sur la porte
du malheur' (pp. 1164–6).

The general situation here is very like the one which provokes the flow
of metaphor in 'Le Vent à Djemila': an individual is telling about the
effect upon him of a specific condition of the weather to which he is
exposed by the special nature of the landscape. The man is Meursault
instead of the *persona* of the poet; the weather condition is intense heat
instead of a wind; the landscape is a beach instead of a basin in the desert.
But these substitutions are local and hardly affect the linguistic conditions:
metaphor is still involved with the contact between nature and the human
epidermis.

The organization is different, of course. In the 'Djemila' passage we
noted first a cluster of images which had to do with the *behavior* of the
wind, and then a second one in which emphasis shifted to what the wind
did to the individual. Here the two themes are mixed: the metaphor about
the panting sea follows two which link heat with its effect upon the head
and the eye; then three more translate the man's physical responses to heat
before the more objective reference to the 'great hot breath'. Next the
image of the 'sword of light' introduces the motif of a blade, the first
of three more physical responses as well as a first suggestion of the
psychological equivalence of flashing light and cutting weapon which
will become decisive a bit later in the passage. Now come a series of three
figures in which physical reaction is not concerned, one in which it is
dominant, and another connecting the light—already fluid in an earlier
metaphor—with the Arab's knife . . . This alternation continues, at almost
the same rhythm, through the rest of the passage. At Djemila weather has
an importance of its own. Here we cannot separate it from its effect.

Meanwhile, the individual himself is passive until, only at the very end,
he reacts. As at Djemila, he feels his contact with the force of nature to be
one with a liquid, the difference being, of course, that in this later instance
the contact does not exhilarate but causes discomfort. The quality of
hallucination, of metaphor confused with literal reality, is even stronger

here than in the part of the Djemila passage where the speaker identifies himself with wind and landscape.

But in *L'Etranger* the relation of the metaphors to literary form is entirely different. They become a principal instrument of psychological analysis. For by following the play of metaphor we also follow the play of hallucination in Meursault's mind, and among the hallucinations is hidden, for all to see, the motive for the otherwise inexplicable shooting of the Arab.

It is essential to the story, of course, that the motive should be adequate to explain the murder to the reader, but inadequate to explain it to the exclusively rational legal mind. In court such a statement as that he killed 'because of the sun' is too elliptic to be meaningful. What the metaphors do, for him and for us, is to fill out the ellipsis. What Meursault told the *juge d'instruction* was the literal and exact truth. If, so to speak, he had been wearing a hat and sun-glasses he would not have shot the Arab.

We have been prepared for this, much earlier in the story, by information planted here and there about the hero's sensitivity to bright light. The glare of an unshaded bulb bothers him at his mother's wake. He finds the sunlight painful when he is on his way to the funeral. And we see, on this occasion, a first instance where bright light confuses not only vision but the mind also. Some of what critics[33] have called the internal distance between Meursault as narrator and Meursault as actor may have the memory of such discomfort for, at least, one of its causes. In any event, the weakness of Meursault's eyes is what seals the Arab's doom.

Even before Meursault discovers his adversary in the shade of the rock he has been dazzled by light reflected from the sand, and his head throngs with hallucinations. Heat is 'raining' on him. His head is full of clangor and he feels it swelling from the beating of the sun. The heat, now personified, weighs him down and holds him back. Naturally, when the light stabs his eyes, his interpretation of it is another hallucination: 'une épée de lumière.' It is the Arab's misfortune that he has, and draws, the knife. The light reflected from it strikes Meursault's eyes as if it were another 'long, glittering blade'. Now the other hallucinations disappear and there remain in his mind only two, the clashing noise inside his heat-struck skull—which he interprets as coming from the heavens, 'the cymbals of the sunlight'—and this one of the flashing blade. So he shoots —because he now has had the hallucination of being attacked by the

[33] For example Brian T. Fitch, 'Aesthetic Distance and Inner Space in the Novels of Camus', *Modern Fiction Studies*, X, no. 3 (Autumn 1964), 279–92.

actual weapon which has already harmed his friend Raymond. Nothing could be simpler nor, given the confused state of Meursault's mind, more comprehensible: he shoots in self-defense.

Critics have alleged that this murder is 'pure Hemingway'. Actually it is very impure Hemingway indeed. The tenser the action gets in a Hemingway story, the less likely metaphors are to appear, and most especially so at the moment of killing. Except perhaps by chance Hemingway does not permit any veil of unreality to hang between his hero and what his hero is doing. For example, as he performs the final murder in *To Have and Have Not*, Harry Morgan reminds himself that he must be light-fingered on the trigger because the clip holds only twenty rounds—a burst of five for each of the four men he must kill. He wishes he could have a steadying drink; he chides himself for procrastinating; he reaches down his Thompson gun from the cabin bulkhead and slips it out of its case. Then the gun comes up and he has the back of the first man's head clearly in his sights.[34]

It is essential that the hero's mind should be clear because killing, in Hemingway's view, is a tragic event: violence is a part of man's destiny, and in pulling the trigger the hero tacitly acknowledges the nature of his human predicament: men have to kill and he is here being a man. Any blur at this point would seriously violate Hemingway's aesthetics and possibly his ethics as well.

Actually, the American influence most clearly suggested in the passage from *L'Etranger* is not Hemingway's but James M. Cain's. In *The Postman Always Rings Twice*, echo is utilized for a climactic effect, much as by Camus, at the end of the passage where the murder, which is again the crucial point of the story, takes place. Nick, very drunk, leans out the car door and shouts toward the overhanging hills, and as he does so Frank Chambers smashes his head with a bottle. Nick slumps in his seat, dead. And then back from the hills comes the echo of his cry.[35] The echo of Meursault's four shots is less crudely handled, but in each case we have the echo introduced just as the murder is committed, with the intention of emphasizing the finality of the event which has just occurred. But, as with Hemingway's hero, Chambers is entirely clear about what he is doing, and there is no need to convey his motive through any such indirect means as metaphor.

However pervasive the influence of the Americans may have been, and whether or not Camus got from them the idea of the unemotional

---

[34] *To Have and Have Not*, Scribner ed., p. 170.
[35] *The Postman Always Rings Twice*, Grosset and Dunlap ed., p. 67.

and paratactic style which has caught the attention of so many critics, comparison of the prose of *L'Etranger* with that of the so-called 'behaviorists'[36] leads to a new realization of how completely Camus's achievement is unique, and his alone. The style of the Americans, dictated as it is by the presence of almost analphabetic—not to say Neanderthal—characters as first-person narrators, is not conspicuously tolerant of metaphor. We have just been watching Camus contrive, on the other hand, to use metaphors in abundance for a narrational and psychological purpose, without stirring his reader to object to a change in style or to his making his speaker appear to have stepped 'out of character'.

At least two possibilities suggest themselves as reasons why the metaphors do not distract. One is, simply, that their narrative and psychological function corresponds so entirely with the kind of interest the reader feels at that juncture in the story. (Why under heaven does not Meursault turn about when he sees the Arab and go away?) The other is that in a sense Meursault's language is not so far out of character as it may seem when studied out of context: this man has regularly shown himself deficient in feeling about other people, but he has always shown himself completely alive to his own physical comfort and discomfort. One may feel that even the experience of this intolerable heat might well not have expanded his vocabulary to include a phrase like 'cymbals of the sky' and still admit that, if any subject could move him to such an utterance, this one could. But neither explanation, nor the two taken together, can provide an entirely satisfactory answer.

Yet perhaps we do learn, from studying this passage, what Camus meant by one of his pronouncements about *L'Etranger*: 'C'est un livre très concerté et le ton . . . est voulu. Il s'élève quatre ou cinq fois, il est vrai, mais c'est pour éviter la monotonie et pour qu'il y ait une composition.' However much difficulty the student may experience in identifying all 'four or five' places in *L'Etranger*, this one offers none: its prose is meant to contrast with that of the preceding episodes and, perhaps, in addition, to mark the distinction between an episode which has an immediate meaning for Meursault and those whose meaning dawns on him only later. In view of his remark about the place of such heightened passages in his notion of structure, we should expect to find a piece of correspondingly elevated prose in the corresponding position, at the end

---

[36] So far as I know, no one has actually shown that an identifiable 'behaviorist style' exists in American writing. The concept itself is unfamiliar to most American students of the subject.

of the Second Part and one where again an immediate meaning comes home to Meursault.

We have it, of course, in the pages which follow upon the interview with the prison chaplain, who has come to offer the consolations of religion—and of accepting the idea of one's own guilt.

> Lui parti, j'ai retrouvé le calme. J'étais épuisé et je me suis jeté sur ma couchette. Je crois que j'ai dormi parce que je me suis réveillé avec des étoiles sur le visage. Des bruits de campagne montaient jusqu'à moi. Des odeurs de nuit, de terre et de sel rafraîchissaient mes tempes. La merveilleuse paix de cet été endormi entrait en moi comme une marée. A ce moment, et à la limite de la nuit, les sirènes ont hurlé. Elles annonçaient des départs pour un monde qui maintenant m'était à jamais indifférent. Pour la première fois depuis longtemps, j'ai pensé à maman. Il m'a semblé que je comprenais pourquoi à la fin d'une vie elle avait pris un fiancé, pourquoi elle avait joué à recommencer. Là-bas, là-bas aussi, autour de cet asile où des vies s'éteignaient, le soir était comme une trêve mélancolique. Si près de la mort, maman devait s'y sentir libérée et prête à tout revivre. Personne, personne n'avait le droit de pleurer sur elle. Et moi aussi, je me suis senti prêt à tout revivre. Comme si cette grande colère m'avait purgé du mal, vidé d'espoir, devant cette nuit chargée de signes et d'étoiles, je m'ouvrais pour la première fois à la tendre indifférence du monde . . . (p. 1209).

This is Meursault's moment of special perception, of understanding, and illumination. He has been pulled away from the priest, and now, with the relaxation of his nerves, he sees the true nature of his human situation.

After two sentences which state objective facts—renewal of calm, exhaustion, lying down, dropping off to sleep—in the typical paratactical manner of earlier chapters, the third introduces a causal connective such as is rare in the mouth of Meursault, and a slight change in the nature of the language: 'étoiles sur le visage' says more than just that the stars have come out; it implies a feeling of connection between man and nature. The following sentence, about the rising night-sounds, is another statement of fact, but the next one contains a *correspondance*: he feels the night-smells cooling his temples, exchanging an olfactory for a tactile sensation. In turn this leads into a metaphor: peace floods into him. After this is inserted a motif reminiscent of Malraux: the steamer whistles symbolize, for Meursault as for T'chen, a world from which the act of killing has excluded him. His mind turns to his mother and his syntax enlarges to admit the use of an augmentative repetition, 'là-bas, là-bas aussi', followed by the explanatory 'où des vies ...'. This repetition is followed by a second: 'personne, personne ...'. And the last sentence quoted contains a parallel absolute construction: 'purgé du mal, vidé d'espoir ...'

These unusual syntactical and rhetorical features are accompanied by a striking expansion of Meursault's vocabulary. Expressions like 'été endormi', and 'à la limite de la nuit', 'où des vies s'éteignaient', 'trêve mélancolique', 'chargée de signes et d'étoiles', and 'tendre indifférence du monde', appear unexpectedly in the lexicon of the man who, before his trial and imprisonment, has seemed hardly capable of the mental effort they would demand, or of the emotional sensitivity they assume. Yet perhaps the movement of the prose itself is even more striking. Everyone is agreed that Camus's style in L'Etranger is radically paratactical, and that each sentence is 'an island'. Yet these sentences, after the first three, are hardly 'islands' and can hardly be said each one to start 'over again from zero'. In a combination of sentences like: 'Des odeurs de nuit, de terre et de sel rafraîchissaient mes temps. La merveilleuse paix de cet été endormi entrait en moi comme une marée', the absence of grammatical connectives is purely formal; one sentence flows into the next.

It is as if, in his new perception of his relation to the world, the relation of one part of experience to another had also become clear to him so that each was no longer to be encapsuled in its own independent statement. And, at the same time, his metaphors here are not so many attempts to describe a physical effect—like that of heat and light on his body—but his relationship to the natural world and, almost, to the universe. This style is an index to the change that has taken place within Meursault, and his ability to use it here is a part of his story.

To judge by the criticism, this change, like the change at the end of the First Part, has not produced widespread feelings of shock by making the protagonist speak implausibly 'out of character'. Doubtless it is not the speech of the man who begins his story with the remark that his mother died today, or perhaps yesterday, he is not sure. We accept the change because he is not the same man.

Another reason for the acceptance of the change in style has to be suggested—the fundamental rightness of Camus's feeling of form—of what he meant by 'pour qu'il y ait une composition'. The First Part had ended on an elevated tone, and symmetry would demand that the Second Part should also end on one.

This view is, unfortunately, in conflict with the brilliant reading of

Carl A. Viggiani.[37] He argues from the major change in the style we have scrutinized that in reality there are not two parts to *L'Etranger* but three. Were the question one to be settled with reference to style alone, we should be absolutely wrong not to grant his point. But looking at the problem from the angle of literary form as well as of style, the necessity for a Third Part seems much less urgent. On the other hand, a contrast of tone at the end of one part, matching a similar contrast at the end of the other, obviates the need of a third and at the same time grants that Camus was craftsman enough to have done what he said he wanted.

As to the nature of Meursault's epiphany, and the actual content of his final perception, one is forced to speak with diminishing assurance as the years pass. Most of the criticism that has dealt with this story has been concerned with its meaning, and each critic has discovered in it one obviously satisfactory to him—and obviously unsatisfactory to his successors. Camus's revelation of his character as allegorist in *La Peste*, as well as the relation all his interpreters recognize between *L'Etranger* and *Le Mythe de Sisyphe*, doubtless make this inevitable. And so does the recurrence of such motifs as law, lawyers, trials, and such themes as Justice and Guilt, throughout Camus's fiction.

From the very persistence of the interpreters one concludes that the search is difficult and not particularly fruitful. Professor René Girard has recently given us reason to think that it will continue to be futile: there is, according to him, a fundamental flaw in the data of the story: Meursault has to be guilty and not guilty at once.[38] If this reading is correct, of course we cannot expect to find a coherent allegory and the epiphany itself will be impossible to restate rationally.

This will distress, however, only those critics who would reduce such fictions to rational discourse—and who do not recognize that epiphanies are rarely rational. In the case of Camus the interpreter is left in the same position as are chronic admirers of Rimbaud and perhaps the later Victor Hugo, certainly of Malraux and Bernanos, and quite possibly of Sartre. The hero attains a state of special awareness, conscious illumination or, in the existential sense, 'lucidity'. But what is lucid is his vision, and this we must take more or less on faith; his statement of the vision does not necessarily, or even frequently, achieve the same lucidity.

In other words, we are forced to treat such writers as if they were poets and the novels somewhat as if they were (obscure) poems. According to one of the persistent theses of these present chapters, such a procedure is

---

[37] 'Camus's *L'Etranger*'.
[38] 'Camus's *L'Etranger* Retried', *PMLA*, LXXIX, no. 5 (Dec. 1964), 519–33.

forced upon us by the nature of the most admired French fiction of the second quarter of our century.

Pseudo-Third Persons

It is not a paradox that *La Peste* should claim attention in a discussion of first-person narrative, or that it should be compared with Malraux's performance in *Les Noyers de l'Altenburg*. Both use a third-person narrator, but to tell a story which might be told by a first-person narrator with no loss of naturalness, and perhaps with a smaller expense of literary ingenuity. And in both, it would seem, the decisive factor in the choice of the third-person form is a concern about tone.

The change of focus in *La Peste* is hardly so dramatic as is sometimes suggested. True, the experience of the plague is, almost by definition, a group experience. Those involved are forced together: efforts to combat the epidemic and efforts to run away from it are knit in the same fabric. But *La Peste* is a moral and metaphysical allegory, and the central moral consciousness is the narrator, Dr. Rieux. The reader's understanding of what happens comes—except for some side illumination from the diary of Tarrou—from this one source.

Camus's notes show[39] clearly that Rieux's revelation, late in the story, that he has been the narrator, is not intended to surprise. Clues were to be scattered through the text. And indeed, had there been none, the amount the nameless narrator knows, from the beginning, about Rieux's intimate feelings would probably alert a reflective reader. In a similar way, Vincent Berger's son knows a surprising amount about the emotions his father has experienced in the course of an adventurous life.

But Berger is an extraordinary individual, whereas the allegory (as Camus perceives it) of *La Peste* would be pointless if its hero were not a representative man. For the latter to be a gifted writer would be more than mildly unconvincing. Hence a technical problem.

Camus adopts the obvious solution, making Rieux surbordinate everything else to the sober, direct reporting of what he has witnessed. Hence, in turn, a style deliberately muted, marked (symptomatically) by an absence of evocative adjectives, and here and there by turns of phrase intended to identify the narrator as the opposite of a literary man. He is given, for example, to the use of the first-person plural possessive in expressions where it connotes a conventional sense of community:

[39] Pléiade ed., p. 1932.

'notre ville', 'nos concitoyens'. One recognizes in this the practice of certain provincial editorial writers, and one which is also in favor among some conservative groups, not necessarily provincial, that are not averse to sounding old fashioned (cf. the 'nos maisons', 'nos écoles', etc. of a part of the Catholic press).

Such procedures set the fundamental tone, the level from which degrees of elevation must be measured by a reader who comes upon such passages as the one where, after Tarrou's long explanation of his desire to attain a kind of un-churched, un-religious sanctity, he and Rieux decide to go for an evening swim:

> ... Ils passèrent et à travers les terre-pleins couverts de tonneaux, parmi les senteurs de vin et de poisson, ils prirent la direction de la jetée. Peu avant d'y arriver l'odeur de l'iode et des algues leur annonça la mer. Puis, ils l'entendirent.
>
> Elle sifflait doucement au pied des grands blocs de la jetée et, comme ils la gravissaient, elle leur apparut, épaisse comme du velours, souple et lisse comme une bête. Ils s'installèrent sur les rochers tournés vers le large. Les eaux se gonflaient et redescendaient lentement. Cette respiration calme de la mer faisait naître et disparaître des reflets huileux à la surface des eaux. Devant eux, la nuit était sans limites. Rieux, qui sentait sous ses doigts le visage grêlé des rochers, était plein d'un étrange bonheur. Tourné vers Tarrou, il devina, sur le visage calme et grave de son ami, ce même bonheur qui n'oubliait rien, pas même l'assassinat (p. 1426).

The special nature of the occasion is suggested by a quickening of the senses, the alertness to smells: fish and wine, iodine and seaweed. This alertness increases as the sentence proceeds: first comes the smell of iodine, afterwards the smell of seaweed—of which iodine is characteristic.

'Sifflait', at the beginning of the new paragraph, again translates a sense impression, and the same sentence also contains the two metaphors in which the sea is first materialized (thick as velvet) and then animized (supple and smooth as an animal); and we observe that a different sense has become active, touch rather than smell. Presently the sea is again represented as an animism, behaving like something that breathes. Another metaphor now follows, if we are willing to grant metaphoric force to the adjective 'huileux'. (By itself such an adjective need not, of course, be a metaphor; 'sugary' applied to candied fruit would not be one, but what of 'sugary' qualifying 'voice'? 'Huileux' may acquire metaphoric force from its functioning in the 'field' of other metaphors.) It is followed in turn by 'visage grêlé des rochers', in which the metaphorical content, and the literary intention, are much clearer: 'grêlé' itself is already a latent metaphor, since rocks are not literally hail-dented or pock-marked, and in addition the expression is certified to be metaphor by the otherwise redundant 'visage' that functions only as re-enforcement of the analogy.

How far such linguistic behavior is from the intemperate metaphor-making of the early essays like *Noces* need hardly be emphasized. The change in literary behavior has been imposed on Camus by the character of the hero-narrator he has chosen. These discreet metaphors are conspicuous only because they contrast with the normal language of Dr. Rieux, which is even more discreet. But, ultimately, it must be conceded that they have their source in his particular conception of the novel.

In contrast with Camus in *La Peste*, Malraux in *Les Noyers* finds himself in the situation of telling the story of a fictional character very like himself—in fact so like himself that he is forced into a literally duplicitous literary behavior. Such aspects of Vincent Berger's career as the acquirement of special knowledge, the subsequent protracted absence from Europe, the life of violent action in Asia, and the eventual return to find himself the subject of a prestigious legend, are also aspects of Malraux's own. But how, in a time that finds the grand manner only a source of uneasiness, is a writer to employ the elevated language required by what I have called 'the epiphany of the walnuts' to treat an experience admittedly his own? Malraux's solution, after an opening chapter (dated 1940) about his later experience and written in a straightforward first person, is to adopt what, for all intents and purposes, is a first person acting as third-person narrator, telling a story alleged to have the narrator's father at the center. Vincent Berger thus appears to be a device for obtaining distanciation, for making elevated language permissible: the son-narrator can do what Rieux, telling his own story, cannot.

Is it exaggerating to say that Bernanos and Céline, Sartre, Camus, perhaps Giono and certainly Malraux, discovered new possibilities in narrating in the first person?

CHAPTER SEVEN

Continuities in the 'New Novel'[1]

It may not be literally true that by 1960 more had been written about the so-called 'New Novelists' than had been written by them, but there is every reason to suspect that few new movements in French literature had ever been more sympathetically observed and reported. Friends of French fiction everywhere, including some of the most gravely erudite of academic critics,[2] had lavished attention on each new development; no genius had been allowed to come to light unannounced, no new text to stay unglossed; criticism had been difficult to distinguish from midwifery. One cannot avoid the conclusion that those who knew the subject best had come to the conviction that the kind of novel we have been discussing had run its course and were eager for something new to emerge.

The exigencies of the literary life, as well as the normal psychology of authorship, at first led authors like Nathalie Sarraute, Michel Butor, and Alain Robbe-Grillet to emphasize their differences.[3] Robbe-Grillet's 'neo-realism', Mme Sarraute's 'tropisms', and Butor's 'novel as research' have been amply and even elaborately expounded not only by the novelists themselves—each of whom would be a considerable critic even if his novels were unknown—but also by very competent interpreters.[4] But now that individualities have been preserved it becomes appropriate to return to the question raised by those who attended the 'New Novel' at its birth: in what is it different from the novel that preceded it?

It was clear from the beginning that the emergent novelists differed from their predecessors on at least one major point: they thought of themselves as being primarily technicians. Mme Sarraute and Claude

---

[1] This chapter enlarges 'Introduction to Butor', *YFS*, no. 24 (Summer 1959), pp. 54–62 and 'Faulkner and the "Roman nouveau", an interim report', *Bucknell Review*, X, no. 3 (March 1962), 186–93.

[2] See for example *YFS*, no. 24 (Summer 1959), the whole of which is devoted to the discussion of the new trend under the comprehensive title 'The Midnight Novel'.

[3] See Mme Sarraute's *Ere du soupçon*, *passim*; Robbe-Grillet's *Pour un nouveau roman*, *passim*; and, in Butor's *Répertoire*, I, 'Le Roman comme recherche' (pp. 7–12), 'Balzac et la réalité' (pp. 79–94), and 'Les "Moments" de Marcel Proust' (pp. 163–73).

[4] For example Bruce A. Morrissette, *Les Romans de Robbe-Grillet*.

Simon had been experimenting for years[5] before they were recognized, in their maturity, as representatives of the young and new. Butor's first novel renewed techniques of Dos Passos and of Vicki Baum's *Grand Hotel*. In *Les Gommes* and *Le Voyeur* Robbe-Grillet rang ingenious changes on the basic formulae of the detective story. In the essays they wrote when not writing novels, the tones Mme Sarraute, Butor, and Robbe-Grillet naturally adopted were those of craftsmen defending their craft with theory.

It was also clear that the central characters—the word heroes will not always do—in these new fictions were different: they tended to become devices for registering sensation and for recording the effect of the impingements of the world outside on the psyche within. Robbe-Grillet would carry this eventually to the point of suppressing the character altogether and presenting only the sensations registered: in *La Jalousie* a special perspective on reality replaces the jealous husband, and in *Dans le labyrinthe* the reader literally does not know by what consciousness the detail of events is being apprehended.

The material of such novels is the immediate data of consciousness. A study of Mme Sarraute's imagery, for example, shows that it operates on the level of the first recognition of phenomena, rather than on the level of evaluation, and thus identifies a kind of psychic activity very rare in earlier fiction.[6] The protagonist in Butor's *La Modification* has difficulty separating memories from fantasies, and these in turn from such present realities as the bouncing of a crumb on the vibrating metal floorplate of his railroad carriage. In this sort of accounting attention may wander and return, but the experience itself does not break up into fragments of which some are more significant than others.

At first blush the 'New Novelists' appear to reject the formulae of their immediate elders much less than they do those of a slightly older generation. Mme Sarraute's rejection of depth psychology, Robbe-Grillet's explorations of surface detail, and Butor's preoccupation with his characters' enslavement to meaningless minutiae, all contrast much more violently with the practice of the age of Mauriac than with that of a group already affected, directly or indirectly, by the influence of behaviorism. Many moments in the lives of Sartre's Roquentin and Camus's Meursault might not sound greatly different if narrated as a series of the tropisms proposed by Mme Sarraute.

[5] Their birth dates are 1902 and 1913, respectively.

[6] The subject has been explored in John A. Fleming, *The Imagery of Tropism*, an unpublished doctoral dissertation in the Harvard Archives.

But this impression is delusive. If all consciousness has the same value, the mighty upsurge of Malraux's Altenburg walnuts and the tender indifference of Meursault's world are no more or less significant than the dance of Butor's crumb, instances of heightened perception have the standing only of psychic states, and the notion of epiphany makes no verifiable sense. The hero whose life reaches climax, once or repeatedly, in a blinding flash of special insight is at best a victim of his own imagination. The great difference between the 'New Novel' and these others is that it sees experience as a continuum.

Style and form differ accordingly. Form is no longer determined by the necessity of bringing the protagonist to his moment of privilege. Tonal variations conforming to the intensity of the experience are out of order. Procedures like Malraux's inserting the picture of the exit of Katow or the descent of the wrecked aviators from the mountain have no place. Nor, in short, has poetry; confusions of identity between the 'New Novel' and poetry of almost any identifiable sort are most unlikely. Consequently the 'presence' of the novelist in his work (except in Flaubert's sense) once more becomes undesirable, and we need no longer be concerned with techniques of intervention. The novel becomes once again a domain of prose.

These differences from the novelists who came before them are confirmed by the kind of use the 'New Novelists' have made of the precept and example of William Faulkner.

Even on a basis of still partial returns,[7] it is reasonably sure that Faulkner's position in France has passed through three different phases and into— if not yet through—a fourth. There was first the Faulkner discovered simultaneously by Valery Larbaud and André Malraux—both, through some confusion in the house of Gallimard,[8] writing prefaces to *Sanctuary* —early in the 1930's. This was the 'tragic' Faulkner. According to Malraux this American had succeeded in combining Greek tragedy with the modern detective story; Larbaud found him to be dealing in obsessed characters and dark fatalities, and thus not unlike the Malraux of *La Condition humaine*.

The second phase began, just before World War II, when Sartre[9]

[7] Stanley D. Woodworth, *William Faulkner en France (1931–1952)*, was presented as a Paris University Doctorate in 1957, and thus does not cover the most recent developments.

[8] The subject has been abundantly documented in Vincent Milligan, *Valery Larbaud, Anglicist*, a Columbia University dissertation (1953), unpublished so far as I know.

[9] See especially the articles reproduced in *Situations*, I, 'Sartoris', pp. 7–13, and

and others got some notion of Faulkner's feeling of time: even through the translations they could see how the present could be the front edge of the past pushing into the future, in such a way that the future is continually becoming the past—without ever being the present except in that infinitely brief moment when we are aware of it as such. This phase also saw the first imitations including, eventually, Sartre's own. (As Butor has pointed out,[10] this is a conjectural attribution because one is never entirely sure whether the writer imitated is Faulkner or a Dos Passos who has surprisingly lost his grip on indirect discourse and *style indirect libre*). This phase overlapped in time with the third, in which metaphysical exegetes like Claude-Edmonde Magny[11] identified the theological Faulkner, with his conviction of the evils of the flesh, his Pauline suspicion of women, his awareness of pervasive sin and guilt and of the capacity of ordinary, feckless individuals like Percy Grimm to become for no reason the agents of utter horror: this was Faulkner the Puritan Dostoevski.

Ultimately, in his fourth stage, he becomes one of the liberators (what Maurice Blanchot has called[12] one of the 'exceptions'), from whom, as from Proust, Joyce, and Kafka, the 'New Novelists' have derived techniques, strategies, and the authorization to depart from tradition.

The situation of Faulkner *vis-à-vis* the French in this fourth phase is one rare in the history of literary relations between national literatures—perhaps unique. This is not an ordinary case of 'influence' of the kind in which a writer in one country 'borrows' an idea, a theme, or a fragment of plot from one in another, like, for example, Balzac's taking from J. F. Cooper the idea for the novel that became *Les Chouans* after being *Le Dernier Chouan*. Faulkner has provided the French with a manner of treating themes and subjects—matter—not his but theirs; ultimately we have the rare spectacle of French writers altering the syntax of their French because of the way he writes his English.

The most readily apparent consequence of the new development is also one of the most elusive and difficult to talk about, that is, the necessity of a fresh critical term, Voice. A novelist may reduce character, as Mme Sarraute does, to a bundle of impulses, or, as Robbe-Grillet does in one instance, to a significant absence situated at the convergence of a number of angles; there is still a source of words that sets distances, defines

[10] In a lecture.   [11] *L'Age du roman américain*, pp. 196–252.
[12] 'D'un art sans avenir', *NNRF*, 5ᵉ année, no. 51 (March 1957), 488–98.

'La Temporalité chez Faulkner', pp. 70–81. See also Jean Pouillon, *Temps et roman* and Claude-Edmonde Magny, *L'Age du roman américain*.

relationships, and establishes what we were once satisfied to call point of view. Faulkner is perhaps not the lone reason for our needing something to call this source: the unceasing talk of the character 'who says I but is not completely me' dominates *A la recherche du temps perdu*, just as a narrator we do not fully recognize dominates Kafka's *Castle*. The narrator in Proust's novel is, after all, a character in the story—despite Louis Martin-Chauffier's attempt[13] to discriminate what are alleged to be four different roles the 'je'-character is called upon to play. But the Voice that narrates in Faulkner is not that of a character, and its tones are much the same from novel to novel. The French have no doubt accepted Faulkner's example in this matter more completely than they have his precept. Characters, he is said to have declared in one of his rare theoretical pronouncements, need not be characterized by the words in which the novelist makes them speak and think.[14] But the tradition of making characters speak always 'in character' remains so strong in France that the 'New Novelists' tend to evade the full issue: Butor avoids the shock by identifying the Voice with a man writing or preparing to write; Robbe-Grillet hides the owner of the Voice; Mme Sarraute works toward ending the distinction between vocal and subvocal dialogue. Only Claude Simon is inclined to accept the liberation from dramatic characterization that the autonomous Voice provides.

Some of Simon's novels follow Faulkner's so eagerly as to obscure whatever originality they have, to the extent that translation of his work has set American reviewers to crying 'Poor Faulkner'. He uses a full gambit of Faulkner's devices. He witholds essential information, as Faulkner does, in such a way as to turn an otherwise naturalistic story into a search for the sources and meaning of action. He confronts youth, which does not 'understand life', with age, which either 'understands' or purports to do so, in situations similar to Quentin Compson's hearing from his father about Sutpen's Hundred, or Chick Mallison's drowsing through Gavin Stevens's oratorical explanations of the background of events. He delights in action that makes his dramatis personae stumble about in the literal as well as the figurative dark. He is aware as Faulkner is of the capacity of the ordinary human for mindless violence. In *Le Tricheur* he even contrives a piece of Faulknerian humor when two of his

---

[13] 'Proust ou le double "je" de quatre personnages', *Confluences*, tome 3, nos. 21–4 (1943), 55–69.

[14] I have not seen Faulkner's statement in print; it may be in one of the transcripts of interviews recorded at the University of Virginia, which I have not been able to consult.

characters turn a dishonest penny by unscrewing the tops of lamp poles and carting them off to the junkyard under the eyes of a sleepy *agent de police*.

He is balked at only one point: being French he has no substitute for Yoknapatawpha County, no local habitation for the hundred years of race, class, and clan rivalries compressed under the weight of the Civil War that are the sources of the twisted motives and thick atmosphere of Faulkner's work. Simon's attempt to use the political events of the Resistance and *Epuration* as a similar source has been hampered by the impossibility—in the nature of things—of being the 'Sole Prop'[15] of such intangibles to the point of making the reader into Ortega's 'provincial in the country of the author'.[16] He is unable to exploit characters like Ratliff and Tull, who are so familiar with their locality that they know why what has not yet come into being must come, and must be, because they know that forces at work for a century generate events today—forces once working in the South, for example—that now cause the suicide of an undergraduate at Harvard.

The inherent conservatism of the French language also prevents Simon's appropriation of Faulkner from being complete: he has no way of getting new meaning out of old words[17] or of using words that have never quite found a place in the dictionary, and thus cannot give the feeling Faulkner does of reaching out toward a meaning of experience that is just beyond the meaning of available words.

On the other hand, his style is a remarkable example of the taking over into one language of a stock of stylistic devices first developed in another. In an extremely perceptive study,[18] Jacques Guicharnaud has pointed out that Simon's style has three dominants: a superabundance of 'logical tools' such as 'donc' and 'de sorte que' which, he affirms, reveal 'the desperate effort of reason to affirm order' and are 'actually the debris of reason's defeat'; another superabundance of comparisons 'made up of terms that do not exactly coincide', introduced by 'un peu comme' and 'à peu près comme', continued by alternative comparisons beginning 'ou plutôt comme', and completed by negative comparisons, that is similarities suggested and simultaneously rejected by a formula like 'non pas comme'; and a third superabundance of present participles, replacing clauses which

---

[15] See the frequently reproduced map, drawn by the sole proprietor himself, entitled 'Yoknapatawpha County, William Faulkner Sole Prop'.

[16] Ortega y Gasset, 'Notes on the Novel', p. 90.

[17] For example, the word 'defunctive', which Faulkner uses repeatedly and never quite in its dictionary meaning although always understandably in its context.

[18] 'Remembrance of Things Passing: Claude Simon', *YFS*, no. 24 (Summer 1959), pp. 101–8.

K

in any normal style would be in the past definite. The devices Professor Guicharnaud highlights here turn out not only to abound in Simon's writing but also to be extremely common in Faulkner.

A typical sentence from *Le Vent*, for example, comes remarkably close to sounding like pastiche.

Non par défiance d'ailleurs, ni mauvaise volonté, mais parce qu'entre temps (un ou deux jours plus tard) se produisit ce second fait, une seconde intrusion, mais celle-là pour ainsi dire de l'intérieur, non seulement du fait que, cette fois, le protagoniste était l'un des pensionnaires de l'hôtel, mais encore parce que celui-ci n'agit en somme que comme une sorte de catalyseur, de révélateur: le personnage lui-même, ce Maurice qui par la suite devait jouer un si grand rôle dans toute cette affaire, des plus falots en apparence, du moins tel que Montès me le décrivit, avec ses cheveux frisés et cosmétiqués soigneusement peignés, son élégance laborieuse, affectée: un de ces jeunes vendeurs de parfumerie ou de nouveautés, pensa-t-il la première fois qu'il le vit, c'est-à-dire le remarqua, ou plutôt fut forcé par l'autre de le remarquer car, me dit-il, il y avait déjà un bon bout de temps qu'il était installé à l'hôtel et il ne l'avait même pas encore vu (ou ne se souvenait pas de l'avoir vu) quoiqu'il prît ses repas à quelques tables de lui (et sans doute, j'imagine, à la lumière de ce que l'on sut plus tard, l'observant depuis le début, l'épiant peut-être, le regardant—assis parmi les autres jeunes gens impécunieux et nonchalants qui se balançaient sur leurs chaises à la terrasse du café à l'heure de l'apéritif—tandis qu'il trimbalait ses deux gosses du manège au marchand de beignets et du marchand de beignets à la petite boutique où l'on vendait des bouts de réglisse, des baigneurs et des moulins à vent en celluloïd multicolore, et ayant probablement déjà essayé à plusieurs reprises de lier conversation, Montès répondant distraitement par oui ou par non, étant même capable, comme chaque fois qu'un visage ou un personnage ne retenait pas spécialement son intérêt, d'avoir soutenu poliment un de ces longs dialogues sur le temps ou les difficultés de la vie sans y avoir prêté plus d'attention—c'est-à-dire méfiance éveillée, et même pas méfiance: étonnement, et même pas étonnement, même pas simple curiosité— qu'au chat de la maison ou à cette nourriture de gargote qu'il avait dans son assiette et se dépêchait d'avaler sans même savoir, sans même se demander si c'était bon ou mauvais, en pensant à autre chose).[19]

An opening 'non par' connects the sentence with the thought-process of the preceding one, aligning it in the position of a qualifier of an idea already expressed and thus contriving a kind of flow, as Faulkner so often does, of the second sentence out of the first by weakening the full stop of

[19] *Le Vent*, pp. 68–9.

the period. The opening movement in the sentence is a search among several possibilities for the motive of conduct previously reported; two are rejected in phrases beginning one with the 'non par' and the other with 'ni'; a second is tentatively accepted with 'mais parce que'; but this second one is amplified by a distinction between outer and inner, introduced by 'mais celle-là'; then follows a distinction as to the sense of 'inner', involving a construction balanced by the presence of 'non seulement . . . mais encore'. Thus, the beginning of the sentence moves through a maze of negative and affirmative causal constructions which have the effect of trying out and then rejecting imprecise in favor of more precise statement.

This is followed by a movement into an explanation of the possibility that has survived the rejection of the others, that is, of the sense in which the character Maurice has played a role of 'catalyst' or 'photographic developer'. This, however, brings back the memory of what Maurice was like, and his figure moves into the foreground of the reader's attention. This proceeds to another set of qualifiers which occasion a renewal of rejecting the vaguer one in favor of the more precise: 'saw' is less precise than 'notice', but this is not exactly right, either, and gives way to 'force his notice'. There are even two more progressions of this sort: 'he had not yet seen him' is corrected by 'he did not remember seeing him', and 'observing' changes to 'spying' and then is altered again to 'looking at'.

This is the practice which Professor Guicharnaud identifies by describing another of the forms it takes, the use of comparisons 'that do not quite coincide'. Whether or not comparison is involved, the essential process is the movement from a less exact to a more exact statement. It is resumed toward the end of the sentence in two additional instances, 'méfiance éveillée . . . méfiance . . . étonnement . . . même pas simple curiosité' and 'sans même savoir . . . sans même se demander'. After this, the sentence returns to the thought with which it opens, 'non par méfiance'.

Meanwhile the use of the present participle in the function of a gerund that Professor Guicharnaud identifies as characteristic turns up in one place: 'ayant probablement essayé à plusieurs reprises de lier conversation, Montès répondant distraitement par un oui ou par un non, étant même capable . . .'. I owe an alert graduate student[20] the suggestion that Simon tends to use the participial form for *showing* the reader the action, while reserving the finite forms of the verb for *telling* what happens without making him see it. The perception may be verified in Simon's writing,

[20] Mr. Peter Fitting, in a seminar paper at Harvard, 1964. 'Showing', in this context, is little different from what Conrad, James, and Ford Maddox Ford appear to have meant by 'rendering'.

passim, but does not emerge clearly in the present passage. The part of the sentence where the participles occur is about two pieces of behavior and one condition of possibility (trying and replying; being capable) repeated or continuous in an imagined past. The principal usefulness of the gerund would seem to lie in its not locating the action in time, of naming action rather than reporting its taking place. We are more aware of the unfolding action than of the moment of its unfolding.

What Professor Guicharnaud calls 'logical tools' are not represented here, to be sure, by 'donc' and 'de sorte que' but rather by conjunctions like 'parce que' and expressions like 'c'est-à-dire' that serve a conjunctive purpose. We have already recognized their role in the dynamic effort toward increasing appropriateness, exactness, and specification which animates Simon's sentence.

Now any experienced reader of Faulkner will testify to the frequency of the same devices in the novels, and most especially in passages where some character is reliving some experience and trying to worry out its meaning, and in sentences too long to lend themselves to quotation. The end of one such sentence (characteristic in its length—two and one half pages—as in its use of 'logical tools' and by the presence of a progression toward more precise statement, even though the 'present participles' are gerundives and not gerunds) is apposite here because it terminates in a statement which reveals the connection between Faulkner's use of this style and his feeling of time:

> . . . a Face, the composite face of his native kind his native land, his people his blood his own with whom it had been his joy and pride and hope to be found worthy to present one united unbreakable front to the dark abyss the night—a Face monstrous unravening omnivorous and not even uninsatiate, not frustrated nor even thwarted, not biding nor waiting and not even needing to be patient since yesterday today and tomorrow are Is: Indivisible . . .[21]

This particular prose is following the consciousness of a very tired, strained, obsessed boy who is badly in need of sleep; the reduction of punctuation to an absolute minimum may be an attempt to follow him into an only half-waking state. But it may also be taken to follow a flow such as resists letting the thought break into parts. In this latter case the form of the sentence confirms the sense of the final clause: to this consciousness time cannot break into parts, either.

In this passage, we must conclude, experience is an unbroken continuum: at any moment it 'is'. 'Was' and 'will be' are only modes of

[21] *Intruder in the Dust*, p. 238.

consciousness of it, for if experience is a continuum time must be a continuum also. The value of the 'logical tool' and of the progression toward greater exactness of statement (sometimes accomplished by a series of what Professor Guicharnaud describes as inexact comparisons) lies in their permitting an increasingly narrowing focus upon one minute area of the experiential continuum. The value of the gerund, as Faulkner uses it, is that it catches experience in the form of our awareness of it, temporally unconditioned.

The adoption of such devices by Simon attests Simon's sharing Faulkner's feeling of experience as a continuum.

What Simon seems not to have done is to put Faulkner's devices to serving purposes immediately distinguishable from Faulkner's. Other 'New Novelists' have been able to adapt rather than adopt; this has worked to make the influence of Faulkner less dramatically striking, of course, but at the same time suggests that the interest in Faulkner corresponds to the fundamental preoccupations of the practitioners of the new form.

We cannot, of course, attribute all the experimenting of recent years to Faulkner's influence alone. We do not know, for example, that Michel Butor's reading of Faulkner led him to base the structures of two of his novels on familiar myths. The hero of *L'Emploi du temps* finds his own predicament pictured in the tapestries of the Theseus story hanging in one of Bleston's two cathedrals, and the hero of *La Modification* is guided toward his recognition of the change in himself by myth figures, including the Wilde-Jäger and the Cumean sybil. Butor has written knowledgeably about Pound and Joyce, both of whom have used myth material more overtly than Faulkner, and the difference between Butor and Faulkner in regard to the use of myth escapes no one: the mythic-structural element in Faulkner is so deeply hidden that it has to be revealed by industrious and imaginative exegetes[22] whereas Butor introduces his myths quite ostentatiously. We cannot come upon such things in his books without thinking of Faulkner—but we think simultaneously of the other possible sources also.

Just so with numerous other innovations in the novels of a generation characterized by boldness in matters of technique. A group of characters sit around a table together and talk and think without the reader's ever

[22] A useful general bibliography is Edmund L. Volpe, *A Reader's Guide to William Faulkner*, pp. 412–22. For an example of specific research see Carvel Collins, 'A Pairing of *The Sound and Fury* and *As I Lay Dying*', *Princeton University Library Chronicle*, XVIII, no. 3 (Spring 1957), 114–24.

seeing them; to compensate for the lack of visual characterization the publisher issues a diagram of the dining room with every copy; and as the story emerges from the talk and thought of one character after another the point of view necessarily moves in a circle around the table.[23] One is strongly reminded of *As I lay Dying*, but nothing else in this novel would make one suspect that its author had ever read Faulkner.

Similarly, a watch salesman murders a shepherdess, and the reader reconstructs from the more or less meaningless events of the day the one fully meaningful one at which he has not been present.[24] The story also has superimposed upon it fragments of another similar incident. The way essential information is witheld from the reader is reminiscent of Temple Drake's experience in the corn crib in *Sanctuary*: in both novels the reader is purposely frustrated in his desire to know what, exactly, has happened.[25] But some witholding of information is indispensable in every detective story, so that although the strategy is part of Robbe-Grillet's regular stock—is there or is there not a murder in *La Jalousie*, and who is the narrator in *Dans le labyrinthe?*—we can only say that Robbe-Grillet's behavior reminds us of Faulkner's.

This continues to be the case as we review other 'New' novels. One is cast in the form of an interminable letter from a father to his dead son.[26] Another is about a woman who becomes so obsessed by a murder in her vicinity that she allows it to modify her whole life.[27] Each new subject seems to have commended itself by promises to test the novelist's dexterity. Such is the climate—and in such a climate Faulkner, the experimenter rather than the regionalist proprietor of Yoknapatawpha or the theologian, would seem to have become part of the common domain. Yet we conclude this only on the grounds that so much smoke must betoken some fire.

For more precise evidence we have to go to the cases where influence is reflected not only in subject and novelistic form but also in the style itself—Claude Simon's and, if I am right, Michel Butor's.

Butor is particularly aware of the conditions in which present-day fiction is written, and especially that other forms of entertainment, such as

---

[23] Claude Mauriac, *Le Dîner en ville*.   [24] A. Robbe-Grillet, *Le Voyeur*.

[25] I have been reminded by Cameron D. E. Tolton that the murder of the little *valet de ferme* in *Monsieur Ouine* produces a similar effect. I am not sure that, in the case of Bernanos, it is a completely calculated one.

[26] Robert Pinget, *Le Fiston*.   [27] Marguerite Duras, *Moderato Cantabile*.

television and cinema, now compete with literature for the attention of all but an elite. This elite is not necessarily small, and may well have the discrimination, sophistication, and homogeneity to make it an extremely satisfactory audience; and Butor obviously proposes to take advantage of the change in nature of the literary public. He has said that the novelist who turns his back upon formal innovation, who does not upset the fixed habits of his reader and require a special effort from him in the form of a re-examination of the positions he has long since made his own, may meet early success but in the long run will merely help deepen the profound intellectual discomfort of our time. This is very much what James Joyce said to an earlier generation of readers: a writer can expect as much collaborative labor from the man who reads his book as was required to write it.[28] He sees the novelist's job to be a long research among novelistic forms to the end of finding one that corresponds to what he calls 'the new situation of human consciousness'. This makes him, like so many of his generation, an experimenter.

Passage de Milan (1954) shows him taking up where writers like the Sartre of *Les Chemins de la liberté* left off, in an attempt at *simultanéisme* which follows the varied doings of the occupants and guests in a large apartment house, between one evening and the following dawn: a coming-of-age party takes place in one apartment, a literary review is founded in another, several sinister characters and some emotionally disturbed young men move from floor to floor, and before morning there is a murder. To date this is the only one of his novels not to use a 'central moral consciousness', and perhaps too many characters who are not central are required to be aware of too much; no device (such as indirect discourse in language characteristic of the character momentarily entrusted with the point of view) alleviates the strain upon the reader who has to tell the various consciousnesses apart. Although it did attract the attention of Leo Spitzer[29] this novel seems to have discouraged most critics.

L'Emploi du temps (early 1957) is less demanding and more rewarding. The young Frenchman who comes to work in the dull English city of Bleston—which sounds like Manchester—is so bewildered by subsequent events that eventually he has to sit down with pen and paper to reconstruct what has happened to him and dig out its meaning. Since he has been going through a trying initiation to English life, two abortive love affairs, an attempted murder, an attempt to identify the pseudonymous

[28] *Répertoire, I*, 8. Butor's tone, however, is polite.
[29] 'Quelques aspects de la technique des romans de Michel Butor', *Archivum Linguisticum*, XIII, no. 2 (1961), 171–95, and XIV, no. 1 (1965), 1–24.

author of a detective story that takes Bleston for its scene, the activities of a pyromaniac, and the unscrambling of a very intricate set of personal relationships, this *prise de conscience* is not very easily achieved. There are two time-plans: episodes from the past are narrated in the order in which the first-person narrator perceives their meaning rather than the order of their original occurrence, but meanwhile the narrator is also living in the present, sitting down day after day in the order of calendar time, fretting with haste because he must solve his puzzle before he leaves Bleston and his days are running out. Thus each discovery of the meaning of a past experience is also an event in the narrating present. Tension is high because each piece of the puzzle that falls into place marks the winning of a battle against the amorphousness of experience. The hero's anxiety, general malaise, and effort to escape these by writing about them, are reminiscent of those of Roquentin in *La Nausée*, and the struggle to discover an order in past experience gives *L'Emploi du temps* some similarity with Simon's *Le Vent*.

Another story of internal struggle, *La Modification* (1957; Prix Renaudot), rapidly became the most discussed of Butor's writings. The man who rides the train from Paris to Rome, where he intends to find his mistress and bring her back to Paris, sits face to face all the way with all the aspects and meanings of his situation past and present, and finally becomes aware that somewhere on the way he has realized that this attempt to run away from his wife and advancing age simply will not work. Time is again complex: various past trips between the same cities—with his wife, alone, with his mistress—crowd into his mind with the present one: the past impinges on the present. The protagonist passes through various levels of consciousness, from full waking to slumber state. Manipulation of point of view, through narration in the second person plural—Butor's now famous 'vous'—adds another dimension of experiment.

A later novel, *Degrés* (1960), provides no further material for the discussion of the use made by the 'New Novelists' of Faulkner's example, and so will not be considered here. *Degrés* is like the two previous novels in that it is one that only he who sits, and sits patiently, may read.

Butor has defined the novel as a new kind of 'epic and didactic poetry', such that every new subject calls for a correspondingly new discovery in technique; conversely a new discovery in technique should reveal a new 'aspect of reality'. Hence by his own logic there should never be a recognizable Butor manner as there is, say, a Mauriac manner—and no Voice, much the same from novel to novel, can speak in his work as it does in Faulkner's. Logic, however, can mislead.

In actual fact, a typical form of sentence that occurs frequently not only in his novels but in his essays on travel in *Le Génie du lieu*, is so instantly identifiable as Butor's that it plays something very like the role of a Voice. Its most striking feature is its length, which is frequently comparable to that of the sentences of Simon, Faulkner, and, of course, Proust. Another, almost as striking, is one these other writers do not offer: the habitual use of indention within the sentence. As Butor manages it, indention becomes a means not of gathering together sentences containing related ideas but of organizing the material of which the sentence is made up. It is thus a powerful adjunct of punctuation. The sentence from *La Modification* quoted here is indented seven times (and so contains seven paragraphs); it is by no means an extreme example.

Vous n'aviez point encore cette assise, cette situation, ces habitudes dont vous cherchiez par ce voyage à vous défaire; vous n'habitiez point dans ces murs, quinze Place du Panthéon, que vous vouliez quitter pour vivre ailleurs à Paris avec Cécile, mais que vous ne quitterez pas, auxquels vous êtes condamné maintenant jusqu'à votre mort, parce que Cécile ne viendra pas vous rejoindre, que vous ne la ferez pas venir comme vous en aviez si fermement l'intention en partant de la gare de Lyon ce matin, comme vous en aviez encore si fermement l'intention jusqu'à. . ., comme vous pensiez encore en avoir si fermement l'intention jusqu'à . . ., parce que vous ne la ferez pas venir à Paris, sachant trop bien désormais que cela aboutirait, malgré tous les efforts que vous pourriez tenter pour la tromper et vous tromper à ce sujet, à vous séparer d'elle peu à peu mais inévitablement, peu à peu mais de la façon la plus pénible et la plus détériorante pour vous deux, et que, si vous l'abandonnez (et vous l'abandonnerez, malgré toute la sincérité de votre amour, rapidement), cette situation que vous lui avez dénichée à Paris se révélera un pur mirage, qu'elle n'y pourra rester sans votre protection que vous lui refuserez alors, parce que vous ne voudrez plus la revoir,

donc vous n'habitiez pas encore dans cet appartement auquel vous êtes condamné jusqu'à votre fin parce qu'il n'y aura pas d'autre Cécile, parce qu'il est trop tard maintenant, parce que c'était votre dernière chance de rajeunir, cette chance que vous avez tout fait pour saisir, voici au moins une justice que vous pouvez vous rendre, mais qui s'est défaite entre vos doigts, qui s'est révélée comme inexistante en réalité, comme n'apparaissant que grâce à l'oubli, à la lâcheté de votre intelligence,

vous n'aviez point encore ces meubles qui décorent votre salon parce qu'ils étaient encore chez vos parents ou ceux d'Henriette ou que vous ne les aviez pas encore achetés,

vous n'étiez pas encore père de ces enfants: Madeleine, Henri,
Thomas, Jacqueline, parce que vous veniez de vous marier, que
c'était votre voyage de noces et la première fois que vous alliez à Rome,
cette ville dont vous rêviez depuis vos études secondaires et vos premi-
ères promenades dans les musées,

au printemps, toute la banlieue parisienne étant en fleurs d'arbres
fruitiers, un temps exquis faisant sentir son air à travers la fenêtre
entrouverte, avec Henriette à côté de vous, tout heureuse dans sa robe
fraîche à la mode de ce temps-là, qui s'émerveillait des moindres collines,
tenant dans ses mains le guide bleu de l'Italie dans cette édition ancienne
que vous possédez toujours sur l'un des rayons de votre petite bibliothèque à côté de la fenêtre qui donne sur la coupole illuminée le samedi,
tandis que vous vous efforciez d'apprendre par cœur les exemples d'une
grammaire italienne,

la forêt de Fontainebleau toute en pousses vives (et n'est-ce pas elle
qui vous a parlé à ce moment-là de ces promenades qu'elle y avait
faites toute jeune avec ses sœurs, terrorisées dès que tombait le soir d'y
rencontrer le Grand Veneur les interpellant et les emportant?)

les averses vous précédant, faisant briller toits et trottoirs, les prairies
éblouissantes sur les montagnes (pp. 190–1).

In *La Modification* these sentences are especially frequent in the Third
Part—in which the fatigued protagonist, approaching the end of his
journey to Rome, realizes that the modification has taken place and that
his mind, freed by boredom and fatigue from conscious control, is now
working on the assumption that he will not take his mistress back with
him to Paris, leave his family, and set up a separate establishment. The
external world, consisting mostly of the people in his compartment and
places flashing by outside, is becoming less real to him; he is approaching
the borders of sleep. Behind him and above, on the wall of the compartment, is one of the ubiquitous travel-advertisement photographs, showing
the Arc de Triomphe with outmoded taxis waiting on the pavement
around it. This he has just seen reflected on the spectacle lenses of the old
Italian sitting opposite him. The age of the taxis has triggered the rumina-
tion in the sentence quoted, they being contemporaneous with his first trip
to Rome.

Hence the imperfect tenses in the two opening verbs refer to different
times: 'n'aviez' refers to the moment of, or else just preceding, his
marriage, while 'cherchiez' reverts only to the beginning of the present
journey. Similarly, 'habitiez' reaches back to the earlier time and 'vouliez'
to the later one. And now the future, 'quitterez', moves his mind from the
two moments in the past to his present situation, a present that contrasts

with both imperfects, of course, but more with the one referring to more recent time since between that moment and the 'now' of the sentence the essential 'modification'—less a decision than the mere becoming aware of certain implications—has taken place. He does not know exactly when it did so: each repetition of the imperfects, 'aviez l'intention', 'aviez fermement l'intention', 'pensiez en avoir si fermement l'intention' leads to a blocking of the mind indicated by a printed ellipsis. All that he can affirm is that, at some time between that of the more recent imperfect and the present, the change has taken place.

But he is perfectly aware that it has indeed done so. The series of roughly parallel clauses, each introduced by 'parce que', and each constituting a recognition of the new situation, has already begun. The 'donc' at the opening of the new paragraph is not a logical tool introducing the consequence of a preceding argument, but instead marks an effort of the mind to return out of its divagations to the main line of its thought; the reasons for his present situation, rehearsed just before it, are cogent and coherent but have diverted the flow.

The time of the opening main clause will eventually dominate the rest of the sentence, but not immediately: after 'habitiez', in the remote past, comes the present that repeats the idea of his being irrevocably caught in his present domestic predicament, and the verbs that follow refer to the time during his present trip when the nature of the predicament has become clear to him. With the next indention, however, he moves back to the time before his marriage, and in the paragraph that follows in turn (the fourth) the marriage has only recently taken place.

Thus the burden of the principal clauses of the first four paragraphs goes: 'you were not in your present situation ... did not live in that apartment ... did not have that furniture ... were not the father of those children'. Meanwhile his attention has been solicited in the first two paragraphs by the comparison of the then-and-now and the problem of what has made the difference. In the third and fourth paragraphs the causal explanations, still introduced by 'parce que', refer to the time of the more distant of the imperfect tenses. In other words, the thought of the time before his marriage, which is the time of the taxis in the photograph, has captured his attention, and he now trails off into reminiscences of his wedding journey. This in turn disintegrates into something like free association as, in the paragraph beginning 'la Forêt de Fontainebleau ...' the thought of the forest revives that of the Grand Veneur-Wilder Jäger. This last fantasy has been a frequently recurring motif throughout the story, and now he wonders—for the first time—if his awareness of it is not associated with his wife. The final paragraph of the sentence continues with only a barely perceptible change in time which the verbs themselves do not show; the geography of France has to supplement them—the hills that shine in the light must be further on, toward the confines of Burgundy.

At the end of this sentence, the protagonist is far gone in fantasy. He is still following the wedding journey to Italy, but his memory leaps ahead to the train's arrival at the frontier where a customs guard puts his 'old Italian face' into the compartment. He seems to be the same old Italian whose glasses have reflected the picture of the Arc de Triomphe that set this whole sequence in motion. With a 'smile of commiseration' he murmurs the words of the cry of the Grand Veneur: 'Où êtes-vous, que faites-vous, que voulez-vous?'

The repetitions of 'parce que' in the first four paragraphs here are somewhat reminiscent of the 'logical tools' of Faulkner and Simon. The insistent reiteration can be interpreted as reflecting a more or less desperate effort to establish causal relationships, and thus grasp meanings, in experience. (If so, the disappearance of these forms in the paragraphs following would suggest a kind of renouncement of the effort and a releasing of the consciousness to wander where it will, undirected.) Otherwise Butor is not using the same grammatical mechanisms as the others: we do not find the progressions toward more exact statement or the disproportionate use of the 'present participle' in a verbal function where normally a finite form of the verb would be called for. And yet the mechanisms he does use work to ends that are certainly very similar to theirs and perhaps identical. The elaborate treatment of time—bringing together two widely separated moments of the past with a situation which exists in the present because it is already clear what (because of the past) the future cannot but contain —presupposes a feeling such as Faulkner expresses in 'yesterday today and tomorrow are Is: Indivisible'.

For Butor as for the others, experience is a continuum.

Since the different techniques in a literary work must be related to each other in some way, routine methodology requires examining whatever relation there may be between Butor's feeling of experience and his choice of the second-person plural for the narration of *La Modification*. His subject is a consciousness feeling its way through past experience that is just as real as the present, with reference to a future that is already determined. (Even the future events which would regularly be handled by a contrary to fact conditional, for example, 'if you did bring her to Paris you would abandon her', are couched instead in a future tense which imagines them as actually having happened.) This consciousness treats itself as 'vous'.

No one, Butor least of all, has ever claimed that narration in the second-person plural is something he invented *ex nihilo*. Much of the lively discussion his novel has stirred has been devoted to identifying his predecessors, and an article by B. A. Morrissette[30] names an impressive number, in France and elsewhere, who have experimented with this technique. Among those mentioned are so many who have also displayed an interest in 'interior monologue' and 'steam of consciousness' as to justify the suspicion that such a device is likely to tempt any writer who wants to explore new levels of awareness.

This observation may prove at least as instructive as Butor's own remark that he understands the pronoun to be a 'vous didactique'.[31] In what sense didactic?

Each of Butor's protagonists, after *Passage de Milan*, starts to tell his story under the impression that he knows something of the meaning that will emerge and, at the same time, that his present understanding is incomplete. But a new and unexpected meaning—the real meaning—begins to show its outline as the story goes on. In a sense he does teach himself in the process, and this fact may be taken to authorize the adjective 'didactic'; the use of the 'vous' would admit some kind of imaginative distinction between the consciousness-as-teacher and the consciousness-being-taught. All this seems more than a trifle tortuous.

Butor, himself, has admitted before friendly witnesses that such a formula fitted his novels little better than it fitted those of Faulkner. Questioned on the subject, he acknowledged the special interest, for him, of *Absolom, Absolom*—Quentin Compson discovering as he talks what the story of Captain Sutpen is really about.[32] A re-reading of *Absolom, Absolom* inspired by this testimony reveals how thoroughly Butor has assimilated the lesson of the master.

Faulkner's novel does not, of course, use a single narrator. Quentin Compson talks with his friend Shreve about the Sutpens, and the story comes out through their dialogue. But at the same time what both speakers

[30] 'Narrative "You" in Contemporary Literature', *Comparative Literature Studies*, II, no. 1 (1965), 1–24.

[31] *Répertoire*, II, pp. 66–7.

[32] Summer 1961, at Harvard. No written record was kept of Butor's informal discussion of his work.

say is shot through with the tones and harmonics of Faulkner's celebrated narrative Voice. Here is a quite typical passage.

> But Luster didn't budge, sitting there in the rain and inventing reasons not to go into the house—that the roof would leak or that you would all three catch cold with no fire or that you would all get so wet before you reached it that the best thing to do would be to go straight home: and your father laughing at Luster but you not laughing so much even though you were not black like Luster was, you were not any older, and you and Luster had been there that day when the five of you, the five boys all of an age, began daring one another to enter the house . . .[33]

The 'you' here is of course not an exact equivalent of Butor's 'vous': the number of persons it designates changes from 'all three' to one in 'your father' and 'you were not any older' and to five 'boys all of an age', as it links different moments in the story to each other. Also, this is not Quentin talking to himself but his friend Shreve speaking to him. These differences should not be overlooked.

But at the same time, Quentin is the 'central moral consciousness'; this talking registers on him, and moves him forward on the way to understanding the events of the story. Furthermore, even though Shreve is the speaker, his speech is not highly characterized: in the four gerunds, the anaphoric 'that . . . or that . . . or that', and in the refusal to let the voice drop and the sentence come to an end, one hears the tones not of Shreve but of Faulkner's narrative Voice. It is possible for an absorbed reader not even to realize here that Shreve is the speaker.[34] The rhythms are simply not those of speech.

This impersonality may work to intensify the effect of this 'you' upon Quentin. In any case, the second person would permit Quentin to detach his present self from that of the small boy in the story and, in a sense, to 'objectify' him. The psychological process may be tested by introspection: it is not difficult for me (whoever I am) to see a younger figure of myself as though it were not entirely I, to criticize its behavior as though it were someone else, to be baffled by some of its motives. (We have studied a phenomenon of this sort in Montherlant's *Les Bestiaires*.)

Wherever Butor may have found the idea of his narrative 'vous', his

---

[33] Modern Library Ed., p. 214.
[34] How easily, indeed, was brought home to me by Dr. Robert Hilton Knox III; I am grateful to him for pointing out to me that, in a paper read to Comparative Literature Group I of the Modern Language Association (1961), I had erred in attributing the passage to Quentin.

reading of Faulkner brought to his attention such passages as this, using a 'you' that produces the same *effect* as his 'vous' does—the effect of creating a psychic, or 'internal' distance within the character. Recent criticism has made much of the nonunitary nature of the psyche, although a fundamental awareness of the phenomenon is by no means new: Rimbaud's 'Je est un autre' has been identified as an echo of the German Romantics.[35] A current interpretation of *L'Etranger* alleges the importance of a detachment of the 'narrating Meursault' from the Meursault who is the principal actor of the story.[36] And I have suggested the possibility of something similar in Malraux's treatment of the hero of *Les Noyers de l'Altenburg*. In speech as in number theory the concept *second* posits a concept *first*, without which *second* is meaningless. If someone is spoken to there must also be someone who speaks, either outside the individual psyche (Shreve speaking to Quentin) or else within it, as in the divided ego of Léon. In this case 'vous' creates a divided character, capable of undergoing experience and, simultaneously, of interpreting it and moving progressively toward understanding. An extensive study of this recent tendency to split the ego of a fictional character should one day tempt one or another of the disciples of Georges Poulet.

Meanwhile, one of the originalities of Butor's performance in *La Modification* must be his making his character capable of the internal distance with respect to the present as well as the past. And thus the device becomes one for dealing with the continuum of experience, the past, present, and future that are 'Is: Indivisible'.

One could doubtless approach the style of the 'New Novel' from still other angles and emerge with the same conclusions. The length of so many sentences and their aperiodic nature, the occasional use of punctuation in which periods impose much less a full stop in the thought than a rest for the eye of the reader and from which commas so often disappear, contrast dramatically with (say) the unconnected sentences of Meursault or the disruptive three-point stops of Céline in *Mort à crédit*. The conclusions would, I believe, confirm those we have led to here, and these may be summed up in one: continuity has recently displaced discontinuity in French fiction.

[35] Albert Béguin, *L'Ame romantique et le rêve*, especially 'Les Aspects nocturnes de la vie', pp. 74–86.   [36] Brian T. Fitch, 'Aesthetic Distance'.

Conclusion:
Observations and Speculations

Nothing in these chapters will have weakened the authority of the most durable of literary truisms, the one most immune to challenge, that holds that each new development in literature imposes an obligation on criticism to renew the study of older literature in the light of this newest revelation of what literature can contain. Much that has been said here about the style and form of fiction in France between 1925 and 1950 doubtless would not have been said if fiction written after 1950 had not turned so resolutely in another direction. Not until writers begin to reject what we have come to think permanently characteristic of fiction as we know it do we see quite clearly how fragile the seeming permanence really was.

Aspects of the older literature that have gone unnoticed for years emerge and claim attention. The 'new' novelists, for example, have made much of the autonomy of inert, inanimate objects—Things—and their power to command the awareness of the beholder. The fact that human consciousness is very largely consciousness of 'les choses' can be regarded as one of the major discoveries of neo-realism. And yet, as soon as this becomes apparent, the important status of things in earlier fiction becomes apparent also. The new practice is seen to have definite antecedents in the writing of the Existentialists. For example:

> Les choses sont délivrées de leurs noms. Elles sont là, grotesques, têtues, géantes, et ça paraît imbécile de les appeler des banquettes ou de dire quoi que ce soit sur elles; je suis au milieu des Choses, les innommables. Seul, sans mots, sans défenses, elles m'environnent, sous moi, derrière moi, au-dessus de moi. Elles n'exigent rien, elles ne s'imposent pas: elles sont là. Sous le coussin de la banquette, contre la paroi de bois il y a une petite ligne d'ombre, une petite ligne qui court le long de la banquette d'un air mystérieux et espiègle, presque un sourire.

The novelist is, of course, Sartre (*La Nausée*, p. 159). The differences between his novel and those of, say, Alain Robbe-Grillet need not be emphasized. Sartre's realism is not 'new' because we are seeing the things through the eyes of his hero, and our interest is focused on his response to their presence rather than on the things themselves. Yet one understands why Sartre would have been willing to write the introduction to Madame Sarraute's *Portrait d'un inconnu*; things are the immediate data of consciousness in his novel just as they are in hers.

Once this process of revision has begun, limits are extremely hard to set. The scrutiny of literature earlier than Sartre, aimed at reassessing the value assigned to things, is to be expected. Symptomatically, one of the papers read at the national meetings of the Modern Language Association of America, in December 1965, was entitled; 'Flaubert, intendant des choses.'[1]

Such examples as this one could be multiplied if there were a point in proving that the newness of the most recent fiction is not absolute. And the process would have the additional effect of deepening our awareness of the aspects of older fiction that the younger writers do not want to perpetuate, and among them one that is near the heart of the present discussion.

Nothing marks these novelists more than their determination not to be present in their work, a determination so strong in the case of Robbe-Grillet that we are threatened not only with the loss of the author but with that of the hero as well. Their insistence has the effect of sensitizing the student to the contrast in practice of the fiction written before 1950—not all of it, of course, but of so much that at its moment was hailed as noteworthily fresh and interesting—in which the author makes himself felt either through his interventions or through a character who is a surrogate for the expression of the author's feelings.

In Gide one admires the functioning of a *persona* whose presence multiplies perspectives. Montherlant's performance is similar, and yet different in that he identifies author and narrator; his 'je' is less a *persona* than *propria persona*; he interrupts his narrative to comment in his own name ('Moi, Montherlant qui parle', *Les Bestiaires*, p. 445). His interventions are so many, and so often abetted by palpable manipulations of style such as variations of tone and juxtapositions of contrasting tones, that the ultimate aim of his novels seems to be the definition of his emotional relationship with his characters. Thus where Gide's total effect, in his more ambitious works, is comic, Montherlant's comes closer, in the novels studied here at least, to the markedly lyric.

[1] By Professor Jean-Jacques Demorest, at the Group Meeting devoted to French literature of the nineteenth century.

L

This kind of poetization of prose fiction is even more plainly marked in the novels of Saint-Exupéry. (It should be distinguished from the poetization of the young Giono, C. F. Ramuz, and, somewhat, André Chamson, in which the external world is somehow alchemized into a more hospitable environment for simple, even primitive, characters; it involves an emotional orientation of the novelist-poet toward the natural and social worlds in which he is called to live.) In fiction such as Saint-Exupéry's, imagery, used not so much for ornament and re-enforcement as for extending and completing an expression, acquires an importance it does not have in other forms of fiction; and one which it will not have, some years later, in the new novel.

If the reader lets himself be guided by the imagery of *Vol de nuit* and *Terre des hommes*, he is led to the conclusion that Saint-Exupéry's specialty is no more a 'poetry of flight' than a poetry of man using the airplane as an instrument of self-discovery. This discovery is at times attended by very powerful emotion such as appears to require something beyond purely rational discourse for its expression. Here again, as in the case of Montherlant, style is overtly and very visibly at the service of personal feeling.

Thus, in the sense that Buffon did not intend, style is the man himself. Style is the undisguised translation of Temper.

Without question there have been critics temperamentally unable to stomach the fictions of Céline and Bernanos precisely because of the emotional content. One can read *Voyage au bout de la nuit* and *Monsieur Ouine* as poems in dispraise of life and, as such, expressions of misanthropy and revulsion. We know that Bernanos recognized in Céline a kinship of temperament and disposition.[2] These facts join to add confirmation. Here again style is temper.

It is easier to feel the personal involvement and identification of author with hero in the cases of Saint-Exupéry, Céline, Bernanos, and Malraux than in those of Sartre and Camus. The autobiography in Céline's novels is so thinly disguised that he lets Bardamu practise medicine and follow the same itinerary—War, Africa, New York, Detroit, Paris *banlieue*—as himself. The priesthood of Bernanos's men is a state he contemplated seriously for himself, and he considered his calling of writer to be a vocation to a frustration and defeat similar to theirs. Saint-Exupéry played the roles both of endangered aviator and of supervisor condemned

---

[2] See Bernanos's undated letter in *Bulletin ... Bernanos*, no. 1 (Dec. 1949), 6. I have seen the original; the addressee, not identified in the printed text, was Céline himself.

by his task to send other flyers into danger. The career of the father-character Vincent Berger follows the outline of Malraux's own. We can hardly claim quite the same relationship between Sartre and Roquentin, Camus and Meursault or Rieux.

And yet Sartre's man experiences the revelation that is implicitly necessary for the sharing of Sartre's view of life; it is necessarily antecedent to the discovery that human life begins on 'the other side of despair'. In the same way, Dr. Rieux lives the allegory of the Occupation which Camus knew, literally, from his own experience. If not entirely the same, their relationships with their protagonists must be admitted to be close.

Now that it has been supplanted we are aware of lacking a name for this sub-variety of fiction, and find ourselves in the predicament of students who lack a commonly accepted nomenclature and so are chronically unable to agree upon what it is they study. But would a more accurate nomenclature really help? Certainly finer discriminations between sub-divisions of the genre would be possible, as various German efforts at detailed classification have shown. Yet these have also revealed the weakness inherent in such systems: distinctions too finely drawn lack real meaning. What, in the concrete instance, is the difference between *Entwicklungsroman* and *Bildungsroman*?

What we cannot neatly name is a renewal of the type of fiction Gide called the 'récit': a first-person narrative with the point of view limited to that of the narrator, peopled by a few primary characters however many the incidental ones, focused on one human situation, and thus a 'roman de l'individu'. It is new by its refusal to let the hero-narrator be a literary type, and thus by putting him in the dilemma of needing the resources of a style he is not supposed to command, in order to handle his characteristic emotional experience; he has to write the poetry of the supposedly un-poetic man. The subject of this poetry is, very often, his own epiphany.

'There are no perfect moments', declares Sartre's Anny with the authority of one who has devoted much of her own life to inducing such instants of euphoria. Her *vis-à-vis* Roquentin confirms this, in his way, by denying that 'adventure' is anything more than a delusion created by the perspective of story-telling. Yet the whole point of Roquentin's story is that he does experience the periods of extreme lucidity when the truth of his existence comes home to him. Perhaps, since they are not euphoric, these would better be termed epiphanies 'à l'envers'.

The theologian may be better situated than the student of literary form to appreciate the nature of these epiphanies, for in theological terms most of these heroes—Bernanos's country priest, Céline's little doctor,

Sartre's retired historian, Camus's shipping clerk, Malraux's adventurer-intellectual—are in danger of sinning against the Second Virtue. Bardamu must be considered to have succumbed, if this is the proper interpretation of his finding, at the end of his life-long *fugue*, the one situation that he can tolerate to be one of an attendant in an insane hospital. The others escape: for each there is some equivalent for what Bernanos calls grace.

The student of literature may properly confine himself to the problems created by the fact that attaining a state of grace is an irrational procedure. His special problems correspond to those of the novelist. The nature of his subject forces the latter into various forms of discontinuity: sharp contrasts in tone, and even incoherence, assume special importance. In other words, a number of important novelists tended to use prose fiction for the sort of expression which might just as appropriately have resulted in poetry.

This in itself suggests an answer to the plaguing question why the novelists have not been more faithful to the genre. If the fiction's purpose is not to explore various individual human predicaments (compare Duhamel, Mauriac, Martin du Gard), but rather to concretize and objectify an author's personal response to life, then, as Ezra Pound has put it, 'all that counts is the quality of the affection'. It is easily comprehensible that the novelist-poet should feel no need to repeat what he has already done once to his own satisfaction.

The change that took place after 1950 emphasizes the special nature of the earlier novels. Butor's protagonist in *La Modification* experiences no privileged moments of lucidity. Quite to the contrary, he does not even know at what point on his long journey from Paris to Rome he has awakened to his own situation and realized that nothing will change, that his life will go on drably being what it has been. Similarly there is no perceptible point in *La Jalousie* when Robbe-Grillet's invisible hero realizes that he is the victim of adultery. One searches the new novel in vain for the privileged flashes of lucidity. They are absent because awareness, like time and experience, is treated as a continuum. And so, while it is true that in some ways the new novel proceeds from the slightly older one, in other vitally important ways it does not. The fascination with objects, for example, forms a connection. But the awareness of objects in the new novel is not intermittent, and the verb 'to see' has a different meaning: it does not denote enlightenment and comprehension. This fact alone should be enough to explain why, in the most recent fiction, poetization, whether of the external world or of the situation of the individual, is not a factor.

It would be difficult to bring this discussion to a close without suggesting guidelines for future historians of the French literature of the twentieth century. If a common tendency in the novel of 1925–50 has been to use the form for the direct expression of feeling, then some of the uniqueness of each work will probably lie in the emotion expressed. The individual critic may retain his right to respond more sympathetically to some emotions than to others, but the historian surely enjoys no right to overlook those that may set his teeth on edge and to behave as if they did not exist.

It is hard to see why the appropriate question to ask ourselves about Céline is not how he managed to hate humanity so violently but how he managed to express his hatred, and, once this is granted, why his work does not merit as careful attention as that of Camus. Or why Bernanos should not be read as intently as Malraux. Or, for that matter, why Giono's preference for one kind of life as compared to another should not be studied as the source of motifs, themes, and images rather than rejected on the grounds that the life he prefers does not seem real.

André Malraux has insisted that we misjudge both the Romanesque and the Gothic if we assume that the second is only a perfected development of the first and not a different style generated by different spiritual needs. The observation is one which may be repeated, with profit, with reference to developments in literature.

Bibliography

Agee, James. 'La Condition humaine', *Films*, II, no. 1 (Nov. 1939), 51–61.

Alden, Douglas W. 'Proust and the Flaubert Controversy', *RR*, XXXVIII, no. 3 (Oct. 1937), 230–40.

Atkinson, Geoffroy. *Les Idées de Balzac d'après la Comédie humaine.* 5 vols. Geneva: Droz, 1949–50.

Balzac, Honoré de. *Le Curé de Tours.* Ed. by Maurice Allem. Paris: Garnier, 1953.

Barthes, Roland. *Le Degrè zéro de l'écriture.* Paris: Le Seuil, 1963.

Beach, Joseph Warren. *The Twentieth-Century Novel.* New York: Century, 1932.

Beauvoir, Simone de. *La Force de l'âge.* Paris: Gallimard, 1960.

Béguin, Albert. *L'Ame romantique et le rêve.* Paris: Corti, 1939.

— *Bernanos par lui-même.* Paris: Eds. du Seuil, 1954.

— ed., *Georges Bernanos, essais et témoignages.* Paris: Eds. du Seuil, 1949.

Bernanos, Georges. *Les Grands Cimetières sous la lune.* Paris and Geneva: Palatine-Plon, 1947.

— *Un Mauvais Rêve.* Ed. by Albert Béguin. Paris: Plon, 1950.

— *Œuvres romanesques.* Paris: Eds. de la Pléiade, 1961.

Blanchot, Maurice. 'D'un art sans avenir', *NNRF*, 5ᵉ année, no. 51 (March 1957), 488–498.

Boros, Marie-Denise, 'La Métaphore du crabe dans l'oeuvre littéraire de Jean-Paul Sartre', *PMLA*, LXXXI, no. 4 (Oct. 1966), 446–50.

Brée, Germaine. *Marcel Proust and Deliverance from Time.* New Brunswick, N.J.: Rutgers University Press, 1955.

Brée, Germaine and Margaret Guitton. *An Age of Fiction.* New Brunswick, N.J.: Rutgers University Press, 1957.

Butor, Michel. *L'Emploi du temps.* Paris: Eds. de Minuit, 1957.

— *La Modification.* Paris: Eds. de Minuit, 1957.

— *Passage de Milan.* Paris: Eds. de Minuit, 1954.

— *Répertoire.* 2 vols. Paris: Eds. de Minuit, 1960, 1964.

Cain, James M. *The Postman Always Rings Twice.* Garden City: Grosset and Dunlap Reprint, n.d.

Camus, Albert. *Théâtre, Récits, Nouvelles.* Paris: Eds. de la Pléiade, 1962.

— 'Le Vent à Djemila', *Noces.* Paris: Gallimard, 1950.

Céline, Louis-F. *Voyage au bout de la nuit, Mort à crédit.* Paris: Eds. de la Pléiade, 1962.

Chevalier, Haakon M. 'André Malraux: The Legend and the Man', *Modern Language Quarterly*, XIV, no. 2 (June 1953), 199–208.

Collins, Carvel. 'A Pairing of *The Sound and Fury* and *As I Lay Dying*', *Princeton University Library Chronicle*, XVIII, no. 1 (Spring 1957), 114–24.

Cruickshank, John. *Albert Camus and the Literature of Revolt*. London: Oxford University Press, 1959.

Debluë, Henri. *Les Romans de Georges Bernanos ou le défi du rêve*. Neuchatel: Eds. de la Baconnière, 1965.

Dreiser, Theodore. *A Book about Myself*. New York: Boni and Liveright, 1922.

Faulkner, William. *Absolom, Absolom!* New York: Modern Library Reprint, 1951.

— *Intruder in the Dust*. New York: Random House, 1948.

Fayer, Mischa Harry. *Gide, Freedom and Dostoevsky*. Burlington, Vt.: Lane Press, 1946.

Fernandez, Ramon. *Messages I*. Paris: Gallimard, 1926.

Feuerlicht, Ignace. 'Camus's *l'Etranger* reconsidered', *PMLA*, LXXVIII, no. 5 (Dec. 1963), 606–21.

Fitch, Brian T. 'Aesthetic Distance and Inner Space in the Novels of Camus', *Modern Fiction Studies*, X, no. 3 (Autumn 1964), 279–92.

Flaubert, Gustave. *Madame Bovary*. Edition du centenaire. Paris: Librairie de France, 1921.

Fleming, John A. *The Imagery of Tropism*. Unpublished dissertation, Harvard University Archives.

France, Anatole. *La Révolte des anges*. *Œuvres complètes* XXII. Paris, Calmann-Lévy, 1927.

François, Carlo. *L'Esthétique d'Antoine de Saint-Exupéry*. Neuchâtel, Delachaux et Niestlé, 1957.

Frohock, W. M. *André Malraux and the Tragic Imagination*. Stanford, Stanford University Press, 1952.

— 'Camus: Image, Influence, and Sensibility', *YFS*, no. 2, (1950), 91–100.

— 'Céline's Quest for Love', *Accent*, II, no. 2 (Winter 1942), 79–84.

— 'The Climax of Montherlant's *Bestiaires*', *RR*, XLIII, no. 4 (Dec. 1952), 266–71.

— 'Faulkner and the "Roman Nouveau", an Interim Report', *Bucknell Review*, X, no. 3 (March 1962), 186–93.

— 'Georges Bernanos and his Priest-Hero', *YFS*, no. 12 (1953), 54–61.

— 'Introduction to Butor', *YFS*, no. 24 (Summer 1959), 54–62.

— 'Notes on Malraux's Symbols', *RR*, XLII, no. 4 (Dec. 1951), 274–82.

— 'The Prolapsed World of Jean-Paul Sartre', *Accent*, VII, no. 1 (April 1946), 2–13.

Frye, Northrop. *The Anatomy of Criticism*. Princeton, The Princeton University Press, 1957.

Gandon, Yves. *Le Démon du style*. Paris: Plon, 1938.

Garcia-Calderon, Ventura. 'L'Espagnolisme de Montherlant', *Cahiers du Sud*, 24ᵉ année (Sept. 1937), 484–94.

Gide, André. *Journal des* Faux-monnayeurs. Paris, Gallimard, 1937.

— *Romans, Récits et Soties, Œuvres lyriques.* Paris: Eds. de la Pléiade, 1958.

Gilbert, John K. *Symbols of Continuity in Recent French Fiction.* Unpublished dissertion, Harvard University Archives.

Giono, Jean. *Que ma joie demeure . . .* Paris: Grasset, 1936.

— *Regain.* Paris: Grasset, 1930.

— *Un de Baumugnes.* Paris: Grasset, 1929.

Girard, René. 'Le Règne animal dans les romans de Malraux', *French Review*, XXVI, no. 4 (Feb. 1953), 261–7.

Guerard, Albert J. *André Gide.* Cambridge, Mass.: Harvard University Press, 1951.

Guicharnaud, Jacques. 'Remembrance of Things Passing: Claude Simon', *YFS*, no. 24 (Summer 1959), 101–8.

Hemingway, Ernest. *The Green Hills of Africa.* New York, Scribner, 1935.

— *To Have and Have Not.* New York, Scribner, 1937.

Heppenstall, Rayner. 'The Priest as Scapegoat', *Partisan Review* (Sept.–Oct. 1946), 448–57.

Hindus, Milton. *The Crippled Giant.* New York: Boar's Head Books, 1950.

Hytier, Jean. *André Gide.* Paris: Charlot, 1946.

— *Les Arts de littérature.* Paris: Charlot, 1946.

— 'La Méthode de M. Leo Spitzer', *RR*, XLI, no. 1 (Feb. 1950), 42–69.

Jakobson, Roman and Morris Halle. *Fundamentals of Language.* 's-Gravenhage: Mouton, 1956.

Lewis, Richard W. B. *The Picaresque Saint.* Philadelphia and New York: Lippincott, 1959.

Magny, Claude-Edmonde. *L'Age du roman américain.* Paris: Eds. du Seuil, 1948.

— 'Malraux le fascinateur', *Esprit*, 16ᵉ année, no. 149 (Oct. 1948), 513–34.

Malraux, André. *Romans. (Les Conquérants, La Condition humaine, L'Espoir.)* Paris: Eds. de la Pléiade, 1947.

— *Les Noyers de l'Altenburg.* Geneva, Skira, 1943.

Martin-Chauffier, Louis. 'Proust ou le double "je" de quatre personnages', *Confluences*, tome 3, nos. 21–4 (1943), 55–69.

Maubrey, Pierre. *L'Expression de la passion intérieure dans le style de Bernanos romancier.* Washington: Catholic University of America Press, 1959.

Milligan, Vincent. *Valery Larbaud, Anglicist.* Unpublished dissertation, Columbia University Library.

Montherlant, Henry de. *Demain il fera jour.* Paris: Grasset, 1948.

— *Romans et œuvres de fiction non-théâtrales.* Paris: Eds. de la Pléiade, 1959.

— *Services inutiles.* Paris, Grasset, 1943.

Morrissette, Bruce A. 'Narrative "you" in Contemporary Literature', *Comparative Literature Studies*, II, no. 1 (1965), 1–24.

— *Les Romans de Robbe-Grillet*. Paris: Eds. de Minuit, 1963.

O'Brien, Justin M. 'Gide's Fictional Technique', *YFS*, no. 7 (Spring 1951), 81–90.

Ortega y Gasset, José. *The Dehumanization of Art and Notes on the Novel*. Trans. by Helene Weyl. Princeton: Princeton University Press, 1948.

Paraz, Albert. *Le Gala des vaches*. Paris: Eds. de l'Elan, 1948.

Peyre, Henri. *The Contemporary French Novel*. New York: Oxford University Press, 1955.

Pézeril, Daniel. 'Du nouveau sur *M. Ouine*', *Bulletin des Amis de Georges Bernanos*, nos. 35–6 (April 1960), 1–4.

Picon, Gaétan. *André Malraux*. Paris: Gallimard, 1945.

Poulet, Georges. *Etudes sur le temps humain*. Edinburgh: University of Edinburgh Press, 1949.

— *Etudes sur le temps humain, II, La Distance intérieure*. Paris: Plon, 1952.

Proust, Marcel. *Contre Sainte-Beuve*. Paris: Gallimard, 1954.

Rees, G. O. 'Animal Imagery in the Novels of Malraux', *FS*, IX, no. 2 (April 1955), 129–42.

— 'Sound and Silence in Malraux's Novels', *French Review*, XXXII, no. 3 (Jan. 1959), 223–30.

Richard, Jean-Pierre. *Littérature et sensation*. Paris: Eds. du Seuil, 1954.

— *Poésie et profondeur*. Paris: Eds. du Seuil, 1955.

Robbe-Grillet, Alain. *Pour un nouveau roman*. Paris: Eds. de Minuit, 1963.

Robert, Pierre. *Jean Giono et les techniques du roman*. Berkeley: University of California Press, 1961.

Roche, A. V. 'Les Provençalismes et la question du régionalisme dans l'œuvre de Jean Giono', *PMLA*, LXIII, no. 4 (Dec. 1948), 1322–43.

Saint-Exupéry, Antoine de. *Œuvres*. Paris: Eds. de la Pléiade, 1959.

Sandelion, Jeanne. *Montherlant et les femmes*. Paris: Plon, 1950.

Sarraute, Nathalie. *L'Ere du soupçon*. Paris: Gallimard, 1956.

Sartre, Jean-Paul. *La Nausée*. Paris: Gallimard, 1942.

— *Situations I*. Paris: Gallimard, 1947.

Schlumberger, Jean. *Saint-Saturnin*. Paris: Gallimard, 1934.

Simon, Claude. *Le Vent*. Paris: Eds. de Minuit, 1958.

Sonnenfeld, Albert. 'The Hostile Phantoms of Georges Bernanos: *Sous le soleil de Satan* and *Monsieur Ouine*', *L'Esprit Créateur*, IV, no. 4 (Dec. 1964), 208–11.

Spitzer, Leo. 'Une Habitude de style (le rappel) chez M. Céline', *FM*, 3ᵉ année, no. 3 (June 1935), 193–209.

— *Linguistics and Literary History*. Princeton: Princeton University Press, 1948.

Spitzer, Leo. 'Quelques aspects de la technique des romans de Michel Butor',
    Archivum Linguisticum, XIII, no. 2 (1961), 171–95, and XIV, no. 1
    (1962), 1–24.
Sayce, Richard A. *Style in French Prose*. Oxford, The Clarendon Press, 1953.
Strauss, Walter A. *Proust and Literature*. Cambridge, Mass.: Harvard University
    Press, 1957.
Tarica, Ralph. *Imagery in the Novels of Malraux: An Index with Commentary*.
    Unpublished dissertation, Harvard University Archives.
Thibaudet, Albert. *Réflexions sur la critique*. Paris: Gallimard, 10th ed. (1939?).
Ullmann, Stephen. *The Image in the Modern French Novel*. Cambridge, The
    University Press, 1960.
— *Language and Style*. Oxford: Blackwell, 1964.
— *Style in the French Novel*. Oxford: Blackwell, 1964.
Valéry, Paul. *Variété*, in *Œuvres*, *I*. Paris: Eds. de la Pléiade, 1958.
Viggiani, Carl A. 'Camus's *l'Etranger*', *PMLA*, LXXII, no. 5 (Dec. 1956),
    865–87.
Volpe, Edmund L. *A Reader's Guide to William Faulkner*. New York, Noonday
    Press, 1964.
Woodworth, Stanley D. *William Faulkner en France (1932–1952)*. Paris: Les
    Lettres Modernes, 1959.

Index